D0472162

*A New Design Synthesis*
*for Cities, Suburbs, and Towns*

# Sustainable Communities

*Sim Van der Ryn and Peter Calthorpe*

SIERRA CLUB BOOKS
SAN FRANCISCO

The Sierra Club, founded in 1892 by John Muir, has devoted itself to the study and protection of the earth's scenic and ecological resources—mountains, wetlands, woodlands, wild shores and rivers, deserts and plains. The publishing program of the Sierra Club offers books to the public as a nonprofit educational service in the hope that they may enlarge the public's understanding of the Club's basic concerns. The point of view expressed in each book, however, does not necessarily represent that of the Club. The Sierra Club has some sixty chapters coast to coast, in Canada, Hawaii, and Alaska. For information about how you may participate in its programs to preserve wilderness and the quality of life, please address inquiries to Sierra Club, 730 Polk Street, San Francisco, CA 94109.

Copyright © 1986 by Sim Van der Ryn and Peter Calthorpe
Sierra Club Books paperback edition: 1991

All rights reserved under International and Pan-American Copyright Conventions. No part of this book may be reproduced in any form or by any electronic or mechanical means, including information storage and retrieval systems, without permission in writing from the publisher.

Library of Congress Cataloging in Publication Data
Van der Ryn, Sim.
  Sustainable communities.

  Includes index.
  1. Community development, Urban—United States—Case studies. 2. Autarchy. 3. Renewable energy sources—United States. 4. Social prediction—United States.
  I. Calthorpe, Peter.  II. Title.
  HN90.C6V36   1986          307'.14          83-4676
  IBSN 0-87156-629-X


Cover design by Paul Bacon
Book design and production by Donald Ryan
Printed in the United States of America on acid-free paper containing a minimum of 50% recovered waste paper, of which at least 10% is post-consumer waste

10  9  8  7  6  5  4  3  2  1



Parts of this book were produced with the help of a grant from the National Endowment for the Arts

# Contents

# Foreword: The Vision and its Contradictions

Our fundamental premise is that Industrial Culture has the means to transcend the apparent conflict between material progress and planetary health, between individual gain and common good. What we term 'sustainability' was a reality inherent in many preindustrial cultures. It was usually built into their beliefs, their practices, and the design of their environment. Sustainability is inherent in what earlier people — and many people today — hold sacred, and yet, it has been dismissed, ignored, and desecrated by the idea of progress. Our vision is that what is sacred is our relation to life and living processes, and that this can be made manifest in the design of our everyday environment. We see design not only as the application of science and technology but as an act of faith in humankind's wish to survive, adapt, and find a place of balance in a world that does not permit domination by one species for very long.

The practical and philosophical problems are really one and the same: the issue is, as the anthropologist Gregory Bateson so often put it, "What counts for knowledge?" What must count for knowledge in the design of a sustainable culture is ecology — a balanced connection and adaptive fit between the products of the human mind and the processes of nature. Realizing such forms of adaptation and balance can be the real and necessary wisdom of design today.

A culture's notion of what counts for knowledge is not easily changed. Indeed, our everyday environment imprisons us within its own reality. Every design has an epistomological consequence. Where and how we live—the everyday form, pattern, feel, and detail of our surroundings—is a tangible expression of "what counts for knowledge." The continuity of a culture is carried in its architecture, urban design, and planning. And so our vision carries with it no small mission. Our failures are likely to teach us as much as, or more than, our successes. In trying to remain true to our vision, we are likely to have more than our share of failures. For the practical person, for the doer (and design is doing), vision will always be contradicted by what is considered practical and possible at the moment.

Today, those of us working to build a sustainable society are faced with an ironic dilemma. In a society that does not place a priority on long-term social and ecological health, economic decisions that favor forms of sustainability cannot compete with short-term gain. The destructive pattern is self-reinforcing: as instability and uncertainty increase as a result of a lack of common vision, purpose, and actions, the future is discounted at ever higher rates, and investment in long-term environmental quality becomes unfeasible. A "Gresham's Law" takes over as potential investment in sustainability is driven out by a scramble to maximize short-term gain.

We remember that the origins of economy and ecology come from the same roots and same concerns: "Oikos," or "Ecos," is the old Greek world for household. Economy is the "nomos" or counting side of earth household, while "logos" is the logic of earth household itself. In today's culture, the meaning and means of these two disciplines seem hardly to converge and are scarcely congruent. In our vision of sustainable communities, the original meaning of the two terms would once more be unified. However, this book considers today's reality, as well as what might be.

The origins of the book go back to the summer of 1980, when a remarkable group of 45 people gathered at the Westerbeke Ranch near Sonoma, California. The purpose was a week-long Solar Cities Design Workshop, sponsored by the Solar Energy Research Institute (SERI). The goal of this investigation was to design ways in which three prototype urban communities—an older, inner-city Eastern neighborhood (in Philadelphia), a postwar Western suburb (Sunnyvale, California), and a piece of raw land within a growing metropolitan area (Golden, Colorado)—could be revisioned into places that, over the next twenty years, vastly reduced their dependence on fossil fuel, and increased community self- reliance and and livability. Some might think it foolhardy to attempt something as complex as the redesign of archetypal pieces of the American environment in a week. Our feeling was that this is precisely the kind of problem that doesn't get addressed because it appears so large and unmanageable. Lacking any tangible vision of what the future might be like, the future comes and goes by default. As the biblical quote says, "without vision, the people perish."

The group that gathered at Westerbeke included a dozen architects who have been at the forefront of shaping a sustainable future for a post-Industrial world. But this was to be a design workshop that necessarily included successful entrepreneurs, community organizers, transportation specialists, engineers, biologists, ecologists, agriculturalists, public officials, planners, along with experts in public finance, and design process.

The strategy of convening an "interdisciplinary group" to talk about or tackle a complex problem is not new. But the Westerbeke conference was different. In our experience, interdisciplinary groups, in spite of the competence of their individual participants, often add up to less than the sum of their parts. In such groups, each expert tends to approach and communicate about issues from the point of view of his or her discipline first. But every problem has an "inside" as well as an "outside." Approaching the outside of some condition in terms of the paradigm of a particular science or discipline often results in the inner meaning being lost. The way we chose to avoid this dilemma—and it was a wholly intuitive choice—was to select people who we thought might form a "meta-discipline," sharing an as yet unarticulated but nonetheless coherent image of worldly potential. Perhaps what united us was encircling the whole rather than perfecting the parts. Perhaps it has to do with an awareness of quality and difference as being more significant than the quantifiable properties of a system. A holistic view is an essential part of the emerging idea of sustainable design.

Something else different about the Westerbeke conference was its focus on creating a product, an image of physical patterning in a week of shared work. We have always felt that a positive force in the make-up of any designer is the desire to express and resolve perceived patterns in graphic or three- dimensional form. Of course our perceptions and desire to produce formal conceptions often gets us and the society we serve into trouble. But, at least we put the physical images out there.

The results of the Westerbeke conference—both the case studies and the papers—became the core of this book. However, we wished to round out these theoretical case studies with actual examples, many drawn from our practice, of attempts to carry out the principles of sustainable design into actual projects. Some of these projects are now being built, others were not carried out. But, they are all valuable in illustrating where we believe the focus of environmental design must be centered in the coming years.

Many people have contributed to bringing this volume into being. It is difficult to acknowledge them all. We are grateful to Michael Holtz, who while at SERI, saw the importance of bringing about the initial conference. In addition to the contributing authors, the participants included Don Prowler, Sarah Harkness, Richard Stein, Robert Twiss, Michael Corbett, Judy Corbett, Steve Conger, John Anderson, Claudia Cleaver, Doug Kelbaugh, Peter Berg, Richard Busse, Fred Dubin, Alison Dykstra, Louis Fair Jr., Bob Harris, Ralph Knowles, Wally McOuat, Richard Merrill, Stephanie Pincetl, Bill Press, Ken Smith, Christopher Swann, Wayne Van Dyck, Margo Villecco, and Don Watson. Andrea Ponsi and Lori Thompson assisted in preparing the first version of this work. Jon Beckman and Danny Moses of Sierra Club Books guided us through the often tedious process of bringing manuscript into book. Our colleague, Scott Matthews, has articulately goaded us into facing often unpleasant aspects of reality and forced us to clarify many points of concern. Doug Mahone and Marianna Leuschel assisted in production. Belinda Presser, with unfailing patience and good humour, typed many versions of the original manuscript and assisted with editing and the final production. Finally, we are constantly renewed by the warm support of friends, colleagues, and students with whom we have shared these ideas over the years.

Sarah Harkness, a participant in the Westerbeke conference and an accomplished architect of long experience wrote us afterwards, ''I think we all came to share a vision of the future which might indicate that there could be a future. We've been hearing for years from wise people who say that this and that percentage of energy could be supplied or saved by this and that method. But the question that always goes through my mind is, 'Yes, but how? What will it look like? How will it affect people's lives? How do these things go together?' The only way to find the answer, short of building a new world, is to try things out in design. This, I believe, is true architectural research—a type of research whose methodology is different from the sciences, and which only environmental designers, working in an interdisciplinary way, can do.''

# Introduction: Ecology and the Commons

In the ten-thousand-year history of cities, there have only been two significant transitions that have shaped urban form: the transition to agriculture and the transition to the machine age. A third transition is coming, brought about by a combination of forces. In the past century, it has been the cheap energy and accessible resources which have permitted cities to expand logarithmically. But it is not just the acknowledged ecological limits of these resources which will change our patterns of settlement. The lines of pressure for change are converging from many directions: limits of land, water, and pollution are being felt; shifts of family size and work force are changing our daily activities; issues of environmental and personal health are mounting; costs of capital and time are reordering investments; and, not least, a search for identity, community, and a sense of place is covertly motivating many peoples' lives. Cheap energy was the mechanism which simultaneously aggravated and postponed the need to re-examine our urban forms and behaviors. But its disappearance is now joined by these other forces. If our cities and towns are to thrive, they will have to be designed for sustainability, reducing resource waste, balancing long-term consumption with sustainable production, and producing social forms of integrity and durability.

The old patterns of growth, built on the industrial principles of centralization, specialization and standardization will give way to new forms. The current social, environmental and psychological pressures can produce a new philosophy of design and planning: replacing symbolic gestures and trendy styles with purposeful forms which honor ecology and history; replacing short-term market forces with long-term stability; and ultimately amplifying the unique qualities of each place, rather than standardizing the built environment.

The trends producing this transformation are readily apparent: environmental conservation became a central issue in the 1970s and is a clear expression of public concern for ecology; the limits of water supplies are effecting growth in many areas of the country, as is waste management in others; the cost of developable land is changing the way America houses itself, as average housing densities have climbed from 6.7 units per acre to 7.6 units per acre in the past 4 years, and land costs have risen 25 percent; our agricultural system is approaching a crisis as over three million acres of prime land are developed every year and topsoil erosion extracts 5 bushels of soil for every bushel of corn produced; we are still sacrificing even greater percentages of our time to commuting and even greater expanses of land to parking; women have entered the workforce as the economy has shifted from an industrial to a service base; the small, two-income family is producing a new set of criteria for households and child raising; finally, and not least energy costs have quadrupled in the last ten years. The sum of these trends will set a new direction for urban design: more compact, mixed-use communities, more efficient buildings, diverse transit systems, an ecologically sound agriculture, water and waste conservation, and ultimately, a greater sensitivity to the uniqueness and integrity of each region.

Sustainability implies different solutions for different places. Like the word "appropriate," "sustainability" is qualified by its context. Sustainability implies that the use of energy and materials in an urban area be in balance with what the region can supply continuously through natural processes such as photosynthesis, biological decomposition, and the biochemical processes that support life. The immediate implications of this principle are a vastly reduced energy budget for cities, and a smaller, more compact urban pattern interspersed with productive areas to collect energy, grow crops for food, fiber and energy, and recycle wastes. New urban technologies will become less dependent on fossil fuels and rely more on information and a careful integration with biological processes. This will mean cities of far greater design diversity than we have today, with each region developing unique urban forms based on regional characteristics that have long been overridden by cheap energy, the great leveler of regional diversity and unique character of place. A sustainable community exacts less of its inhabitants in time, wealth and maintenance, and demands less of its environment in land, water, soil, and fuel.

Sustainable communities are not necessarily autonomous or self-sufficient. They aim for a balance between local and regional integrity and trade on a global basis. Today the split between economy and ecology has unbalanced the system and made it "feasible" to ignore the use of small-scale regional resources in favor of large-scale exploitation on a global scale. However, sustainability need not imply a balkanization. Regional specialization based on ecological considerations is compatible with a sustainable approach. Wheat or coffee will continue to be grown in the places best adapted to it. Places with a skilled technical labor pool such as Silicon Valley will continue to produce new information technology rather than the peaches and plums that grew there fifty years earlier.

Our old patterns of growth are built on isolation—an isolation from the environment, an isolation between activities and ultimately an isolation between individuals. Whether city or suburb, these qualities of isolation are the same. Buildings ignore climate and place, uses are zoned into separate areas, and individuals are isolated by a lack of convivial public places. Sustainable patterns break down the separations; buildings respond to the climate rather than overpowering it, mixed uses draw activities and people together, and shared spaces reestablish community.

## The Westerbeke Workshop

This book grew out of an intensive week-long design workshop where thirty of America's leading innovators in ecology and community design asked themselves the question, "What would our cities and suburbs look like if we could redesign them toward sustainability?" The book, through specific design proposals and other contributions by participants, outlines some of the strategies that can transform our cities and towns from machines designed for consumption to sustainable habitats, from commodities to communities.

Taken as complete proposals out of the context of incremental change, the alternatives we propose may seem utopian. They should be seen as composed of a connected group of interdependent options and design strategies that, taken together, define a physical pattern that may ease our transition to a post-industrial culture.

Because it lasts so long, the built environment is a product that lags behind economic and cultural change. Yet, precisely because it represents such a major long-term investment, and because it so largely affects our perceptions and patterns of activities, the design of our everyday environment should lead the way to the post-industrial era. Post industrial architecture will be information rich, more responsive to place, biologically balanced, compact, durable, differentiated, and as in earlier times, will shift its focus from design for purely private consumption to the enjoyment and celebration of what we share in common.

What we mean by post-industrial culture in design terms is developed in the chapters by contributors which accompany our major proposals. Paul Hawken postulates that the shift in our economy and culture from an industrial to a post-industrial base is most clearly described as a shift from a "mass" economy to an "information" economy. This means that a specific cultural and economic function, whether it be providing thermal comfort or personal transportation, will increasingly be met not through the application of more resources and energy, but through more intelligent design—design that replaces materials with higher-quality information. For example, in an information economy, thermal comfort is more likely to result from climate-responsive design that uses the sun and daylight rather than pumping more fossil-derived heat into the space. Smaller, lighter, more fuel-efficient cars get us where we are going in as much comfort and as fast as "petro-pigs." The post-industrial era is one in which the major economic strategy will be carefully matching energy and resources to specific functions and values, rather than designing for infinitely expanding mass markets. The economy is defined by the quality of information and the quantity of energy and resources available to it. The emphasis shifts from design for consumption to design for efficiency, or doing more with less.

David Katz's discussion of sustainable agriculture suggests a striking parallel between today's industrial agriculture and modern land development. The short-term productivity of large-single crop agribusiness is built on the massive application of energy-intensive machinery, fertilizer, pesticides, herbicides, processing, transportation, and water—all highly subsidized. The result is the degradation of complex biological systems, a loss of basic stability through soil and water depletion. Like agribusiness, the modern suburban city appears highly productive, but it is extremely wasteful in its use of land, resources, energy and human beings. It is a zoned monoculture of huge housing subdivisions, industrial parks, office plazas, and shopping malls which demand support systems similar to the food systems they depend on: complex machinery, imported water, polluting waste disposal systems, energy wasting buildings and power grids, and specialized service elites. Both suburban cities and agribusiness are industrial solutions that sacrifice long-term health and sustainability for short-term profit and productivity. Both are increasingly vulnerable, unstable, and short-lived. Both seem to provide products which are tasteless, monotonous, increasingly expensive, and finally, unhealthy.

In contrast, an agriculture based on a diversity of crop species and the use and renewal of on-site soil and water and nutrients increases overall wealth, biological health, and stability, rather than maximizing the production of a single component at the expense of the whole. Similarly, compact mixed-use land planning may compromise the quantity of private land for the separate household, but will reduce travel time, land area devoted to automobiles, and air pollution. The private domain becomes more compact, but the public domain may become more livable and diverse. Just as smaller, highly integrated farms tend not to maximize the use of energy and resources on one cash crop, but use local intelligence to diversify the product and market, the post-industrial suburb will be more site-specific and rely more on local people and local intelligence rather than abstract standard formulations from afar.

Diversity is another key quality of the post-industrial culture. Transportation is a good example. Industrial mass production and cheap energy made private auto ownership feasible for all, and it has effectively replaced all other forms of transportation. Most current transit is by auto, and our land planning reflects and reinforces this. Transit has become an auto monoculture.

Fred Reid indicates that this is unlikely to change in the near future, especially given our current land-use patterns. Smaller, lighter, more efficient autos are the logical result of our massive auto infrastructure. But beyond that, diversification of options will be necessary. This is not feasible with our current forms of land use, and the alternates are interdependent with clustering, density, and mixed-use planning. Given our massive investment in the convenience of the auto, change will be slow.

Beyond these physical and economic forces lie social shifts discussed by Clare Cooper-Marcus. The nature of the work force is changing as women enter the service sectors in increasing numbers. This in turn changes the nature of homes and child rearing. Says Marcus, "By 1990, 80 percent of all preschool children will be in day care, which not only means more provision for day care, it means more work opportunities in or close to residential neighborhoods for both men and women; greater accessibility to public transport." Our existing land-use patterns are built on outdated notions of the nuclear family with one wage earner as much as on cheap oil, land, and water.

David Morris extrapolates these forces beyond physical planning to political forms and the scale of business. In his view, the tendency toward smaller more place-specific enterprises and technologies will tend to decentralize political power. Cities and neighborhoods will gain greater economic and political independence as local self-reliance provides cheaper and more stable services than can be provided by large centralized industries or government. The utilities are a good example: once their monopoly was broken by the Public

Utility Regulatory Policy Act (PURPA), which allows solar-based and small co-generation facilities to use the grid, local energy production has doubled in the last ten years.

A city that relies more on its own resources relies more on the skills and abilities of its own people. Today's urban dweller leads a split existence of eight hours as a "producer" in the workplace and the rest of the time as a "consumer" at home and elsewhere. In the sustainable city, these split roles will be reintegrated. The homeplace, rather than being merely the site of consumption, might, through its very design, produce some of its own food and energy as well as become the locus of work for its residents. The designs of the New Alchemy Ark in Woods Hole, Massachusetts, and the Farallones Institute Integral Urban House in Berkeley, California, are early experiments toward creating sustainable habitats that integrate food and energy production at the small scale.

However, urban self-reliance cannot be an individual affair. In a city, no one is a tight little island, and survival is a collective enterprise. Constructive action must be cooperative. The conditions that are pushing us to seek new ways of living in the city will, if we are creative, cooperative, and not paralyzed by fear, move us to new and richer experiences of community and the natural world.

## Between Public and Private

Our modern technologies and forms have not only deadened us to the natural world, they have largely eliminated the common ground of our communities. As cheap energy isolated buildings from their environment and the auto disbursed urban life, the shared domains—from courtyards, porticos, and arcades to semiprivate streets, common yards, and neighborhood stores—were largely eliminated. As a result, our public space lacks identity and is largely anonymous, while our private space strains towards a narcissistic autonomy. Our cities and communities are zoned black and white, private or public, my space or nobody's space. The auto destroys the joys of urban streets, the shopping center destroys neighborhood stores, and depersonalization of public space grows with the scale of government. Inversely, private space is strained by the physical needs to provide for many activities which were once shared, and is further burdened by needs to create some identity in a surrounding sea of monotony.

With the new potential for unparalleled ownership and seemingly endless wealth made possible by industrialization, the private domain quickly overtook many of the functions of the public realm. Transportation moved from rail to car, recreation moved from park to yard, entertainment moved from circus to TV, housing moved from townhouse to ranchette, child care moved from neighborhood and extended family to nuclear family, and commerce moved from the public street to the private mall. The traditional balance and tension between public and private was overthrown, the middle ground was eliminated. The most intimate of the public domains were consumed by the private realm.

The notion of a "commons," not unlike its British ancestor, is a central element of design for resource conservation and environmental stability. Our current patterns of settlement, focusing on private space, are quite resource-inefficient: land use, transit demands, energy, and material needs are greater for low-density, single-family developments than for higher-density mixed-use equivalents. The clustering imperative born of these environmental constraints inherently raises the issues of common space and shared facilities. It is the shared ground, responsibilities, and systems at the community scale which offer the potential for a more benign form of human settlement, both socially and environmentally.

Underlying the technical aspects of the case studies there is a question of what is private and what is shared in our settlement patterns. In all case studies, there are dominant features: the clustering of habitats, a highly developed common ground, and shared facilities. In each case, precious land is wrested from the auto to provide multi-use shared space. In the Philadelphia case study, the east/west residential streets are closed to provide common green space and playing areas. In Sunnyvale, the mat suburban grid is broken down into roads for primary traffic and local streets dominated by pedestrians and plants. In Golden, new construction allowed a clear set of zones: auto driveways small and slow, pedestrian paths and play areas connecting front doors to village services, and green space backing each cluster. For each case, the effect is the same: the clustering saves land, resources, and energy; the common open space is usable, personalized, and productive; and the pedestrian ways are safe, human-scaled, and nonpolluting.

At the building scale, similar common spaces are critical; the courtyard, for example, offered an identity and generosity rarely matched by our modern lobby and elevator. The shared parts of a building, once the most important, have shriveled into narrow corridors and boiler basements. We are now discovering that such shared spaces as atria and courtyards, played an important part in the building's natural energy systems as sources of light, as buffer zones moderating between indoor and outdoor temperatures, and as thermal storage. At the community scale, the common space has also atrophied. Pedestrian streets and squares have been reduced to parking lots and freeways by the same technology—cheap energy.

The identity of a community is often based on its common ground, whether a piazza, square, or parking lot. The English commons identified a village and its people as much as its church and castle. The Enclosure Acts not only robbed the people's access to productive land, it eroded their common identity and therefore their power. The same awareness persists today: after the People's Park and anti-war demonstrations in Berkeley, then-Governor Ronald Reagan requested that university designers avoid spaces large enough for such unruly gatherings. No common space, no common action.

Setting aside the social consequences, the abandonment of a meaningful 'commons' at the community scale has sacrificed many valid technical alternatives. For example, in each of the case studies we found community energy and waste systems operating at a more responsive scale than current utilities. These community systems are more efficient because they serve multiple needs. In the revisited Sunnyvale, a biological sewage treatment plant doubles with garden areas and a recreation lake, turning the wastes into fertilizer and food while recycling the water and providing a park. In Golden, a village-scaled woodchip gasifier produces methane for neighborhood co-generation plants. This local electrical production and waste heat utilization is based on the region's renewable biomass, involves smaller capitalization, and is more energy-efficient than common utility practice. The recycling and processing of solid wastes in all cases become a source of local employment and small business opportunity. This is certainly more desirable than the tax burden of regionally based and potentially polluting landfill operations and sewage dumps.

Perhaps the most romantic and most consistent features of each scheme are the neighborhood stores. Economically a thing of the past, these small retail shops played an important role in sustaining local identity as well as providing personal service and convenience. Like utility companies, the corporate chain stores are remote, rarely reinvest in the community, and are highly fossil-fuel dependent: for auto access only. Twenty-four percent of the trips of an average family are for shopping, education, and recreational activities, and 15 percent are for services (bank, post office, etc.) and personal business (dry cleaners, doctor, etc.). In an environment structured for the auto, there is no disincentive for large and distant facilities. However, in the pedestrian environment postulated in each case study the local store would benefit from convenience and energy savings. As walking is not always comfortable, perhaps deliveries would become a tradition once more. Given local densities, pedestrian networks, and a critical mass of services such small-scaled stores could do much to reduce our dependence on oil and to enhance our sense of community.

Local employment, and for that matter productivity, is central to each scheme. The Schuylkill River front in Philadelphia is redrawn lined with small businesses that convert abandoned warehouses and turn old barges into fish farms. Sunnyvale rediscovers its not-too-distant agricultural past and redistributes its growing electronics industry into neighborhood centers along the old strip commercial zone. And Golden develops orchards, greenhouse propagation, and fish farming along with studio and office space attached to housing. Once again, the implications for reduced transit are just one of many; on average, 33 percent of all trips are work-related.

In each case, the community takes responsibility for primary services now relegated to large, inefficient, and unresponsible bureaucracies. These services—energy, water, waste, and transit—are more site- and climate-responsive. The soft services—education, protection, and recreation—are integrated in ways rarely pursued at the municipal scale. The Golden site design boldly places the school straddling the main street. The classrooms, gym, and library will be multipurpose, providing for adult education and day care, along with elementary and high school levels. The library is a public space, and the playing fields (as in many communities) are a central feature for community recreation.

None of these strategies are new. Jane Jacobs postulates the same mixed-use urban village based on social criteria. The difference here is the justification and perhaps the feasibility. The Westerbeke Charrette arrived at the same conclusions from the criteria of conservation, environmental quality, and energy. By investigating the technologies and social systems scaled for limited resources, the concepts gain a long range of economic viability. If such human settlements can truly reduce our dependence on foreign resources, limit pollution, and create socially robust places, they will not only become desirable, they may be inevitable.

Today, many of these proposals are becoming commonplace: higher densities, mixed use, passive solar buildings, and environmental impact reports. But something is missing from these trends. Part of what is missing has to do with our interaction in the ecosystem. Beyond material efficiencies and simple conservation, our communities must express a reverence for the nature of a place. This reverence bespeaks a greater everyday understanding of our regions, its watershed, climate, geology, plants, animals, and most importantly, its activities—its life. This understanding must go beyond static preservation in which "nature" is placed in large outdoor museum. We need to move towards a sense that our place is a habitat within, rather than a settlement beyond, the ecosystem. The other aspect missing is the notion of the commons, that the public domain must become richer as the private domain becomes more frugal; that success and well-being must be a shared, rather than a private, affair. It is the missing sense of ecology and the commons that makes places real, turns ''housing'' into dwelling, ''zones'' into neighborhoods, ''municipalities'' into communities, and ultimately, our natural environment into a home. Emerson translates this into a kind of individual ethic:

''. . . to live content within small means; to seek elegance rather than luxury and refinement rather than fashion; to be worthy, not respectable, and wealthy, not rich; to listen to stars and birds, to babies and sages with open heart; in a word, to let the spiritual unbidden and unconscious grow up through the common.''

# Part One:
# Case Studies

# The Urban Context

*Peter Calthorpe*

There is a special kind of wisdom in our cities born of time and its shifting forces. Each age brings with it a new set of priorities to which the city responds by constantly modifying and adjusting its form and character. For the environmentalist, the city is a mixed metaphor: on the one hand symbolizing the congestion, pollution, and waste that modern culture has created, and on the other, a compact alternative to the constant invasion of open space (wilderness) represented by modern sprawl. The old pattern of the city, with its mixed use, active pedestrian streets, public transit systems, and public spaces had a human dimension born of technical and environmental necessity. The form of many cities evolved before cheap gas and the auto dominated the pedestrian, before electric lights replaced windows, subdivisions replaced neighborhoods, and before shopping malls replaced local stores. Originally, cities demanded less of the environment in terms of land and energy simply because accessible land and cheap energy were not available. In this sense, they are a model of conservation and material frugality.

In older cities and towns, the framework and traditions for compact and efficient communities are already in place. Not to reuse them not only wastes the material, energy, and ingenuity that created them in the first place, it squanders our history and depth. By reuse, we are forced to relearn many of the traditions and disciplines lost to modern architecture and planning. These lessons range from how to daylight a building, to how a street becomes a neighborhood; from how to shelter the pedestrian and make common areas that work, to how certain building forms respond to the local climate. Many of these older urban patterns were born of climate and community as well as technologies and style. The city of old Charleston is a good example. Its one-room-thick houses, naturally ventilated, lined with porches for shade, and overlooking narrow tree-lined streets, create a town of great beauty and sensibility.

While respecting these old traditions, we must modify them according to our current needs and knowledge. We know more about passive solar heating and cooling, we have different requirements for housing types and workplaces, and we have new techniques for transportation, utilities, and services. The challenge is to synthesize the relevant pieces of the past with the progressive ideas of the present. Cities have always offered the opportunity for such combinations. Their old dense cores must be humanized: that is, made livable in current terms while maintaining their diversity, compactness, pedestrian networks, and local commerce. Many strategies can be used to bring this about. We can build new buildings on vacant lots and we can rehabilitate the old. In some cases we can add new workplaces or retail area; in others, more open space or street amenitities are needed. In all cases, the goal is balance: a balance between uses, between climate and the needs of the building, between the community and the individual. The examples used in this chapter represent two primary approaches: Sacramento is a case study in infill for urban rehabilitation; Philadelphia, a study in rehabilitation of existing structures.

The old buildings of Charleston, South Carolina, are socially and environmentally intelligent.

2

# The Form of American Cities

Urban development in the U.S. did not follow the traditional patterns of Europe or other older cultures. The pre-industrial towns did not evolve over time in a balanced relationship with the land, but were laid out with a surveyor's rational grid. They were generally located for commerce, first on bodies of water, later at railheads. The medieval fortifications which contained most European cities before the Renaissance were missing, as was the ecological sense of limits which bound the scale of the feudal village to local food production. Our pioneer town was based on growth, not stability, mostly an economic monoculture rather than a polyculture. In contrast to most European towns, many U.S. towns were built around extracting resources quickly: minerals, lumber, single crops, and wildlife. Their form was fashioned after the Roman garrison town and the Bastille, a French settlement for occupation. The gridiron plan implied many things: that the town could grow quickly and had no man-made limits, that one place was as good as the next, and that land was a standardized commodity to be traded and speculated on.

This pioneer culture set up a distinct quality for urban America. Topography was ignored as land was divided for allotments of abstract equality rather than evolved quality. Lacking age, the towns had a temporary quality reinforced by the unmatched mobility of the new world. Much of this ethos, the interchangeability of place and its disposable character, has returned to haunt us now that the borders are fixed and the limits set.

Along with this abstract relationship to the land, there was a new social structure that emphasized the individual and private property. Although many of the early English settlers carried with them the tradition of the commons and the village green, these land allocations withered away with the movement west. Land was designated in the grid as street or private lot, with some area for public development, but little for common open space. New York City evolved for 230 years before land was designated for Central Park.

The early Spanish towns had a different quality. They applied the 1573 settlement directives' 'Laws of the Indies' to the U.S. as its first planning code. The code called for a main square with all its public buildings to be established first. This square was to have a unified architectural appearance, and future development was to progress symmetrically from this center. The idea of the commons, a central public space not dedicated to movement, did not take hold as the dominant pattern, however. For better or worse, the grid in its many forms is urban America.

The gridiron urban pattern is a strange American mixture of abstract idealism, surveyors' expedience, and urban flexibility. It is a paradox: on the one hand implying the placeless expandability of our modern ideal, while on the other reinforcing the common ground of street life and form. For Americans, it symbolizes the city in its negative aspects while also harboring our remaining mixed-use neighborhoods. Its uniformity is often broken by the mix of different building types and ages, while the curving cul-de-sacs of suburbia often create sameness from forced variation. Its equality belies single-use zoning because its universal structure is adaptable to any use: once warehouses, then studios, then houses or offices. This layering of uses in time as well as space is the basis of a city's vitality.

Exceptions gain power from the 'normalcy' of the grid. Broadway cutting through Manhattan, La Font's system of diagonals and plazas, the interruptions of parks in Savannah, and the hierarchy of Philadelphia's cross axis are all amplified by the background of the grid. Variation is also created by differing use-patterns: active commercial streets, quiet residential areas, and civic or recreation zones. The grid itself has a subtle order of corner, base, entry, alley, and interior. Because the typical urban block was mostly laid out before the auto, it has a pedestrian dimension while being large enough to create a neighborhood. Its internal hierarchy of corner, street front, stoop, alley, and interior sets up a progression from public to private that is missing from its successor, the superblock or subdivision. Nature's topography and forms are strangely highlighted by the grid's order. San Francisco's hills distort and interrupt its streets, while the grid provides long views to the bay and delineates the form of the topography. Rivers and streams running through the grid carve out special views and parks. And waterfronts always create a special excitement. The interaction of the natural and abstract can in many cases reinforce and strengthen each other rather than diluting and compromising their order.

The negative image of the grid city has mostly to do with its recent history. The flight of wealth to the suburbs left the poor to control much of the inner-city fabric. And the invasion of the auto destroyed the quality and life of the street, the central asset of the urban fabric. Inner-city redevelopment tended to destroy mixed-use areas, substituting freeways, parking structures, office complexes, and shopping malls for the fine grain of the old city pattern. The street was the glue of urban neighborhoods, and its destruction led to the images of danger, desolation, and abandonment.

Perhaps there are better forms for the city — more personal, site-specific, romantic, or efficient. But the gridiron is the dominant pattern for the American city and must therefore be the genesis of future evolutions.

New York City's grid appears rigid in plan but in use is very diverse and complex.

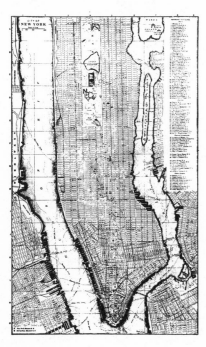

# *Case Study 1 — Sacramento: Transforming the Urban Tissue*

Sacramento is a classic American city. Its grid street layout is interrupted by a miniature version of the four-park symmetry of Philadelphia, designed by William Penn in the eighteenth century. The smaller parks, forming the focus of different neighborhoods, are arranged around the large Capitol building and its remarkable park.

This stonecut from 1870 highlights the historic importance of Sacramento's riverfront.

The Tower Bridge over the Sacramento River starts a grand axis that terminates at the Capitol. The neighborhood blocks have a north-south primary orientation with an alley system running east-west. The old housing pattern of large, closely-spaced Victorians facing the street was traditionally punctuated by corner shops and small service buildings on the alley. The streets are blessed by large elms and magnolia trees which form a complete street canopy modifying the hot summers and sheltering the pedestrians.     Since World War II, Sacramento has been attacked by many typical suburbanizing forces and destructive attempts at urban renewal. The growth of the suburbs first drained the residential population away from its employment center and dislocated the market for the downtown retail. The corrections applied were more devastating than the problems themselves:

5

freeways for commuters destroyed more neighborhoods and cut the city off from its waterfront; the retail area attempted to battle the shopping malls by imitation, closing the main shopping streets to cars, which just made the district more inaccessible and dangerous; and finally, the state created a high-rise master plan for its forty square blocks in the heart of the city. This plan was never completed, but it demolished more neighborhoods and left vast wastelands to be converted to parking lots.

This Ville Radieuse plan for state buildings was superseded by an 'urban village' plan developed by Governor Jerry Brown's administration. This plan attempted to correct the mistakes of the recent past by emphasizing conservation and diversity. Conservation meant more

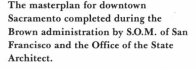

The masterplan for downtown Sacramento completed during the Brown administration by S.O.M. of San Francisco and the Office of the State Architect.

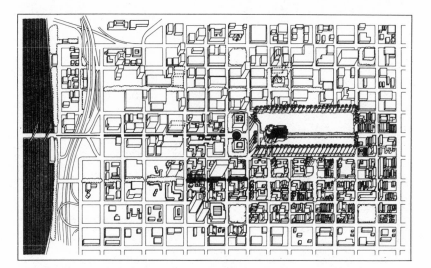

The masterplan called for diversity and mixed use within a city block. State offices, parking structures, and housing were to be developed in quarter block pieces.

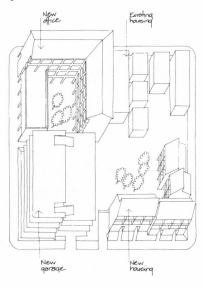

than simply saving a few worthy buildings or saving energy, but conserving the older qualities of the city: the mix of housing, local stores and workplaces, the 24-hour community, and the scale and diversity of old Sacramento neighborhoods. To recreate this mix and fulfill the requirements of the state for office space, the plan called for an incremental growth of low-rise new housing, rehabilitation of existing housing, and construction of new energy-efficient office buildings. Adding new housing for all income levels along with local restaurants and service retail, was seen as an opportunity for workers to live near their jobs. While reducing the need for commuting, the plan gave special attention to pedestrian amenities and solar access. Streets were designed for more than cars, and buildings had to respond to more than their internal needs. A four-story height limit and requirements that all new buildings use passive solar and climate-responsive design combined with the 'old' idea of mixed-use neighborhoods and with the 'old' idea of buildings that were less dependent on fossil fuels. Finally, the plan called for the new buildings to be compatible with the old. This requirement to fit meant that buildings contributed to a coherent whole rather than standing autonomously. It meant that they must maintain the scale and identity of the place rather than constantly redefining the neighborhood.

## *Housing*

Within this area, a one-block development of 106 affordable housing units was designed to meet the requirements of the master plan. It utilizes passive solar strategies at what may be the highest densities possible (43 units per acre) in combination with commercial space and a day-care facility.

The old Sacramento pattern of large detached dwellings, mid-block alleys, and commercial corners is reflected in the site plan. The massing offers three scales to the city: a 'hard' 3 1/2-story wall relating to the denser development on the north, a 2-story townhouse mews reconstituting the traditional alley, and a row of detached apartment buildings reflecting the scale of old Victorian buildings across the street. These scale shifts reinforce a sense of identity for the occupants while allowing a natural social zoning. The one- and two-bedroom units enter from the street, while the family units enjoy private yards and the safety of the inner block location. A variety of landscaped areas, unified by a bosque, provide for recreation, privacy, and cooling microclimate effects.

The buildings are oriented to the south and are spaced to allow winter solar access to each unit. Passive solar features are simple decorations and amenities: canvas shades, balcony overhangs, night

The masterplan for Sacramento invisioned a human scaled live-work neighborhood of low rise buildings. Pedestrian activity is encouraged by street treatments and residential infill.

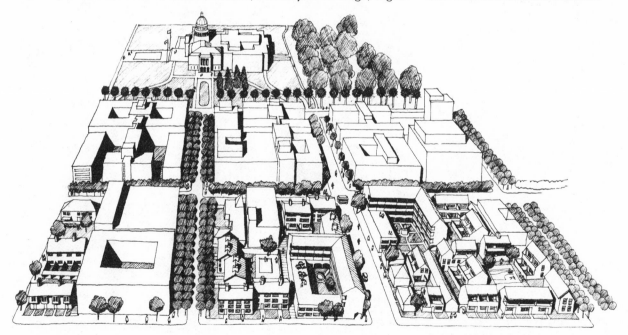

insulation curtains, and plaster on interior walls. The one-inch plaster acts as the thermal mass for cooling and heating while providing fire and acoustic separation. Beyond reducing the energy demands of the buildings, the simple act of creating housing in an area close to jobs and services helps to complete a neighborhood and dispel the 'bureaucratic monoculture' that Sacramento had become. Respecting the street life and configuring useful community space within such projects generates the shared domains so important to city life.

Although the project appears fairly standard, it manifests a significant deviation from current housing types, both suburban and urban. The mix of unit plans, from three-bedroom family townhouses through two-bedroom apartments designed for co-ownership to one bedroom units for elderly or single people, represents a cross section of the population combined in one neighborhood. This mix of different age groups and households is a reversal of our current segregated housing patterns: subdivisions for families, retirement villages or high-rises for the elderly, and condominiums for swinging singles. Such mixes were once the norm of cities and contributed to the synergy and wisdom of the social fabric.

The costs of the dwellings make them available to several income groups. One-third of the project is subsidized for low-income groups,

(Above) The passive solar system for Somerset Parkside involves no complex technology; south facing windows, canvas shades, cross ventilation, and plaster interiors for thermal mass are strategies for natural heating and cooling.

Somerset Parkside is a mixed income, mixed use development of 107 units of housing and six retail stores on a city block in Sacramento. At forty three units per acre it demonstrates that passive solar can function at urban densities.

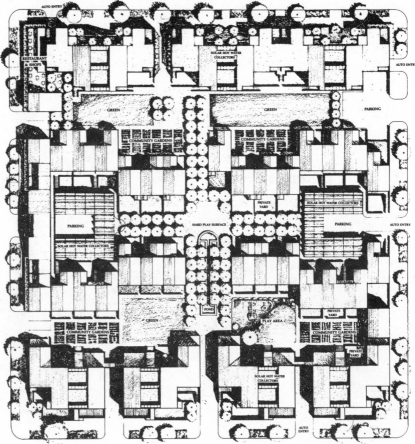

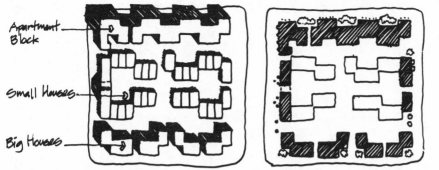

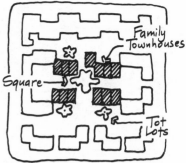

A. The overall plan includes a variety of Housing types and forms.

B. Single and double units are placed on the perimeter for street and urban orientation.

C. Family housing is clustered at the interior, a children's play area is nearby.

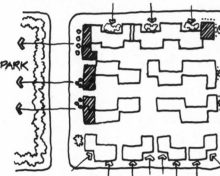

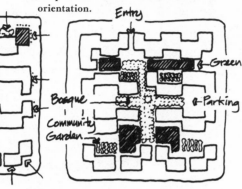

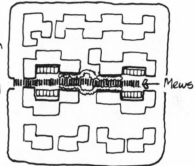

D. Shops face the parkside and front doors face the streets to enhance pedestrian activity.

E. A 'Bosque' of trees links various open spaces; greens, community gardens, entries and parking.

F. The Mews reinforces the Sacramento tradition of mid-block alleys.

one-third is priced for first-time buyers, and one-third is priced at the standard market rate. The income mix reaffirms a basic philosophical commitment to equality of opportunity and a rejection of the kind of economic segregation that breeds discrimination. Gentrification has become the standard result of much inner-city redevelopment. As proximity to work and to the vitality of the city is rediscovered by the middle class, the tendency has been to crowd out poor people left behind in the last swing to suburbia. But many studies have demonstrated that dense developments that take advantage of existing infrastructures are potentially extremely affordable. Therefore they are a unique opportunity to provide for all income groups, which should not be squandered. The health of a community rests on its ability to satisfy divergent needs rather than cater to a select elite.

The physical configuration of the block demonstrates several principles not widely incorporated in housing design. First, the project does not turn away from the street for security but attempts to reinforce its activities and identity. Housing entrances, overlooking balconies, corner commercial stores and restaurants, and landscaped streetside sitting areas all contribute to the life and ultimately the safety of the street. It is such affirmations of the street, attempting to make it more than a corridor for cars, that binds neighborhoods and

The fountain and Bosque of trees are a response to a hot summer climate.

ultimately cities together. The alternate is the fortress condominium, a monocultural island in a sea of cars, little more than a dense suburbia. This is a key environmental and social issue. One ecological purpose for higher-density living environments is to make a pedestrian life possible again, thereby reducing the energy, land, and pollution demands of the auto. But the pedestrian and most mass transit systems, for that matter, need paths that are safe and lively. If we build as if the environment is hostile, it undoubtedly becomes so; if we build for a sense of community, with public spaces that are shared and active rather than anonymous, we may not need tons of steel on wheels to protect us.

Walkable streets need not exclude the auto; in fact, it may be detrimental to do so. We do need a feeling that we are watched over, that there are activities and people around, that one will not be alone and vulnerable. Mixing alternate forms of transit helps: we always feel more comfortable walking on a streetcar route; it promises people and interest. Similarly a street with a bikeway tends to buffer the cars and slow them to a more cautious pace. Thermal comfort also plays a part. Walking across a hot parking lot could never match the cool comfort of old European arcaded streets or tree-lined boulevards. Pedestrian shelter is climate-dependent. In extremely hot desert climates, the street is apt to be fully covered, while in wetter climates, glass shelters such as the galleria in Milan are in order. For Sacramento, trees seem to be just right, providing shade in summer, allowing breezes to pass, and opening to the sun in winter. Such care for the pedestrian helps surrounding buildings with shade and cooler microclimates.

Walking needs to be interesting, and there is nothing more interesting than people or stores. Mixed-use planning is necessary not

Mimicking the old housing of Sacramento, the stairs and balconies reinforce activity on the street, increase security thru surveillance, and shade the large south facing windows.

only to bring activities closer together but also to line our paths with 'on the way' activities and chance meetings or rendezvous. Without the random meetings and local enterprise, it is hard to imagine a community or neighborhood existing. It is such personalization of public space and recognition of a special kind of possession of common ground which ultimately transforms our environment from a commodity into a community. Such possession is not legal or financial but has more to do with use and identity. A neighborhood must maintain a kind of squatters' rights relationship to the local public domain. In making it theirs, they render it more accessible to all.

In another project in Sacramento, the same attitude to the street is evident. A new light rail line is planned to link downtown Sacramento to its outlying areas with a station across the street from the project site. In response, two spaces for retail activities face the station, one a sidewalk cafe. Above, dwellings overlook the street with balconies over the cafe. A bank occupies the corner. The design works intimately with the new transit system, providing activities and meeting places for travelers, as well as eyes on the street for surveillance. In return, the light rail delivers customers for the stores, activity for spectators above and below, and an easy way to get around. The interaction between the two, public and private, may transform a street that had been merely an access to parking lots into a street for people.

Jane Jacobs, in **The Death and Life of Great American Cities**, advocates such streets, alive with diversity and density, as the panacea

Heilbron Place, a project designed jointly by Batey & Mack of San Francisco and VCM, addresses the street with a bank, stores and cafes at the ground level and residential balconies above.

The plan for Heilbron Place shows the diversity of building types and open space. The small site includes private yards, a shared court, private balconies, and a sidewalk cafe.

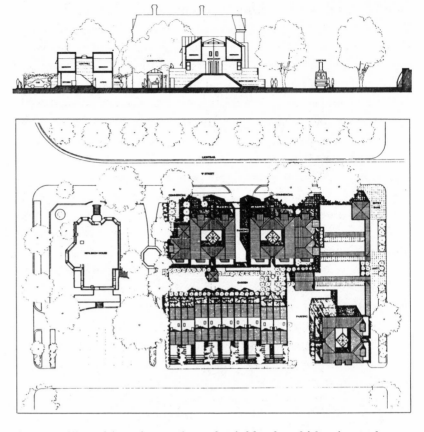

A housing unit spans a driveway in Somerset Parkside to transform a parking area into a semiprivate court.

for our ailing cities, the catalyst of neighborhood identity and community safety. Hers is a valid attack on the absurdity of high-rise apartments in superblock developments and the commercial destruction of finely grained local stores and neighborhoods.

But beyond the reaffirmation of the street, we are now challenged to reconstruct the structure of the block itself, respecting its history while addressing new demands for housing. Unlike the traditional housing in the city, there is now a justifiably greater demand for private open space and semiprivate zones in addition to active streets and common places of the neighborhood at large. The Somerset Parkside project develops a range of exterior places rarely found in Sacramento: from semiprivate entry courtyards, passive shared green space, and active commons such as the bosque and fountain, several barbeque areas, or the community garden areas, to private yards and decks. Even the parking areas are configured into courtyards. Formal gateways translate what are traditionally either completely private garages or public street parking into a semiprivate court.

A similar range of shared and private domains is developed in a project for 120 dwellings over two blocks in San Francisco, called Wisconsin Street Houses. The project works with the traditional housing type of the neighborhood, two- and three-story row houses, but manages to create more diversity than the typical public street and private yard.

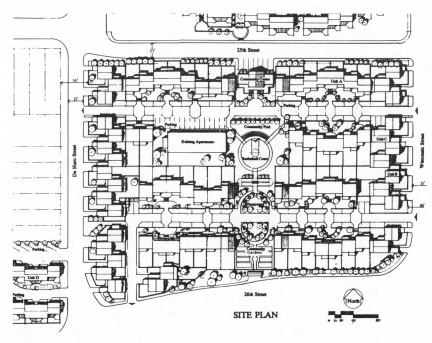

SITE PLAN

The plan of Wisconsin Street Houses shows the narrow private streets to be shared by pedestrians and cars. A central park bisects the site dividing the site into two smaller blocks more in keeping with the traditional neighborhood scale.

The interior streets are narrow and constantly interrupted by pedestrian bumps. Kids love to play on streets, whether safe or not. By making these streets alley-like, they become more private and safer than the larger neighborhood streets. The front yards of each housing cluster are shared. Overlooked by kitchen windows and decks, they become another area for kids or adults to get together. Maintaining the grid of the city, a large central park covers an abandoned right-of-way at the center of the project, with an amphitheater, basketball court, tot lots, community gardens, and a system of terraces and ramps. At its top is a community building and day-care facility. Built at the same density as the surrounding neighborhood, this project offers a larger variety of useful spaces and perhaps a more accessible community.

Another new criterion for housing infill should be energy efficiency. Given that heating and cooling can represent as much as 40 percent of a family's income, there is no reason that our current understanding of passive solar systems and conservation should not be applied to every new dwelling constructed in the U.S. — especially since most of the strategies make for more pleasing and livable buildings. Sunlight, good ventilation, adequate daylighting, sensitive landscaping, and sufficient insulation do more than save energy; they improve the quality of our lives and health. Differing climates obviously demand different design strategies with a positive effect of reinforcing the identity of place and people's connections to climate. Part of the rallying cry of the modern movement in architecture was to replace the unhealthy buildings of the past, lacking adequate ventilation, light, or heat, with a new generation of efficient social housing. Unfortu-

13

Community Center

The elevation of Wisconsin Street shows the primary facades facing south with windows providing views as well as passive solar heating. The Community center is located at the top of the central park.

nately, cheap energy and mechanical systems numbed their sensibilities, producing monotonous buildings based more on style and abstract form than on place or climate.

The requirements of solar access and adequate ventilation draw into question many modern and traditional housing types. The new design concerns are orientation, solar envelopes (building massing that doesn't shade adjacent buildings), quantities of glazing and thermal mass, landscaping, shading, and ventilation. Solar access defines an upper limit to housing densities for moderate latitudes of approximately 45 units per acre. This may be lower than some in cities, but matches others, such as Savannah, Georgia and Palladio's hometown Vincenzo, Italy, and can certainly maintain the finer aspects of urban life. The configuration and spacing can take many forms, but the criteria of intimate streets and open spaces imply low-rise forms. Two-to four-story building masses with human-scaled courtyards and parks between them can define a rich urban fabric with the added benefits of more accessible open space and light. Such densities are certainly adequate to maintain a local market for retail, a balance with employment, lively streets, and many options for mass transit.

The Somerset Parkside project demonstrates several housing forms that employ passive solar heating and cooling while maintaining urban densities and useful open space. The spacing allows winter sun to enter the primary living spaces of each unit. Each dwelling type, from row

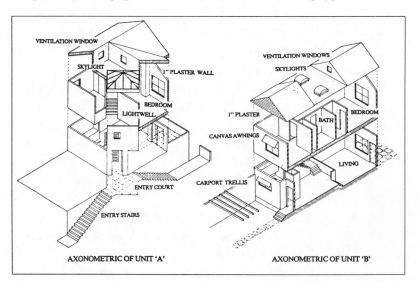

Energy efficient design for high density housing involves simple shaded south glass, cross ventilation, and thermal mass in the form of plaster interiors.

14

house to apartment, has cross ventilation from south to north exterior walls, as well as generous daylighting. In Heilbron Place, two-story spaces with clerestories at the roof provide ventilation and solar access for apartments with only one exterior wall. Some housing types are very difficult to adapt to such climate-responsive strategies. Apartment buildings with double-loaded corridors, for example, necessarily have half the dwellings with a poor orientation, and generally cannot provide cross ventilation. Older tenement forms are simply too dense, one building shading the other. Modern high-rises typically have double-loaded corridors, and their long winter shadows define wastelands of unusable space.

A more difficult problem is orientation. Often, the street calls for one orientation, while solar heating requires another. Luckily, most of the American grid cities were laid out on a simple north-south axis. The surveyor generally used magnetic north for simplicity, being oblivious to other forces — including, ironically, the sun. Throughout North America, this is within 20 degrees of true north. Sacramento is a case in point, as are New York, San Francisco, Chicago, and many others. This leaves the problem of the inevitable east and west streets. At the lower densities of the San Francisco project, approximately 20 units per acre, simply staggering the row houses allows south windows and yards for each house, while the front doors face the street completing the neighborhood. In denser conditions, roof apertures can supply solar heating for buildings with no south walls. Ultimately, a certain percentage will have to depend primarily on conservation. In Sacramento, the site plan for a complete block leaves only five out of 106 dwellings facing east or west. The city will never be a pure system; exceptions represent minor losses in relation to the overall economies of compact communities.

Many of these social and environmental design concerns can by summarized as an expansion of the now accepted philosophy of contextualism. For architects, contextualism is a retreat from the vain modern ethos of casting aside history and the influences of local concerns. For the progressive modernist, the function of a building was to define its form rather than its relationship with its neighbors or its responsibility to the larger urban framework. But contextualism is seen largely in formal terms by architects. The results are, in some cases, buildings which fit into their surroundings with more grace and modesty, but in others ,a Disneyland type of historical allusion, a caricature of the past without a real redefinition of the present.

All three of the housing projects take care to respect their surrounding buildings without specifically imitating them. Heilbron Place sets up a relationship of massing and bays to compliment the old Victorian mansion next door, while Somerset Parkside deals more generally with the surrounding building types. The San Francisco project uses

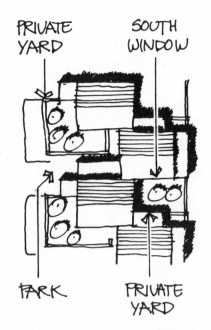

Difficult orientations for housing facing streets to the west or east can be overcome by jogging the units to provide south yards and windows.

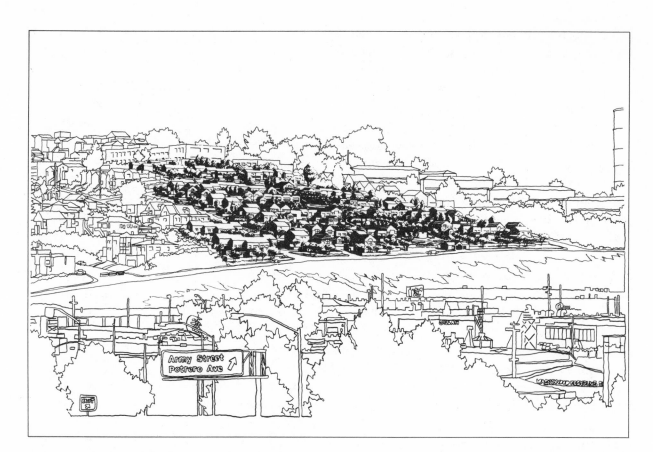

The overall design for Wisconsin Street matches the texture and scale of the surrounding neighborhood in order to reinforce the identity of the place.

the familiar form of gable roofs and identifiable houses to match the qualities of the surrounding area and to help complete the neighborhood, rather than stand apart from it.

A broader interpretation of context would move beyond the visual to the social, environmental, economic, and climatic context of a place. Buildings then respond to the public needs as well as their private function, participate in creating a larger whole rather than expressive piece, and respect the uniqueness of the place rather than the mechanistic universality of modern industry. The neighborhoods described here begin to demonstrate such a contextualism: responding to the needs of the neighborhood by reinforcing the street while providing for the private needs of the inhabitants with internal spaces; responding to the specifics of the local climate while respecting the urban traditions; fitting in visually by using sympathetic forms while modifying the plans to satisfy current household types. In effect, the future as well as the past is taken as the context of our built environment.

## The Workplace

Like the design of the dwellings, the design of our workplace in the city will undergo radical transformations. Once the segregation of work and home is broken and the freeway link reduced, the form and criteria of the workplace will become a part of a neighborhood again, rather than floating as the focus of many dispersed and incomplete bedroom communities. Once again, our cities can nurture new forms, similar in scale and type, but different in content and environmental function. Such buildings can be of a variety of sizes, from small storefront offices integrated with housing to larger buildings that still respond to the needs of the user, street, neighborhood, and climate.

In fact, there is a synergy between social, environmental, and individual concerns. The courtyard, for example, used as a thermal buffer for energy conservation, offers an identity and generosity rarely matched by our more modern lobby or elevator core. The low-rise building tends to be more compatible in a mixed neighborhood, to have a more human scale on the street, avoiding large shadows, and is more walkable than its high-rise counterparts. Similarly, balconies and porticoes that provide shade serve social as well as energy ends. Under the pressure to maximize rentable space, the shared parts of a building have shriveled to double-loaded corridors and boiler basements, and the public edges have been reduced to oversized parking lots or windswept plazas. The alternates are clear: buildings that respect their climate and neighborhood as well as corporate image and productivitity.

There is an interesting contrast in Sacramento between several state office buildings, some built in the 1960s and some in the '70s. State Office Buildings 8 and 9 (called OB-8 and OB-9 in bureaucratic jargon) are two identical high- rise buildings set back from the street by a partly walled plaza. Their height casts winter shadows over three blocks to the north, making housing in those areas undesireable, and reinforcing the single-use urban strategy implicit in their design. Though they are unusual in having exterior shades, their tinted glass eliminates the possibility of natural lighting and necessitates an interior bathed with fluorescent illumination. The buildings are symmetrical, ignoring the implications of the sun or the qualities of different streets around them. This indifference to climate results in annual energy loads of approximately 150,000 BTUs per square foot. The lobbies are grand but offer no place to linger, meet, or socialize. The plaza to the north of one of the buildings is cold and uncomfortable most of the winter, and, because the street trees were eliminated, too hot in the summer. From a distance, the buildings are an identifiable monument looming above the tree canopy, but from the street, they present no life and offer no shelter or public activity. Like most modern buildings, they ignore the climate, the neighborhood, and the qualitative needs of their occupants, favoring an abstract expression of uniform space.

In contrast, the state office building across the street, called the

**Two state office buildings contrast two design philosophies; towers OB-8 and OB-9 set back from the street with equal facades and equal floors of artificial light and the Bateson building low rise, energy efficient and daylit.**

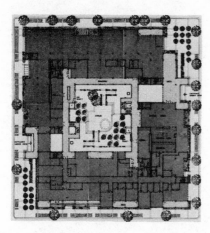

The plan of Bateson Building shows the courtyard which organizes the space and provides light to the interior.

The section drawing calls out the climate responsive features of the building. These include movable shades, concrete construction for thermal mass, the courtyard as thermal buffer and night ventilation.

Bateson Building after the renowned anthropologist Gregory Bateson, attempts to respond to a broader range of concerns. Its plan is nearly the inverse of OB-8 and 9: built to the street edge, at four stories high, with a solar courtyard in the center. The courtyard is warmed in the winter by the sun, cooled in summer with night ventilation and shades. The building is friendly to the pedestrian, offering small sheltered plazas located at two of its corners, the maintenance of the existing street trees, and a small landscaped buffer along the sidewalk. The courtyard has become a special place for workers and the public to meet, have lunch, listen to speakers or performers, and generally socialize. Simultaneously, the courtyard acts as a thermal buffer for the building, reducing heat loss and heat gain through the walls, and providing daylight to the interior. On the exterior, balconies provide shade, add life to the street, and give workers easy access to the outside at each level. A large dining balcony is located over the main entry overlooking the park. Each facade is different in response to its solar orientation: the south is shaded by deep trellises and decks, the east and west have canvas shades that retract, and the north has simple clear glass for daylighting. This facade variation, along with the decks, wood infill siding, and landscaping, make the building more compatible in a mixed residential neighborhood. Many of its climate-responsive systems, which reduce annual energy consumption to

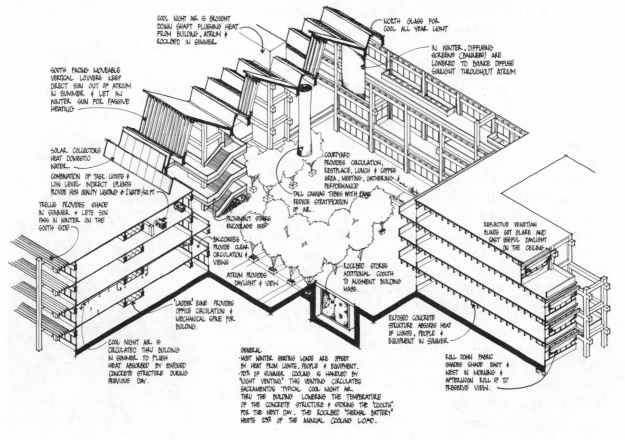

The courtyard of the Bateson Building has no artificial heating or cooling but remains comfortable year around with passive solar heat from the south facing skylights and night ventilation.

25,000 BTUs per square foot per year result in a more varied and satisfying work environment. For example, the use of the concrete structure to store the night's coolness eliminates the typical low ceilings and natural lighting may be in some unquantifiable way more interesting and humane than the homogeneous consistency of artificial light.

Two other office buildings built at the same time demonstrate the same principles. Both are built around courtyards and maintain an intimate relationship with the street. The courtyards, shaded by a canvas structure in one case and open in the other, are important social points, both for the workers and the city at large. As in housing, semiprivate places such as these support the conviviality necessary for healthy city life. Without places such as these, people retreat into their private world, losing any common identity or responsibility.

The courtyard is a traditional urban type. It seems to be the natural consequence of buildings that follow the street and need natural lighting. The notion that they serve an important social function was abandoned when cheap energy eliminated the need for windows to ventilate or light the interior of buildings. Without the hierarchy of public street, courtyard, and private room, our cities become anonymous, one place much like the next, with both the individual

The California Energy Commission building has a courtyard shaded by a canvas tensile structure. This partially interior space serves as a social gathering point and the primary circulation of the building.

19

Site 1-C uses fixed shades on the exterior which give it a highly textured, massive feeling. Its interior has an open air courtyard shared with a parking structure.

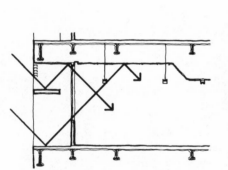

The high ceilings along the perimeter, the external light shelf, and the shading allow deep penetration of natural lighting without the glare and heat of direct sunlight. The ceiling is an unobstructed plane which will reflect daylight to the workspace.

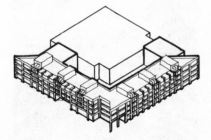

Fixed horizontal and vertical elements shade the building from direct sunlight while reflecting daylight into the building. The vertical elements prevent penetration of low angled morning and afternoon sun.

and the community losing the locus of identity. In some intractable way, climate-responsive design forces buildings to become more locally and socially responsible.

Another example of such design is a project for the General Services Administration in San Jose. In this case, a large shaded pedestrian street with overlooking balconies reduces the building's cooling loads and provides a comfortable place for worker and public interaction. Lined with shops at the ground floor, the semisheltered space is a gift to the city at no expense to the individual building. Once again, mixed-use buildings help make the city more livable and are more compatible in a residential area.

The use of daylight in commercial buildings also transforms their social and urban identity. The simplest daylight building is narrow from wall to wall, with high interior ceilings. This implies smaller working groups in more spacious environments with better views. The site 1-C building in Sacramento follows this pattern. There, facades are richly textured by the shading devices necessitated by the use of clear glass. Such buildings ultimately maintain a responsibility to admit natural light to their surroundings. Such access implies a low-rise though dense pattern of contained urban 'rooms.' Mirror glass faces and high-rise wind effects give way to sunshades and landscaped courtyards. In every case, the environmental concerns reinforce the common spaces — in some cases creating places that had been eliminated by 'the building as machine' ethic; in others, making existing domains more habitable.

It seems obvious that all buildings, and especially those we work in, should integrate with their neighborhood, be energy-efficient, and support a sense of community as well as privacy and concentration. The industrial vision was of buildings for efficient production. Even dwellings were reduced to an abstract list of functions: eating, sleeping, shitting, talking. The built environment was seen as a kind of factory to manufacture the desired products. We now find that the resources to maintain such a simpleminded view of existence are overwhelming. And that even in succeeding, too much has been left out.

20

# Case Study 2 — Philadelphia: Urban Conservation

In contrast to Sacramento, Philadelphia's residential neighborhoods have not been subjected to devastating urban renewal programs or large scale reconstruction. Its turn-of-the-century buildings and urban patterns are largely intact, though decaying. Like many sections of our older urban centers, it represents an opportunity for rehabilitation and adaptive reuse. The neighborhoods are in need of sensitive repair and updating rather than redesign. The common transit systems need to be reinforced, the energy efficiency of the dwellings upgraded, the economics of local business stabilized, the quality of open space and the strength of the community increased. Here, as in the other examples, improving the ecological character of the place goes hand in hand with solving some serious social and economic problems. Philadelphia's time frame is not the future but the present: the social and economic needs of the site's inhabitants are severe and current, and the neighborhood evolution must begin now if it is to survive.

## Context

The site is an aging residential/warehousing neighborhood in the central section of the city. On its north side, Schuylkill Park, rehabilitation of this extremely valuable (economically, historically, and aesthetically) portion of the city is under way. This 'gentrification,' while certainly improving both the physical and economic health of the city, also has negative side effects, such as the displacement of the original inhabitants and speculation on land and housing stock. Its south side, not yet attracting outside investment, remains a 'rundown' neighborhood with a poor and largely unemployed population, an intrinsic lack of identity of place, and a decaying infrastructure called Gray's Ferry. Within this context of change, the patterns of resource allocation and energy consumption within the site are inequitable, wasteful, and unsound. Schuylkill Park South's population is primarily upper-middle-class and white. Its urban fabric is a well-maintained pattern of two- and three-story attached row houses, aligned along a regular street grid, with east-west alleys bisecting each block. The beauty of the historic townhouses and the intimate scale of streets still paved with brick and lined with rows of trees are making the neighborhood one of the more attractive residential sections of the entire city, continuing the pattern set by the revival of Rittenhouse Square and Society Hill.

The study site is on the west side of central Philadelphia along the Schuylkill River and bridges two distinct neighborhoods; Grey's Ferry and Schuylkill Park.

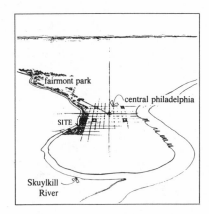

21

Schuylkill Park South is an area of fine old townhomes and brick paved streets which has undergone 'gentrification' for some time.

In the Gray's Ferry neighborhood, the pattern of street grid and housing type is identical, but a sense of decay is predominant. Repeating another tragic but familiar pattern of urban reality, the unemployment rate exceeds 20-30 percent, housing ownership is low, and the crime rate high.

The neighborhood, however, has several physical assets which, over the next few years, will bring opportunities for change. First is its location. The railroad right-of-way bordering the river is scheduled to be converted to a linear park, connecting the recently completed park at the west end of the site to the Museum of Fine Art and Fairmont Park, lying to the northwest of the City Center. This link, and the neighborhood's walking-distance proximity to the campuses of the University of Pennsylvania and Drexel University as well as several medical schools and teaching hospitals will surely bring an influx of young professional families seeking inexpensive but sound houses to renovate, and the inevitable speculation that accompanies gentrification.

## Energy Consumption

The site's major energy consumption characteristics were estimated by extrapolation from data for the entire city of Philadelphia. The site's residential neighborhoods are the area's major energy consumers. Most houses are heated by natural gas furnaces, and approximately 10 percent have one or more window air conditioners (air conditioners are more prevalent in the partially gentrified South Schuylkill neighborhood). Over 60 percent of the neighborhood's nontransportation energy comes from natural gas, 25 percent from

A map of the area shows a similar building pattern and street system for the two very different neighborhoods. The park along the river will link the two socially distant areas.

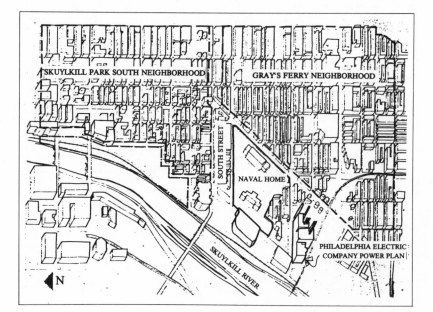

oil, and 11 percent from electricity. Space and water heating, therefore, are by far the neighborhood's greatest energy cost. Space cooling would also be significant if all the site's residents could afford air conditioners. Currently, most make do with window fans to alleviate the muggy heat of July and August.

The energy consumption of the industrial and commercial sector has a small impact, given the limited number of active commercial and industrial buildings. Energy used in transportation, however, is a significant source of consumption on the site, probably approaching 50 percent of the site's total consumption. Since the neighborhoods are well-served by mass transit, this sector's consumption is likely to be reduced only if service and light manufacturing businesses are attracted to the site, thus allowing the neighborhood's residents to walk to work.

It must be noted that the energy-related problems of the site's two neighborhoods are quite different: South Schuylkill's residents can and will attach storm windows, and will have furnace tune-ups, hot-water-heater blankets, and expensive but fuel-efficient cars. Gray's Ferry residents must generally make do with gas guzzlers, leaky windows, and elderly furnaces much in need of repair. Consequently, although the site's poorer residents live, often literally, lower on the hog than their neighbors to the north, they often must consume more energy to do it.

Grey's Ferry neighborhood has not experienced 'gentrification' as yet, but as the pressure for housing near the city center grows, renovation and repairs may be accompanied by displacement.

## Design Goals

Any attempt to address the physical problems that this site presents must first be informed by an understanding of the main socioeconomic factors and patterns of energy and resource use which generated the existing conditions.

The decayed building stock, worn out infrastructure and ghetto social condition of much of the urban fabric surrounding the commercial/financial district of our older cities is a residual condition of, among other factors, an investment policy. This policy directed the nation's major capital investments in housing and commercial activities mainly into the city centers on one side, and into suburban sprawl on the other. The poorest stratas of the cities' population, usually nonwhite ethnic groups, were the recipients of the left-over portion of our cities, namely the peripheral center city.

Beginning in the late '60s, private investment in rehabilitation began to trickle into several of these run-down neighborhoods, the process being fueled by the growing appeal of the central city. Initially, 'urban homesteading' and gentrification appealed to the growing number of childless married couples desiring a small home more conveniently located to the cultural amenities of the city than suburbia. Following the OPEC oil embargo of 1974, the increasing cost of energy, and, consequently, the desire to lessen dependence on the automobile further undermined the avantages of living in the suburbs. Finally, in several cities, there has been continuous expansion, vertically and horizontally, of the central district, pushing far outside its own boundaries.

This pressure for rehabilitation has even spread to such hard-core ghettos as Harlem, where 60 percent of the remaining residential property has been abandoned by its owners to city ownership. A recent lottery for the disposal of twenty-four boarded-up but structurally sound and architecturally handsome brownstones brought two hundred and fifty applicants.

The past and present reality of the process of rehabilitation and physical improvement of an inner-city residential neighborhood has been the de facto eviction of its population. Consequently, a strategy for intervention which would not automatically displace the existing population from the neighborhood, while improving its environmental and economic health, is a major goal.

From a social point of view, Gray's Ferry currently has no unique identity or sense of cohesiveness, and consequently little political influence over its future. A primary political goal, therefore, is to instill a sense of community in the neighborhood. Such a stake in the future has no hope of taking hold while the neighborhood's people are themselves without hope for their future. Therefore, the initial work of the 'bootstrapping' of the neighborhood is the improving of the economic health of its residents by helping them to reduce their cost of living and creating sources of employment. A substantial part of these actions would be concerned with the neighborhood's building stock: the 'do-it-yourself' and 'sweat equity' upgrading of the housing stock, aided by some outside entrepreneurial investment and 'pump priming' from government, would not only reduce utility bills and improve comfort but would also start a market for small local construction-related businesses.

The second phase of the project would involve the improvement of the environment between the buildings, both to serve as the neighborhood's summer 'living room' and to attract new investment. A visually improved neighborhood would in turn attract the wider market and investment needed to adapt the neighborhood's largest physical assets for new purposes, thereby stabilizing both the neighborhood's economic base and physical environment.

The phases of the physical upgrading of the neighborhood described above may lead to its economic and political self-sufficiency, but also constitute its gentrification.

This is a very real worry to neighborhood residents of modest means. In Harlem, for example, many applicants for the surplus brownstones were white professionals seeking center city housing but unable to find or afford even so much as a flat south of 110th Street. The site's real challenge, and one only partially met by the team, was the design of a process for control of the neighborhood's future by its community. This may not be possible, as the imbalance in the allocation of resources extends far beyond the neighborhood's influence, but the general failure of the trickle-down tradition to improve the lot of the neighborhoods such as Gray's Ferry requires that the neighborhood organize itself as a community and move to help itself if it is to survive.

## Design Solutions

In the design of an urban sustainable community, its energy conservation ethic, the creation of on-site jobs, and the improvement of its physical and environmental condition are interdependent elements. For example, mixed-use neighborhood planning has been shown to reduce transportation energy consumption. Similarly, on-site food production would create jobs, reduce energy consumption for food transportation, and enliven and regenerate the physical environment (street farming, community gardens, etc.). Local light industry, producing energy and conservation tools and components for the rehabilitation of the neighborhood, would also create jobs, as well as provide a market for small service businesses, thus tending to recycle income several times through the community.

The rehabilitation of the residential block identified three simultaneous goals: generating jobs, conserving resources and energy, and 'reinhabiting' the physical environment. One of the first elements to be considered with these goals in mind is the street itself. In planning for a future in which we all have to do more with less, the current organization of the street patterns seems disfunctional and obsolete. A large amount of space is taken over by parked cars, thus making the asphalt area unnecessarily large. Every neighborhood street, independent of the amount of traffic carried, is equally dimensioned. There should be a hierarchy in traffic patterns, reflected in the use and the dimension of the neighborhood streets. Streets running north-south and carrying more traffic should be maintained much as they are: multilaned arterials with parking along both curbs. The streets running on an east-west axis could be treated to leave only a paved path for drop-offs and emergency access with few parking spaces provided. Such streets would be similar to the 'woonerfs' or 'street-yards' widely used on lightly traveled streets in the Netherlands. The necessary additional parking spaces would be provided along adjacent north-south streets, or concentrated in one area serving the entire block. Such areas could be created by displacing the ground floor

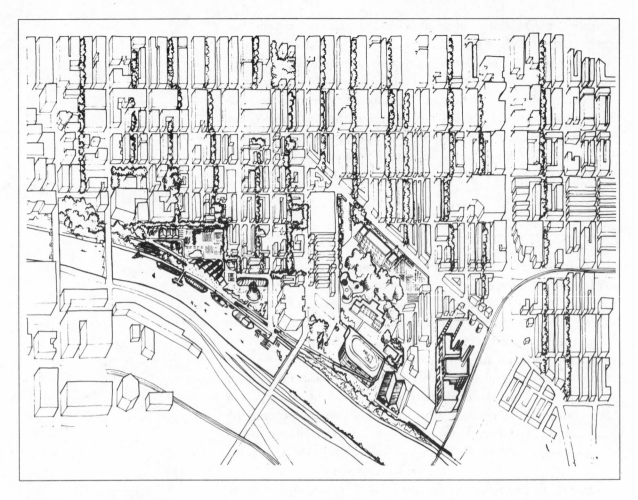

An overview of the modifications proposed for the two neighborhoods; limited access residential streets, waterfront park, renovated Naval Home, and aquasystems developed on the river.

A greenhouse addition on the south facade serves a townhouse as entry vestibule, insulation, a passive solar heater, and can produce vegetables year round.

of one or two townhouses, located in the 'courtyards' within the interior of each block or in parking structures.

The cross streets, freed from the function of warehousing immobile cars, can be 'reinhabited' several ways. Their northern sidewalk, being the sunnier, can be widened to allow enough space for the installation of attached greenhouses and of food-producing gardens. Trees, playgrounds, and benches would be added to provide a summer living room for those living in the adjacent houses. These features, often considered the trappings of gentrification, are actually among the most important to a neighborhood population that moves onto the front stoop on summer evenings while their unair-conditioned houses cool off. In planning for the future, when it is likely that there will be fewer auto trips per resident and more pedestrian activity, the urban front yard and the immediate neighborhood should invite outdoor activity and neighborhood communication, rather than present the passerby with the cold shoulder we have accepted in the past.

While such strategies may seem quixotic in an alienated, high-crime neighborhood, there is a precedent, even in Philadelphia. The city sponsors an existing and successful 'urban gardens program,' which

helps community groups to trace the owners of vacant lots, and get permission to use the lots for gardens, and also gives technical advice from a professional staff. In Gray's Ferry this activity would be extended to almost every unused flat area: backyards, front yards, sidewalks, and even in plastic greenhouses on the roofs of houses able to support the load of plants grown in boxes of compost.

The 'reinhabiting' of the neighborhood's side streets, while certainly improving the ambience of the neighborhood, also serves another, more pressing need: security. A street that has become a 'front yard' and a 'turf' under the eye of the block's residents will have fewer cases of street crime than a no-man's-land 'owned' by the city.

The building stock of the neighborhood is sound but sadly in need of repair. By far the most attractive means of improving the energy efficiency of the neighborhood's houses and thereby reducing their inhabitants' cost of living, is through basic rehabilitation: installing attic insulation, repointing brickwork, rebuilding and caulking wood windows, adding storm windows and doors, and all this done by local businesses. These actions taken together, would reduce a Gray's Ferry row house's annual heating bill by almost 45 percent.

A large percentage of the remaining space-heating and water-heating needs of the row house could be met by solar energy. The limited height of the two- to three-story row houses, the generous street width (generally 40-50 feet), and the favorable east-west block alignment allow adequate solar access. The roof and at least one facade of each row house can usually be counted on for winter solar access (the second-

Limited access residential streets would mix pedestrian and autos while creating room for play areas, gardens, and greenhouses. Such streets, called "Woonerf" in Holland, have been used with much success in Europe.

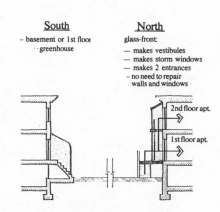

Greenhouse additions can serve on both north and south facades; on the south they act as passive solar heaters and extra space, on the north they can act as entry vestibules and replace detailed weatherization.

27

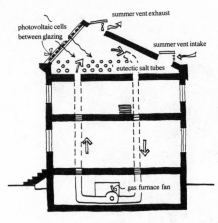

photovoltaic cells between glazing

summer vent exhaust

summer vent intake

eutectic salt tubes

gas furnace fan

The 'solar attic' is a way of utilizing roof areas as passive solar heaters. A south facing skylight heats a phase change material in the attic which stores the heat until distributed through the forced air furnace system.

floor facade only on some narrow blocks). The 'trombe wall' system and/or the installation of attached greenhouses would be the most favorable strategy for passive solar heating in these conditions, the necessary thermal mass being conveniently provided by the existing masonry exterior wall of the houses. Additional thermal mass can be added within the house in the form of phase-change thermal storage (eutectic salts), a material particularly appropriate for solar retrofit.

Additional thermal storage would be useful in summer as well. Coupled with a large attic or window fan, the storage would help the house remain cool during the day by absorbing heat to melt the salts. At night, the house would be continually ventilated to provide cooling air movement for its occupants as well as carrying away the heat stored in the thermal storage.

An energy conversion system suited to the neighborhood's climate and density is the block-scale co-generation plant or 'total energy' system. Such a system would be built around several generator sets powered by internal-combustion engines. These machines, currently marketed abroad by Fiat and Mitsubishi, combine a water jacket heat exchanger with the engine/generator set, thus allowing the machine to produce hot water as well as electricity. In the case of the Philadelphia site, each block of 40-50 row houses would be served by several TOTEMs (Fiat's brand name: Total Energy Module) connected to both the utility power grid and, through a pumped piping loop and heat exchanger, to each house's furnace and hot water heater. Each block has at least one or two houses in particularly bad shape and subject to demolition, which, if rehabilitated, could house the TOTEMs. These rehabilitated spaces would also provide space for other community services: a laundromat, a Mom and Pop store, a play area, and a community garden toolshed, thus becoming a major meeting point for the neighborhood.

The TOTEMs themselves would be owned by a limited partnership of investors, with the neighborhood's block members, church groups or community organizations serving as general partners. The outside investors would supply the investment cash in return for investment tax credits and accelerated depreciation deductions. The operating costs of the system would be covered by natural gas costing $2.40 per million BTUs to generate electricity that is sold to the local utility at its marginal generating cost of 5-6 cents per KWH ($14.50-$17.50 per million BTUs). This 600-percent markup would show a modest profit, as well as cover the system's operation, maintenance, and repair costs by a neighborhood-owned firm. The occupants of the block's row houses therefore receive free heat and water in return for their maintaining a community organization active enough to run the neighborhood utility. There are two strategies for operating the block-scale utility, depending on the partnership's goals. One

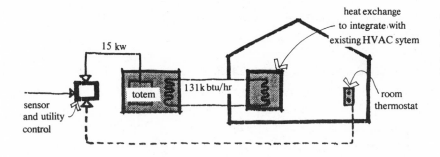

strategy is to run each block's system flat-out all year, in order to generate the maximum return on investment from the sale of electricity. This option's drawback is the accelerated wear and tear on the systems themselves and the relatively low thermodynamic efficiency of the process. While all of the electricity generated would be used, only 30-40 percent of the system's annual heat output would be needed by the block's houses. The utility's overall input/output efficiency is about 40 percent, which is equivalent to that of the electric utility combined with the gas furnaces that presently serve the block.

An alternative strategy is to use the TOTEM only when heat is needed by the block's houses or when electricity can be sold at peak rates, typically on summer afternoons. This option would be less profitable to the partnership, but would be substantially more energy-efficient: over 85 percent of the TOTEM's natural gas input would be converted to usable heat and electricity.

In new developments, physical form can, to some extent, encourage the social interactions that foster community. In Gray's Ferry, the restoration of the community must precede physical changes, for without a strong local organization, physical improvements will not benefit the neighborhood's current inhabitants: they will already have been displaced. Ironically, the cohesiveness necessary for the neighborhood to survive will not center around energy but around the 'benign neglect' of the neighborhood by city government in the form of inadequate police and fire protection, street lighting, and maintenance of the neighborhood's infrastructure.

However, once a group is galvanized into action by, say, a rash of vandalism ignored by the police, it can also move to take control of the neighborhood's seat in the city council. With political representation comes the power to change the way things are done to benefit the neighborhood. For instance, following the trend of many cities, Philadelphia could contract many of its maintenance services out to private firms which often can do the job better at less cost to the taxpayer. For example, the Gray's Ferry neighborhood organization could contract with the city to maintain its own streets, using tax funds to maintain them by 'reinhabiting' each cross street.

Open space within neighborhoods, such as the 21-acre Naval Home, should be developed into multipurpose community facilities such as gardens, open playgrounds, recreational areas, and parks.

## Adaptive Re-use of the Naval Home and J.F.K. Building

One of the major challenges of the site is to coherently integrate its separate elements: the residential blocks, the railroad right-of-way, the river, the Naval Home, the J.F.K. Center, and the power plant. The resulting pattern must also relate to the rest of the city: the adjacent neighborhoods, Fairmont Park and the Center City on the north, and the universities beyond the river to the west.

Within the site, the 21-acre vacant Naval Home presents a major opportunity for creating an important focal point. Because of the large park area available and the presence of historic structures within, it seems that a multi-use approach is preferred. An environmental and energy educational center, linked to the power station and the J.F.K. Center is proposed. Specifically, the park could be used for several functions: as an urban horticultural development center with demonstration gardens where technical assistance and training could be offered citywide; as open community gardens for ornamental plants and food production; as a community park enriched by the presence of large existing trees; and/or as a neighborhood community center providing day-care facilities, a health clinic, meeting rooms, a teen center, and a children's playground.

The other structure that merits particular attention is the J.F.K. Vocational Center. Only partially utilized, it is at 1.2 million square feet, one of the largest commercial buildings in Philadelphia. The citywide policies of energy conservation, housing rehabilitation, and job creation are interrelated goals that could be assisted by the existence of light industry connected to these fields. The J.F.K. Center would be an ideal location for such enterprises. The type of production to be encouraged could be that of solar collectors, greenhouse kits, storm windows, insulation materials, etc. Since the building is located at the southern end of a 26-mile bicycle trail, a bicycle factory, modeled on the famous Fiat Building built in the '20s in Turin, could be developed with a testing circuit right on the roof.

## The Schuylkill River Park

The pier across the Schuylkill River at the Water Temple (one mile upstream from the J.F.K. Center) has effectively divided the river into industrial (downstream) and recreational (upstream) uses. The development of the railroad right-of-way into a linear riverside park will open access to the lower river for recreation. A concept extensively tested on a smaller scale at the New Alchemy Institute would be located along the shore to generate visitor activity, provide jobs, and help clean the river: a barge-borne fish farm. Used gravel barges, 200-300 feet

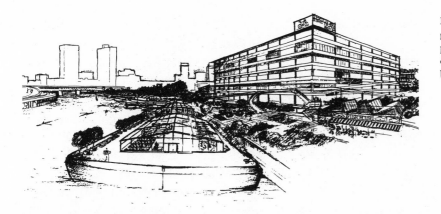

Fish farms located on renovated, used gravel barges would line the river's edge, providing jobs and fresh fish while cleaning the river water with its biological system.

long and 40-50 feet wide, would be purchased at $40,000- $50,000 each and nested along the river bank between the J.F.K. Center and the power plant. Large, translucent plastic cylinders or even free-standing plastic swimming pools would be closely packed in the barges' holds and sheltered by inexpensive poly-covered commercial greenhouses. River water would be pumped into the first barge's cylinder, where a roofed, plant-based ecosystem (water hyacinths, bulrushes, etc.) would strip out the toxic substances, cleaning the water. The purified river water would then be pumped into the following barges, where catfish would be grown for the wholesale market. Each barge, if managed to capacity, might produce up to a million pounds of fish per year. The effluent from the fish tanks would again be cleaned by biological action and returned to the river.

In one of the synergies common to design for sustainability, the greenhouses covering the barges are also excellent environments for the propagation of flats of ornamental and vegetable plant crops for resale to commercial nurseries. Those 'bioshelters' provide a visual focus and center of activity on the waterfront, around which might grow sports facilities, an open-air theater, a cafe, and a canoe rental concession to anchor the southern end of the Schuylkill River Park. Furthermore, the fish farm's proximity to the power station might allow the waste heat from the steam condensers to be used to heat the fish tanks during the periods when the station is generating electricity.

## The Power Plant

One of the major opportunities for the on-site conversion of energy is the existing Schuylkill Generating Station, located at the site's southwest corner. The plant's equipment is obsolete and its inefficient turbo-generators are used only for summer peaking power. However, it has a considerable district heating capability serving, through the existing city heating distribution system, buildings of the University of Pennsylvania and the commercial/financial district. Ironically, no part of the adjacent neighborhood is served by the district heating system.

The plant is currently utilized at no more than 25 percent of its capability. The Philadelphia Electric Company (PECO) has no plan for its repowering, relying instead on projected nuclear capacity to meet its base loads.

Given the insatiable demand of nuclear projects now under construction for very expensive financing, PECO's reliance on the nuclear solution seems ill-advised, especially in a region well served by coal resources. While the Schuylkill station could not be economically repowered to burn coal (which would not be legal within city limits anyway) it could, due to its central location, very efficiently provide both electricity and heat to the downtown area. Using the 'combined cycle' concept, an increase in generating efficiency, from the current 25 percent to 40-45 percent could be economically realized by either replacing the existing boilers or installing gas turbines to generate electricity alongside the boilers. Waste heat recovered from the gas turbines' 700 degrees F exhaust would then be recycled through steam generators to power turbo-generators or to feed steam into the district heating system. The input/output efficiency of such a system might be close to the 85 percent enjoyed by block- scale TOTEMs operated in the same way to follow their 'customer's' heating load.

The question of expanding the district heating system so as to serve the adjacent neighborhood is more complex, since the necessary construction would require a considerable initial capital investment. If, however, the district distribution system is installed in conjunction with the other street work proposed, the incremental costs might be manageable. The use of combined cycle urban power plants to heat their surrounding neighborhoods as well as generate electricity is a common practice in northern Europe. The economics of such stations, however, are based on a somewhat higher building density than the two- to three-story Gray's Ferry neighborhood, and a much colder climate.

## Conclusion

Although these two case studies, Philadelphia and Sacramento, are necessarily unique, the design principles applied to their reconstruction or rehabilitation have broad application. Reversing the flight to suburbs and making cities responsive to our current social and environmental needs is a design, an economic, and a social problem.

As a design problem, it requires reexamining the assumptions of modern architecture, moving beyond simple internal functionalism to a philosophy of contextualism. Buildings have a responsibility beyond their walls. Their location and density control the kind of transportation mix that is viable; their climatic intelligence controls the number of power plants we build and the amount of energy we import; their configuration affects the health of the community; and their sensitivity either raises our spirits or dulls our exuberance.

As an economic problem, redirecting growth away from sprawl implies a basic shift in value. Long-term life-cycle costing and replacement must become the criteria rather than relatively short run profit margins. Irreplaceable agricultural land and wilderness areas must be revalued; the costs of commuting must be calculated in terms of the long-term value of oil, the health costs of pollution, and the time value of the rider; and the costs of housing must be expanded to include maintenance and energy.

As a social problem, reurbanization questions the relationship and proportion between public and private space. The domination of private transportation, private recreation, private open space, and private dwelling must shift. Given a rational physical layout, more of our essential possessions and needs can be shared without compromising livability. This requires that our well-being be based less on commodities and more on community.

In classical Greece, one wasn't considered a complete person unless one were part of a *polis*; the definition of citizen was tied to the notion of city, community, and shared responsibility. Banishment from the city was therefore the ultimate punishment. In a sense, modern industrial culture has banished most of us from that essential connection with our environment, community, and our *polis*. Our future lies in reestablishing those links.

# The Suburban Context

*Sim Van der Ryn*

There is no more important community design problem than the redesign and adaptation of the American suburb — the symbol and logos of American affluence and technology and growth in the past forty years.

Yet, suburbs are alien territory for most designers. They seem to resist the best intentions we have for them. If you've ever watched a hungry teenager hanging on the refrigerator door, then you know the essence of suburbs. Prodigious amounts of energy are needed to maintain and support growth. In fact, suburbs are like noisy, exuberant, troublesome adolescents who seem to deny our values and experience, resisting our attempts to channel and restrict their behavior toward more mature and responsible forms. You find yourself at an impasse, unable to guide change, until you accept the person and situation for what they are: a young being in evolution.

The literature of planning, design, and social history is replete with criticism of suburban sprawl and its social, ecological, and aesthetic effects. There has been little attempt to approach the form on its own terms and imagine what it may become as it adapts to forces that are now at work. That is what we attempt to do in this chapter as we evaluate existing suburban forms and propose design concepts in relation to energy changes and resource use as well as living patterns. Our goal is not to impose new values or invent wholly new forms, but to describe existing trends and anticipate what they imply for the possible evolution of built form.

The suburban pattern is familiar to us, but it is not old — only a generation or so. It is a pattern that began with the large-scale development in the years following World War II of single-family housing on large tracts of raw land — the 'subdivision,' and since has extended to the creation of an entire auto-centered way of life, whose key physical elements include 'the strip,' the shopping center, the workplace, and entertainment, all woven together along a horizontal grid.

Suburbs started as collections of neighborhood formed of single-family houses, with clusters of neighborhood serviced by an existing or expanded town core. Suburbs were located some distance from the central city, which was generally the place of work, entertainment, and major shopping trips. The late nineteenth century, with radial trolley lines fanning out from central city, saw the establishment of satellite towns and suburbs — essentially commuter or bedroom communities. The newer suburban pattern is different from urban pattern in the sense that it is a suburban city and includes all the functions of a city arrayed on an auto-linked grid.

The scene is so familiar that, except for the background scenery and the road signs, we could be almost anywhere. Ten miles out of town, on the Interstate, we pass the first signposts of the suburban city: truckers' gas stations and eateries, auto parts places and junkyards, the remnants of farms, mobile home parks, a drive-in movie, billboards telling us what to look for when we get there. Pretty soon we're there. The frontage roads on either side of the Interstate are lined with wholesale distributors, sprawling manufacturing plants, economy motels, trucking companies — all manner of commerce whose lifeblood is the Interstate. Swinging off the Interstate, we move onto a six-lane

Landslides

The archetypal suburban city: freeway, major arterial commercial street with residential grid filling in between.

35

arterial street, the strip. Mile after mile is lined with franchise food places, gas stations, retail outlets of all kinds, two- and three-story apartment blocks. Each building is set back from the major street by an asphalt parking area in front, on the sides, and behind. We swing onto another arterial, this one punctuated with new office buildings six to twelve stories high, each one set off by its own parking lots and signs announcing its major tenants. At the corner of two major arterials, we come to a major shopping center, one story high, buffered by acres of cars, each large store a familiar national franchise. The sidewalks along the arterials are an anachronism. We have not seen anyone walking, except the short distance from their car in the parking lot to their destination. Background and foreground are the unceasing flow and rhythm of cars, dancing to the lights at each major intersection. We swing off to a side street behind the shopping center onto a sixty-foot-wide street lined with single-family houses, each set back from the street with a front lawn. Each house presents us with a driveway leading up to a two-car garage door, a paved entrance walk, a front door, and a large window facing the street.

It is a weekday afternoon and there is little activity. Two joggers pass by, a man is watering his lawn, a teenager is working on his car in the driveway. We drive down block after block, seeing little more activity. The scale of the residential street is smaller and more intimate than that of the arterial with its unrelieved flat surfaces, its eight-story-high signs, its asphalt, concrete, and stucco, with cars everywhere. The monotony of the residential street is relieved by trees, lawns, occasional personal touches. There is not much traffic, of either cars or people.

This book is not the place to trace in detail the historical forces and ideals that came together to create the suburban city; however, in order to be able to direct its future form, it is important to have some sense of how it all came about. As designers, we believe that form results not only from economic and technological imperatives that reflect and reinforce a prevailing world-view, but also from aesthetic and cultural ideals.

Suburbs have always been with us, but as modern idea of suburb grew out of reaction to the ugly, crowded, inhumane nineteenth-century cities and towns that quickly expanded to accommodate the dispossessed peasantry who became the industrial work force. The suburban city is a late twentieth-century version of the nineteenth-century frontier town built to exploit the bountiful resources of a then virgin continent. Modern suburbs are truly 'pioneer' urban ecologies where little time or thought has been given to the subtleties of place, shared amenities, a sense of community, permanence, long-term costs, or sustainability. The emphasis is on speed ('time is money'), short-run profits, standardized products, mobility, and mass.

England, with its tradition of modest villages and commons, individual gardens and cottages, spawned both the Industrial City and the romantic reformist countermovement toward garden cities. The Garden City, with its curving streets, broad lawns, open space, and horizontal form, was a guiding model for the earlier suburb. In the United States, where the primacy of the individual and family is held supreme, the miniaturized estate that suburbia promised held immediate appeal to the growing middle class. The earliest suburbs developed in the first several decades of this century, but real momentum and the extension of the ideal into the dominant urban form developed after World War II. The war probably had a lot to do with it. Millions of men experienced a mass-produced environment for the first time. Moving became a way of life, and one outpost was much like the last one, even though they were at other ends of the continent, or the world. National corporations and advertising media, fresh from their success in the war effort, asserted a new dominance over local and regional tradition.

In the 1940s, American productive capacity and technological know-how were the mass-industrialized engine that won the war and rebuilt a devastated European economy. Now, that capacity, coupled to the pent-up demand for housing, the dollars saved by families during the war, and the formation of new families, all came together to demand massive amounts of new housing quickly. With generous government mortgage insurance programs and other forms of assistance, experienced builders and new entrepreneurs entered the market, building vast communities almost overnight. The suburban boom was born, and through the next thirty-five years changed the face of America.

There were also other forces that fueled the boom during these next years. Government policy favored decentralization through such programs as the highway building program, the most massive public works program in history. Increasing mechanization and larger units of production in agriculture and improved transportation and food processing reduced the need for the traditional truck farming base around central cities. Farmland was converted to housing and shopping centers with no apparent ill effect to the food supply or cost. For producers, suburbs offered convenient, predictable markets for their products. Indeed, modern marketing researchers can predict consumption patterns from zip codes. The suburbs demanded massive new investments in new energy-supply and distribution facilities, but with plentiful supplies of oil and natural gas, and with favorable long-term returns, utilities eagerly geared up to service the new markets. Their strategy was to encourage consumers to use more energy so that that new capacity would be fully used. (In the 1950s, utility company offices gave away light bulbs.)

For a long time, the suburban pattern seemed to be the perfect expression of the American ideal: a healthy, secure, convenient and pleasing place for young families to fulfill their aspirations for the good life. The frequent moves demanded by the job meant that one could move from one familiar environment to another three thousand miles away. The goal was few surprises, a ready-made community of people with similar backgrounds and jobs, and steady progress toward material well-being: a mass participation in the American dream. Our basic premise is that the present form of the suburban city is grossly wasteful in its use of energy, materials, and land; and thus — under conditions of increasingly scarce and expensive resources — its form must adapt to more frugal and·sustainable patterns. Changing demography and living patterns render the present form increasingly unstable and dysfunctional.

Perhaps it is the persistence of the forces that brought the suburban form into being — forces that are embodied in both ideals and values, as well as physical form and functioning mechanisms — that makes the transformation of suburban form such a challenging problem.

# Redesigning the Suburban Fabric

How can existing suburban form begin to adapt to another set of values — conservation, cooperation, place-centeredness, more expensive basic activities — values which we believe will become more important in the coming years? The acceptance of these values and their expression in built form are the basis for the creation of sustainable communities.

We have articulated the most basic building blocks of the suburban city: (1) the limited-access highway linking together an entire metropolitan region of suburban cities and providing commuter access to industrial and commercial workplaces; (2) the strip arterial lined with commercial services; (3) the regional shopping mall and commercial center; and (4) the block pattern of detached houses designed for nuclear families.

We start by considering the residential pattern and suggesting some adaptive strategies for redesign.

## The Suburban Block

A first strategy is aimed at deemphasizing the importance of the street. In the typical suburban block, much of the total land area is wasted. Streets that serve only local traffic are usually oversized. Typically, there are two lanes for traffic, each twelve feet wide, and two parking lanes each eight feet wide, for a total width of forty feet,

Berkeley's traffic barriers are an attempt to balance the street as a traffic carrier with more convivial neighborhood needs.

not including sidewalks. In most cases, streets transect neighborhoods till they reach arterials. One design solution is to remove many of these through streets, limiting parking to clusters at the end of the now dead-ended streets. Solutions similar to this have been carried out in Europe, while Berkeley, California pioneered the reduction of through traffic in residential neighborhoods by installing traffic barriers. The results of this redesign of streets are fewer accidents, a better use of outdoor space, and a greater neighborliness, in addition to making land available for other uses such as food production and common outdoor activities. A similar approach is illustrated in the Village Homes community in Davis, California. The intention of the designer-developers, Mike and Judy Corbett, was to provide narrow streets and allocate the space saved to commonly shared backyard areas. Their plan was compromised in order to meet local standards. The houses, instead of being oriented to the street, generally have a small private fenced area off the street, with primary private and shared space along common areas in back. These design principles can be applied to suburban redesign with relative ease. The use of narrower and fewer through

Village Homes in Davis, California converts land saved through narrow streets into community food production area.

streets also encourages the use of walking and bicycling within the neighborhood, particularly since, with many streets closed, foot and bicycle paths would offer the most direct path between points. Another implication of narrower streets is the use of low-speed mini-vehicles for many types of local trips that are now performed by full sized automobiles.

## *Density and Diversity Within the Block*

As we have seen, the idea of the suburb was to provide separate homes for nuclear families, once the dominant social form in the country. However, social structure has been changing rapidly, with some regional variation. While the family consisting of man and woman and one or more children is with us to stay, the number of households composed of unattached individuals of one or both sexes has increased dramatically, as has the number of single-parent households. Combined with a vast increase in the number of women in the work force, a lower birth rate, and housing costs that have risen far more rapidly than real income, this is having dramatic effects on housing patterns in the suburbs and elsewhere. People can purchase less space today for the same proportion of their income. Yet, much single-family housing is underused, when it is still occupied by parents whose children have left. Single parents band together to share child-rearing, and singles find that they must share housing and use facilities cooperatively. All of these trends point to opportunities to redesign the suburban block pattern toward greater density of use and more adaptable housing forms. In many parts of the country, housing costs, economic pressures, and changing demography are already producing changes, though perhaps they are not well documented, because they largely exist within what economist Scott Burns has called the 'Household Economy.'

Owners eager for some added income, or to accommodate the housing needs of a child or relative, turn basements, attics, and garages into 'in-law' units, which are generally not permitted in 'single-family' neighborhoods. People increasingly run small businesses out of their home, again violating single-use zoning dictums that were intended to keep 'harmful' or conflicting uses out of exclusively residential neighborhoods.

What we advocate is to indeed encourage these kinds of densification and diversification of the suburban neighborhood. From the point of resource use and sociability, the suburban density of six to eight houses to the acre, or about fifteen to twenty people per acre, means a high per-capita cost of building and maintaining services such as roads, utilities, and any form of transportation. From the point of view of sociability, it is a density that is too low to support corner stores, cafes, and all the kinds of places we associate with conviviality. In the suburb, the locus for neighborhood becomes the backyard potluck and the Saturday TV football game. In the Sunnyvale case study, we proposed that in exchange for closing streets and clustering parking (which might mean in some cases that people would have to walk several hundred feet to their house), zoning would permit 'zero lot line' additions to dwellings and the addition of second units.

Increasing density within the block pattern goes hand in hand with remodeling to add space and improve energy use by reducing energy losses, as well as making direct use of the sun for heating. At the residential scale, conserving energy is always more cost-effective than redesign to capture additional sources of energy supply. So the cycle of remodeling and adding on to the suburban home will be combined with conservation measures such as insulating walls and ceilings, replacing single glazing with double glazing, reducing infiltration by adding vestibules, and providing air-to-air heat exchangers. Once these basic steps to increase comfort and reduce energy loss have been taken, the stage is set to further reduce the need for external energy by capturing the sun. The solar techniques that work best in remodeling or 'retrofitting' existing small buildings include the 'solar attic' and solar greenhouses. The solar attic approach works in houses that have pitched roofs. The rafters and ceiling are superinsulated and lined with black plastic. Double-glazing panels are installed in the southerly slope, together with 'heat rods': plastic tubes filled with salts that have (20x) times the heat-retention capacity of dense materials often used for heat storage such as concrete. The heat captured in the attic is then distributed through a conventional duct and fan system to other parts of the house. The advantage of this system, besides its relatively low

The addition of a solar greenhouse provides multiple benefits such as lower heating costs, a place for plants, improved thermal comfort.

cost, is that it makes use of space that is already built and cannot be used for living. The solar greenhouse consists of a wood-framed, plastic-enclosed addition — often only four feet to six feet wide, built off a south side of the house. It acts as an extra wall, reducing heat loss and capturing heat when the sun is shining. This simple addition, which also serves as a place to grow salad vegetables year round, can be built for less than a thousand dollars. A more elaborate solarium room provides additional living space and thermal capacity in mass walls or floors which hold onto the sun's heat.

In summary, a move toward 'living in place' brought about by a slower growing, more localized economy and persistently high fuel costs will have profound effects on the traditional form of the suburban block. Cars will no longer be the exclusive means of transportation for all trips, and the space devoted to the car will be reduced and turned over to more productive uses, such as gardens or playing areas. People will spend more time at home and spend more of their 'leisure' time on activities such as maintenance, gardening, and improvements. People will band together in cooperative projects involving the use of common space, such as a sauna, or a home cannery, or a basketball court, on what was once street. More people, representing more diverse age grouping and income mix will be living there in a greater variety of living accommodations.

## The Strip

The strip consists of generally one-story establishments lining each side of four- to six-lane arterials filled with constantly flowing traffic. The buildings typically cover only a small portion of their site, with perhaps 80 percent of the area reserved for parking in front, on the sides, and in back. The strip is totally designed to cater to auto access. In addition to easy parking, strip buildings use large signs, bright lighting, and large display windows for maximum visual attention from passing automobiles. The strip is the purveyor of goods and service to the mass automobile culture. Auto supplies, sales, and repair are well represented, along with fast food, gas stations, one- stop shopping stations, leisure, and recreational supplies, and often neighborhood convenience shopping. Older strips often evolved from their earlier function as neighborhood shopping streets, and often still contain a large proportion of local small business, while newer strips present us with a complete catalogue of standardized nationally franchised services and sales operations.

The opportunities for redesign of the strip arise from its low density, its relatively high turnover of businesses (particularly in the older, more marginal locations), and its inherent structure as a channel for movement. The redesign of the strip is closely linked to the redesign of residential neighborhoods previously discussed. One strategy is to make it possible for people to walk to neighborhood shopping, rather than getting into a car and cruising the strip for a number of miles, stopping here and there. This can be accomplished by concentrating housing density in the blocks directly behind the arterial, and turning what is now 'the back door' of strip-oriented facilities into a front door that is reached by foot or bicycle from the residential neighborhood behind it. We have previously discussed closing and interrupting residential through streets. This begins to provide the space to create pedestrian access to shopping and additional housing sites. As neighborhood shopping becomes more oriented to the neighborhood behind it, buildings can begin to cluster together into nodes rather than as isolated elements on a linear auto access route. As activities shift more toward pedestrian, bicycle, or neighborhood mini-vehicle access, need for devoting so much space to parking is severely reduced.

A second strategy involves the gradual restructuring of the single-purpose sparsely-covered strip into a dense linear mixed-use zone that integrates light industry, offices, places of employment, community facilities, housing, neighborhood shopping, and possibly energy and food production. This concept was explored in the redesign of the Sunnyvale El Camino strip into a multi- layered linear mall. The typical width of the strip (600 feet in the Sunnyvale case) provides plenty of room for different configurations. In the redesign, activities are gradually separated from the street, points of auto access are concentrated, and redundant streets are closed. Thus, the arterial becomes 'exclusively' a traffic channel, without the hazards and distractions of the present strip, where cars are constantly pulling in and out of traffic, visual chaos confuses and pollutes the eye (see Peter Blake's **God's Own Junkyard**) and traffic lights impede traffic flow.

The final stage in the redesign of the strip is a reduction in the number of vehicle lanes and a conversion of one or more lanes to exclusive use or light rail use. Once again, the key to more efficient transportation is achieving a density than can support it.

The suburban city embraces the automobile with exuberance and the single-minded devotion of the truly religious. The resulting pattern is a linear horizontal grid that is diffuse and uniformly low-density and undifferentiated. As we shift from total reliance on the automobile to a greater mix of modes, the sprawl begins to coalesce into more distinct nodes and neighborhoods, and the grid and surrounding land uses configure into a clearer hierarchy of density and function and pattern within the existing local fabric. In its complete transformation, the strip becomes a horizontal linear city of mixed-user housing, community services, offices, shopping, and industry serving local 'consumer sheds' behind it, while efficient transit provides access to workplaces and other nodes of activity along its length.

The new light rail in San Diego provides an anchor for a renewed commercial zone.

## The Shopping Mall

Another feature of the suburban city is the shopping mall. These centers — an innovation of the 1950s — are designed to serve regional markets and always include several 'anchor' tenants: major national and regional department stores carrying a wide variety of merchandising. Around the anchors are other major tenants specializing in various kinds of consumer hardware. Rounding out the center are local specialty shops and often a sprinkling of business and professional offices.

The first malls sprang up around the new suburbs and were designed as a convenient central alternative to city shopping areas, which typically were congested, and difficult to park in. The malls quickly achieved success, eliminating long trips to the city, providing adequate parking and bringing together a wide enough selection of goods and services so that consumers could buy in a car-free, relaxed environment. The shopping mall became the closest thing to a town center for many suburbanites.

Our strategy is to turn the mall into precisely that: a town center. The commercial heart is there; what is lacking is housing improvement and a greater variety of activities to provide sufficient diversity.

These key concepts in suburban redesign were explored in the Sustainable Cities Design Workshop as one of three case studies. The example explored at the workshop was Sunnyvale, California, which, because of its location in the industrially dense Silicon Valley, is by no means typical of all suburbs. Yet, most of the strategies discussed here are probably relevant to suburbs built since the 1940s.

A typical shopping mall is a town center separated from its community by a sea of parking.

# Case Study 1 — Sunnyvale:
# A Mature Suburb

Sunnyvale represents a typical suburban tract housing situation bisected by a commercial strip. The pattern is largely built out, and there is very little open space. In San Jose, there are hundreds of square miles of a pattern similar to the piece we selected. The original natural history of the site has been almost completely obliterated. Sunnyvale lies in the center of 'Silicon Valley' — the world center of research, development and production of solid-state electronics. The area is forecasted to lose people and gain jobs, although, because of a lack of housing and space for industrial expansion, electronics firms are moving to other, less built-up places in Northern California. Although suburban housing was largely built for family ownership, at present 50 percent is renter-occupied and family size is decreasing.

The benign climate means low heating bills and little air conditioning. Transportation and air pollution are major energy-related issues.

The Sunnyvale site chosen for redesign comprises approximately 600 acres, including 500 acres of single-family residential housing and 77 acres of commercial buildings, the latter primarily along the major arterial road, El Camino Real, which bisects the study area. There is some multifamily development in the block directly behind El Camino Real, a small amount of industrial buildings adjacent to the railroad which runs at the north edge of the site, two schools, and park sites. Most of the area was built in the '50s and '60s on what was once one of the richest, most beautiful agricultural valleys in the world. The Santa Clara Valley lies at the southern end of San Francisco Bay — an alluvial fan between the north-south ridges of the coast range which form its two edges.

## Climate

Santa Clara County has a Mediterranean climate characteristic of extensive areas along the California coast, influenced by ocean air systems roughly 85 percent of the time and by inland or continental air systems roughly 15 percent of the time. Temperatures generally fall within a moderate range, with lows in the 40s from November through April and highs in the upper 70s in August and September. Extremes in the 20s can be hit in the winter period, causing several freeze days per year with extreme highs hitting the 90s by late summer. Applicable heating degree days (at Moffett Field, located a short distance to the northwest of the site) are 2,969; cooling degree days, 236.

Annual sunshine is estimated at 3,000 hours per year, with sunny

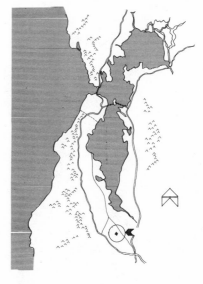

Sunnyvale (circle at bottom) is situated at the northern end of the Santa Clara Valley in the heart of "Silicon Valley".

45

days occurring roughly 50 percent of the time in winter, increasing to 85 percent of the time in July. Winds are generally light to moderate, varying from a north- northwesterly direction from March through November to a southeasterly direction from December through February.

## Goals and Strategies

In the Sunnyvale case, goals and strategies were intertwined. The overall goal is, of course, to enhance sustainability by reducing energy and resource inputs and developing locally available energy and resources.

Because the area is largely built out, the aim was to increase the efficiency of housing and transport while maintaining the essential suburban character by diversifying existing housing patterns and freeing streets and park areas for food and energy production. The goals of the project were to reduce energy use in this type of community by 50 percent. We wanted to show that it is possible to densify this pattern, so we assumed an increase in population of 50 percent, with about half of this increase achieved in the existing residential fabric and the rest through densification in the commercial strip. We hoped to achieve a more sustainable urban culture by linking people directly to land, food, and energy systems. This transition can only come about through a shift in the values and habits of the people in the community, so we have made educational support an integral part of the process.

The plan incorporates a variety of resource and energy strategies, many of them retrofit techniques. A low-cost space heating retrofit is the 'hot attic,' in which sun is admitted into an attic space that is lined in black plastic and well insulated from the living space below. Heat is stored in rods filled with eutectic salts, and the warm air is circulated from the attic into spaces. Domestic hot water is supplied by a flat plate collector or heat exchanger located in the attic.

Bringing back agriculture is an integral part of the plan. Gray water from households would be used in a drip irrigation system along the newly greened streets which would provide some of the local tree fruit for which the area was once famous, as well as vegetables. (Community-scale agriculture is discussed in The Bio-Educational Center section, below.)

In approaching the Sunnyvale site, we identified a number of conditions that became catalysts and opportunities for design. First, the site lies in what was once a uniquely productive agricultural area with deep alluvial soils, an excellent climate, and a long growing season. Reestablishing some measures of local food production became an important goal.

As a typical suburb (there is no 'there' there) one area seems in-

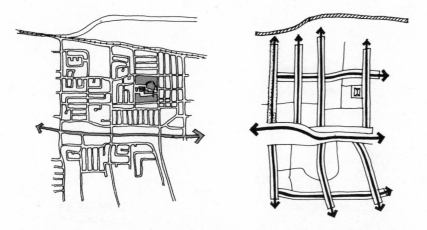

The existing street pattern (diagram at left) is reorganized into a coherent hierarchy of local neighborhood streets, collector streets and a major thru traffic "spine".

distinguishable from another, and there are few natural boundaries. It is a bland horizontal melange of traffic-laden commercial strip with miles of similar detached housing. An important aspect of redesign was to reinforce more recognizable boundaries through a differentiated street pattern, the elimination of local through streets, and the reinforcing of major arterials. Yet, the suburb as a way of life has real value in its openness, green space, and closeness to the ground. These are values worth keeping. Another opportunity is provided by characteristic strip commercial development on major arterials, particularly El Camino Real. The strip is typically low-density, with mostly one-story cheaply-built structures, parking lots front and back, and a high rate of turnover in use. In our plan, the commercial strip designed for auto cruising and access from the four- or six-lane street is redesigned into a dense, mixed-use linear spine, or 'Lifebelt,' which is entered from the back side. The spine becomes a pedestrian place much like a shopping mall and is the center of community activities that include shopping and services, local industry and energy production, multiple housing and community facilities.

## Design Solutions

### A. Denser, Greener, More Livable Surburban Neighborhoods

Achieving higher density while maintaining the integrity of the predominantly detached dwelling pattern combines with the overall goals of improving the productivity of land use and energy efficiency. Less space per person and shared facilities — two features of a housing cost that is outstripping real income, and of a tight land market in metropolitan areas — are themselves inherently energy-efficient. Permitting owners to upzone detached dwellings through zero lot line additions, garage conversions, etc. can be used as an incentive to achieve a better local street pattern by removing parking to the ends of blocks, eliminating through traffic on local streets, and narrowing the streets to 12-foot service lanes, with the rest of the space given over to gardens

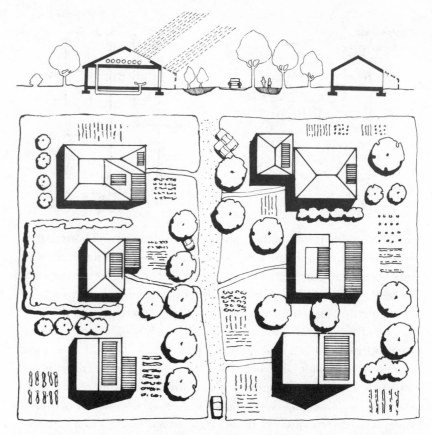

Minimizing street dimensions on neighborhood roads can increase gardening areas.

and orchards for local food production. This type of neighborhood change has been locally initiated in other communities, largely to reduce auto hazards to children. In **Livable Streets**, Donald Appleyard documents many such cases in Western Europe; and Clare Cooper-Marcus has shown us the value to children of auto-free environments. In our case study, the goals are connected to the desire to produce some fresh food and create generally more coherent neighborhoods.

Ralph Knowles developed a series of street planting profiles that beautifully demonstrate the dynamic interactive quality of sustainable design as it integrates seasonal sun path, building and street orientation, and the qualities of different tree types. The criteria include building solar access at rooftop height (12 feet), using fruit-bearing trees, and having shady streets for summer.

On an east-west street, the principle is to locate a high deciduous tree on the south side of the street to provide summer shade. In the winter, the tree's bare armature allows sunlight to penetrate. The deciduous tree is positioned so that its shadow when the sun is at its lowest winter point (December 21) does not shade the roof of houses on the north side of the street.

North-south streets present a different condition, in which the positioning of street and trees can be used to provide afternoon shade on west exposures.

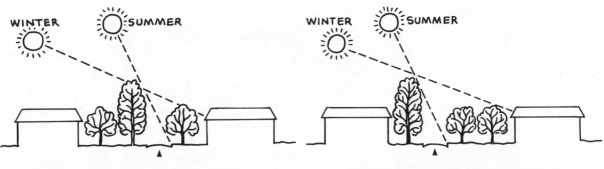

STREET SHIFTS TO NORTH HALF OF PAVING.
COMBINATION OF FRUIT AND SHADE TREES.

STREET SHIFTS TO SOUTH HALF OF PAVING.
COMBINATION OF FRUIT AND SHADE TREES.
TALL TREE SHADES STREET IN SUMMER.

*B. Commercial Strip: From Low-Density Monoculture to Pulsing Polyculture*

The low-density auto-oriented commercial strip of one-story buildings buffered by parking and facing a four- or six-lane arterial is a ubiquitous feature of U.S. suburban and fringe areas. Lined with fast-food franchises, gas stations, and other auto-related businesses — marginal business of all kinds — it is a key symbol of America and one that we consider ripe for revision.

The typical strip — in this case a 600-foot wide swath of El Camino Real and its frontage — presents real opportunities because of the high turnover of its businesses and the low density of use.

The concept we developed envisions the gradual transformation of the strip into a dense, pedestrian-oriented spine of mixed-use which grows out of activity nodes at major intersections and grows along an internal pedestrian spine toward the next node.

The selection and placement of trees relative to orientation can be used to modulate sun at different times of the year.

An overview of "the strip" renewed as a "Lifebelt". Activities are clustered at major nodes lined with parking and a greenbelt.

49

A diagram of a rehabilitated strip center to include pedestrian links to the surrounding neighborhoods and to add recreational facilities.

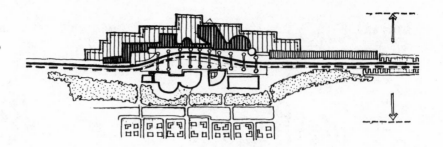

This 'Lifebelt' contains commercial services (now located in marginal neighborhood centers), industrial space, housing, and education and community services, and is buffered from El Camino Real which, without the cruising traffic and driveways every 100 feet, can now effectively fulfill its function as a traffic-bearing arterial. The Lifebelt also incorporates electrical energy generation in rooftop photovoltaics. The Lifebelt is buffered from the residential neighborhood behind it by parking and a 'wild zone' of native plantings.

Through these strategies, we see the dissolution of the strip into a new, efficient, urban linear pedestrian spine that becomes the commercial center of the revitalized suburban pattern.

### C. Bio-Educational Center

People today are marrying less and having fewer children. One result is that many suburbs built in the '50s and '60s are finding themselves with underused school facilities. The school sites present an interesting opportunity for community reuse.

Within the Sunnyvale planning area, there is a 30-acre underused school and park site. The team's proposal was to revise the site as the locus for agricultural reinhabitation and community access to the tools for biological self-reliance and education.

The reintroduction of agriculture and biological systems to urbanized people who have lost touch with the basic roots of their sustenance is going to take several generations at least. The Bio-Educational Center addresses three aspects of this process:

1. **Awareness**: The biological basis for life must be made visible in the immediate environment.
2. **Education**: Learning how (even at the backyard level) must be a conscious, managed process. The skills are not easy to come by.
3. **Production**: Food production is a job for professionals.

While backyard gardening is an important tool for opening awareness and producing supplementary food supplies, producing food in quantity will remain a full-time skill and business.

In this plan, the park site is left as is. Some of the existing schoolyard area is put into two types of agricultural production. One part is developed as a demonstration agricultural center for use by the school, and includes a diversified orchard, a vegetable and flower garden, a small stock area, and a greenhouse. The other portion is used for small-scale commercial production and is coupled to the local waste and treatment facility, which provides nutrient and water input for crop production. In this way, the circle is closed, and locally generated organics — waste and water — are reused on-site.

The waste treatment technology is the 'solar aquacell' system developed by Steve Serfling and his associates. The system creates a polycultural habitat in which a plastic substrate provides a surface for bacteria, which in turn are grazed by arthopods and other marine microorganisms. Floating water hyacinths take up the majority of nutrients in the effluent. The system is covered with commercial double-layered plastic greenhouses to maintain a stable temperature for optimum biological activity. The energy use of the system is far below that of conventional secondary sewage treatment plants; and because the process is entirely contained, it does not present the hazards of airborne viruses, odor, and unsightliness which are associated with conventional sewage treatment systems.

Purified water from the Aquacell is of recreational quality, and in the plan is stored in a pond in the adjacent park. From there, it can be used for landscape irrigation in the park or agricultural zone.

Interior of the Ark at the New Alchemy Institute, Cape Cod. This early bioshelter is an important example showing how food production, water and waste recycling can be combined into the design of human habitat.

### D. Transportation

We did not assume a drastic change in travel patterns over the next twenty years. The commute trip to work will still be there. Our approach to the transportation design was to:

1. reduce the length of trips to local services by densifying housing along the redesigned commercial strip.
2. reduce the number and size of redundant local neighborhood streets

by closing them to through traffic, narrowing many of them, and clustering car parking at one end.

3. strengthen the capacity of major arterials and create a hierarchy of streets.

What these measures do, then, without impeding movement or assuming diminished travel, is to give cohesiveness to blocks and neighborhoods within the study site and encourage bikes and walks for short trips by creating a local pedestrian environment; and, through redesign of the major arterial commercial strip, El Camino Real, uses are rationalized into a 'Lifebelt' or linear pedestrian-oriented multi-use mall.

### E. Waste Disposal

The goal here was to stop exporting sewage — waste water and waste nutrients — out of the area and to recycle it locally. Two options were explored. The first envisions using existing water-based sewage transport and organic wastes in a local solar aquacell biological treatment system at the community bio-educational center site (see the Bio-Educational Center section above), with savings in water, energy, and infrastructure. A second option is to have a split system, replacing the existing system of flush toilets and waterborne sewage disposal with dry toilets (there are many types that are safe and sanitary), and recycling other waste water, called 'gray water,' locally on- site for landscape irrigation.

### F. Energy

The principal emphasis in energy design is the elimination of imported fuel for heating residential and commercial buildings and the eventual provision of local electricity through photovoltaics. Noteworthy is a low-cost retrofit for typical tract homes through the installation of a roof aperture and the storage of eutectic salts. The goal of a 50-percent reduction in energy use seems easily attainable in the building sector, but much less likely in the transportation sector.

### G. Asphalt Eater

As we all know, we live in a technoculture — a landscape filled with sophisticated tools and large machines. The usual image of Appropriate Technology is of a scaled-down, human-sized, slightly funky technology in the hands of smiling neighborhood folks with granny glasses and clean overalls: Western versions of the happy folk you see on the covers of **China Reconstructs**. However, in order to realize the solar biological vision, we need tools that are at least as awesome as the icons of the technofantasy culture. Today we have huge machines to turn living soil into concrete ribbons, and, lo and behold, we have concrete everywhere. So we designed a machine that eats roads and turns them back into productive landscapes. Here's how it works: Up front is a tool like a sod cutter that rips up the roadbed into chunks. Behind it, a chisel plow prepares the subsoil for agriculture. An asphalt catcher and conveyor belt carry the material onto a heating bed or perforated griddle that softens the asphalt, separating it from the gravel. The asphalt oil is burned in the gasifier unit that powers the entire machine, and the waste heat is fed back into the griddle to melt the asphalt. The separated gravel is conveyed off to trucks for reuse in construction.

Behind the gasifier unit is the auger unit, which drills holes for trees. Each hole is automatically injected with sewage sludge from a tank on the machine which is filled at the local sewage plant. Behind the auger boom is the planting platform with workers who are busy placing tree stock in the new holes.

# The New Suburban Fabric

*Sim Van der Ryn and Peter Calthorpe*

Our discussion thus far has focused on redesigning the existing suburban fabric through piecemeal change. Considering the sheer quantity and pervasiveness of suburbs that have been created these last forty years, design innovation that provides the means for the gradual transition of the existing fabric of suburbia toward sustainability will be the major focus of public and private development activity in the next twenty years.

In addition to the strategies discussed, there is another important option for redesign toward sustainability in suburban areas through the infilling of raw land and the redevelopment of other sites at a scale large enough so that a new pattern of activities and of energy and resource use can emerge and infiltrate into the existing pattern. We have in mind not the creation of isolated 'New Towns' or self-sufficient 'planned communities' isolated from their surroundings. We want to focus on converting the scale of new development contiguous to existing suburbs toward the goal of greater social and ecological sustainability, consistent with accepted economic practices. A good deal of new suburban development involves land areas large enough to build complete neighborhoods of from 500 to 5,000 people. This is a scale large enough to design the basic fabric of land use from the ground up. The scale must be large enough to plan the overall disposition of land use, density, roads, services, and utilities. What will be the differences between this type of ecologically planned community and conventional large-scale suburban development? How will this type of design differ from the New Town concept so popular with planners? Here are some of the basic principles:

1. Utilizing residential densities greater than the suburban standard of six to ten dwelling units per acre. This reduces first costs and operating costs across the board and, with proper design, opens up the opportunity for a level of social interaction that transcends the isolation of low-density suburbs and the alienation of high-density cities.

2. Locating everyday shopping and services so that people can meet their daily needs with greater convenience and less stress, with a greatly reduced use of time, space, and expensive energy, and with a greatly reduced automobile dependency.

3. Building in a local employment base within the community, either by providing for work at home tied to communication and information access tied to computer terminals, or through the location of local employment centers.

4. Devising information-efficient and energy-efficient building strategies, including better use of enclosed space and climate- responsive design through building location and orientation, passive solar heating and cooling, daylighting, shared use of capital-intensive facilities, and energy-frugal appliances and equipment.

5. Creating design that encourages the emergence of networks of local people to carry social responsibilities such as crime prevention, fire protection, and home care of children, the elderly, the sick and the disabled.

6. Providing local energy and food production within the community.

7. Recycling water and wastes.

8. Integrating community design with a transportation system that provides balanced options.

Over the past five years, we have had the opportunity to develop and test these brief concepts in a number of real situations. Each of these situations is presented as a case study summary as part of this chapter.

These case studies are not utopian in the classical political or religious sense. Though they are similar to the garden city plans first envisioned in the early twentieth century, there is no overt restructuring of ownership and social equity. They are not conceived of as 'new towns' in the isolated sense, but rather are a kind of suburban infill. They are intended to occupy voids within the metropolitan areas, rather than new sites beyond the existing infrastructure. Inserting dense, mixed-use nodes within the suburban fabric not only reduces pressure for further sprawl, but helps to reorder the surrounding neighborhoods. Internally, they are designed to reduce people's material demands on the environment, and they represent a kind of environmental efficiency that can make growth more affordable to the culture. Inevitably, such conservation has social and political consequences in a culture based on consumption.

In a planning study for 400 acres on the outskirts of Golden, Colorado a mixed-use community was proposed to displace the inevitable sprawl of this high-growth area. The hope is to reconnect home, work, commerce, and recreation. The plan reclaims valuable land from the auto, focusing on convenient pedestrian access throughout. The residential sections of row houses enjoy private yards, courtyards, common open space, and solar access at a density of about twenty units per acre. The neighborhood paths lead to a mixed-use pedestrian spine that provides regional-, community-, and neighborhood-scale facilities. Sections of this street are glazed, providing year round comfort for the pedestrian as well as reducing the energy demands of the individual buildings. This solar street focuses and intensifies the scattered public life of the community, saving energy by localizing activities while heating buildings.

Our proposal for the reuse of a 1,200-acre air force base in Marin County, California proposes a similar reintegration. The shopping center, industrial park, truck farm, and housing subdivision are condensed and combined into a new form. The plan proposes the renovation of existing military offices into a town center, and of existing hangars for light industrial use. The two thousand new housing units, designed for passive solar heating, are configured into five neighborhoods free from cars; yet cars are within 300 feet of each dwelling unit. Open space is divided between a productive truck farm and recreation areas. New office space and a transit center complete this 'town' which, at considerably higher densities than a typical suburban development, has a lower environmental impact.

Similarly, a planning study for 18,000 acres in San Bernardino County, California proposes an even more modest modification of traditional suburban sprawl: pedestrian clusters linking retail services and recreation to housing. In an area destined for shopping malls and subdivisions, the study proposed eight 'villages' at townhouse densities with circulation patterns to allow safe access from house to store and open space. The zoning describes a quarter-mile pedestrian area with schools, over 2,000 dwellings, schools, open space, and a 100,000-180,000 square-foot retail center.

In each case, the environmental strategy is simple: density is increased and land is wrested from the auto and configured for pedestrian circulation and recreation. Mixed use reduces trip distances, party walls reduce building thermal loads, and compactness reduces infrastructure costs. The clustering saves land, resources, and energy. The common open space is usable, personalized, and productive; the pedestrian ways are safe, human-scaled, and nonpolluting.

The social consequences of these configurations are of course unknown. Clearly, the vitality of Greenwich Village will not be matched by such suburban substitutes. The culture of cities cannot be simulated, but the culture of suburbs can be intensified. The isolation of housewives and the need to chauffeur children is minimized. A mix of private and common space at least provides the opportunity for gathering, spontaneous interaction, and perhaps the basis of neighborhood cooperation. The chance meetings on foot, or in the local store, the close play areas, the small offices and studios — all provide a life and human connection missing from the strip and subdivision.

Within the ecological design movement, village has become a key concept, slogan, and password toward the reconstruction and revisioning of human settlement patterns. Developers and subdividers have been fond of naming their products 'villages' for many years so we have 'Country Club Village,' 'Westwood Village,' 'The Villages,' and their counterparts around the country. Used in this way, the term becomes simply an image and a selling tool for a subdivision of houses, something attached to a shopping district. How then, is an 'urban village,' a 'solar village,' a 'meta-industrial village,' or an 'ecological village' something more than simply a collection of houses, a piece of a suburban consumer shed emptying onto a freeway and a shopping center?

In the last years of her life, Margaret Mead suggested that villages are the fulcrum around which people can make major changes in the future. As an anthropologist, Mead may have had in mind that for two-thirds of the world population the village is still the primary settlement pattern. More than that, perhaps the village represents an organic vision of community, because the central theme of village is that of a community directly tied to the productivity of the land. The size of a village is usually defined by how far one can walk to outlying fields. The village is an organism that literally builds itself and feeds itself and today would also grow or collect its own fuel and energy. In the village, everyone is both a producer and a consumer of goods and services to be sold, exchanged, or given freely. The composition of the village includes all age groups living together, not segregated spatially or by institutions. A village might have from a few hundred to a few thousand people. At the latter size, the village's core is its trading center and stores, also containing the centers of local governance, communication, education and religion, the town square or commons, and places to gather together — in other words, it contains coherence, stability, continuity, sustainability.

From this description of the basic morphology, properties, and characteristics of village, we can see that nostalgia for coherence, rootedness, and continuity is behind the misnomer of 'village' applied to designed conglomerations for singles, retirees, military dependents, or other inhabitants of our instant suburbs.

An influential report from HUD and the Urban Land Institute (**The Affordable Community: Growth, Change, and Choice in the '80s**) defines urban villages as 'a form of development that combines compactness, infill and revitalization, transportation options, mixed use, and affordable housing. A central feature of the urban village concept is that location of jobs should be closely linked to housing. Urban villages can be planned and developed in central cities, suburbs, small towns or rural areas.' This statement represents the conventional wisdom on what 'village' could mean in today's context. There is a realization that efficiency of energy and resource use is an important criterion, hence the emphasis on compactness to reduce land and servicing costs, and the call for bringing home and work closer together. It is a move toward social and ecological coherence, but it falls short of proposing a reintegration of production and consumption within the village structure, or of calling for a move toward local self reliance in terms of the production of food, energy, and the necessities of a local economy.

In the Marin Solar Village Plan, the concept is explained: 'The keynote of the plan is *sustainability*. Sustainability implies balance and permanence: a balance between people living in a community and the jobs available there; a balance between renewable resources continuously available locally and local consumption patterns; a balance between maintaining the natural environment in good health and the needs of the human community which lives within it. Like an individual in balance, a sustainable community will be healthy: socially, economically, and biologically....'

Here, the modern notion of villages has been expanded in several key dimensions from that of the progressive development community. Ecological balance and sustainability become key criteria. In the actual Solar Village plan, these goals were only partially achieved. Eighty percent of the space and water heating were supplied by direct solar gain; 30 percent of the food was grown on site; 50 percent of the water was supplied from runoff or from recycling. In other fuels, savings of 25 percent in electrical use, and 40 percent in transportation fuels were calculated.

Another, more important goal acknowledged, but not addressed in the plan, is that true villages grow and change organically over time through the direct participation of their inhabitants. Modern industrial society replaces local knowledge and skills with professional expertise; replaces local investment of time, labor, and indigenous materials with centralized investment, and industrialized wage labor; replaces local governance over suitable patterns of form and growth with centralized bureaucratic authority. In terms of creating villages in the traditional sense, overcoming these mechanisms of industrial development poses a major obstacle. Perhaps the information age and its ubiquitous tool — the small computer — promising everyone access to all types of information, may provide the means to recreate a new type of post-industrial village.

We are entering a new era in which servicing and transport will become overriding factors in the organization of urban form. The decentralization of industry into village-scale enterprises is a trend that is already under way, as large, outmoded heavy industries, particularly in the east and midwest, close down, to be replaced by smaller, more economic, adaptive, and regionally responsive industries. To state one example: while shifting the recycling of steel to large national plants for reprocessing has proved uneconomic, locally based mini-steel plants that can turn scrap into a variety of basic products is proving extremely profitable.

As we have described elsewhere, urban sprawl results in 30-40 percent of the land area being devoted to the automobile, and much of the rest poorly used. The compaction of metropolitan areas into networks of villages and the inevitable shift away from auto-dependency will make possible the conversion of a great deal of land into intensive agriculture. There is a healthy infrastructure of home gardeners developing in this country, and there are increasing numbers of community gardens in central cities and suburbs. These are good signs; they may make a real difference for the future, not because the amount of food presently grown is significant, but because it takes time for people to learn how to grow their own food, and the more people who learn now, the easier it will be to make a transition later on. The more people who reconnect with the everyday magic of soil, water, sun, photosynthesis, and plant growth, the better for the health of our communities as people begin to directly experience the essentials of life support.

These, then, are the issues we address in the case studies that follow. Each case study was designed for a specific site and context. Marin Solar Village was the boldest proposal and attracted a great deal of public attention. The plan did not respond to a specific client but to a specific opportunity: the reuse of surplus Federal property. The plan was developed over a two-year period. The Golden case study was part of the week-long design workshop and is necessarily sketchy in detail. Chino Hills is a design at a larger scale and focuses specifically on land use disposition and density as determinants of energy use.

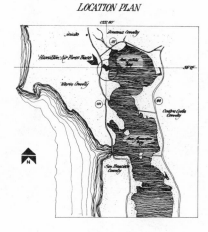

*LOCATION PLAN*

# Case Study 1 — Marin Solar Village

Hamilton Air Force Base comprises 1,653 acres just south of the suburban city of Novato, fifteen miles north of the Golden Gate Bridge. The site is directly adjacent to the freeway, the transportation corridor between the North Bay suburbs and San Francisco. On the east, it is

The former Hamilton Air Force Base,
the site of Marin Solar Village, twenty
miles north of the Golden Gate Bridge.
The Freeway is in the lower center with
San Pablo Bay at the top of the picture.

bordered by San Pablo Bay, the marshy northerly reaches of San Francisco Bay. The base was decommissioned as an active Air Force facility in 1974, and was turned over to the Federal General Services Administration for disposal as surplus property. For the next four years, a political battle raged between factions in the county who wanted to acquire the site for use as an airport and those who opposed aviation but had no clear alternative use. The Marin Solar Village plan was developed as an alternative to aviation use in 1979, and rapidly captured the interests of many people in Marin County and elsewhere.

In November 1979, the issue was put to the voters of Marin County as a ballot measure which asked: 'Shall the county acquire Hamilton Air Force Base for the purpose of building an energy-efficient community such as Marin Solar Village?' The measure lost by a narrow margin, but this was only the beginning. Grants from the San Francisco Foundation and the U.S. Department of Energy made it possible to set up a nonprofit Marin Solar Village Corporation to further develop the plan; and through this means, we did extensive planning studies and a technical feasibility analysis. In addition, the corporation mounted a public information program and began seriously soliciting the financial and community-building talent to implement the plan. In 1980, after a series of negotiations between Marin County,

Peter Xiques

A model of the Marin Solar Village proposal. The existing hangars are in the foreground.

the City of Novato, and the Solar Village Corporation; the joint City-County Commission charged with responsibility for implementing the acquisition of the site failed by one vote to accept the Solar Village development proposal, which by then had received backing by major development firms. At that point, the Corporation abandoned its effort and the site still sits vacant today. The description that follows through p. 83 is taken (with editorial changes) from the final Marin Solar Village Report.

## Assumptions

We recognize that what makes sense in a technical and economic context does not in itself add up to a community.

1. **Solar Village as a concept particularly appeals to a large number of people looking to live in a place in whose design and development they can participate directly — not only as consumers in the marketplace but as individuals who want to help create their homes, workplaces, the physical and social patterns of the village.** We believe this is an important objective. We know that large, planned communities, no matter how skillfully designed, have a certain deadness and uniformity to them. We know that most memorable

towns and villages feel like they grew over time in a process that many hands and generations participated in. At the same time, we react negatively to most patterns of development that are largely unplanned. How to create an organic pattern of growth that many people of diverse values, interests, and levels of skill can help to create in a consensual and participatory way over a long period of time is an important question that our study has not attempted to answer.

2. **The development process must satisfy accepted tests of economic feasibility, but may use progressive financing techniques.** This suggests that the project should aim for incremental innovation in design, land use, and management, rather than radical design and social innovations. While we watch major industries that have failed to see the handwriting on the wall continue to 'decline' economically (utilities, auto companies), large lenders continue to put their money in what has worked before, even though the conditions that accounted for success in the past are no longer there. There is a paradox inherent in this situation. The way toward sustainability can be found only if society is willing to invest its capital and remaining fossil fuels energy in technologies and living patterns that are sustainable. It is our inability to make such investments in a long-term future that feeds uncertainty and instability, causing capital to flee toward speculation in unproductive commodities such as gold. These investments add nothing to our productive or sustainable capacity. This results in still lower productivity. The result is an economic system discounting the future at ever higher rates, creating an unwillingness to invest in projects that cannot pay out in five years or less. Barring economic collapse, we predict that capital will flow toward investment in sustainable technologies and patterns of growth as lenders and investors become aware of the long-term security and value such investments offer.

3. **The plan does not require major life-style changes. Its features are acceptable to a broad spectrum of buyers in the market.** An important motivation inherent in the Solar Village concept is the desire to create large-scale models that demonstrate the feasibility of a nationwide transition toward a sustainable future. Americans are pragmatic. They will adopt what works. The dispersion of ecologically sound design concepts into the mainstream American dream is just beginning. For these concepts to catch hold and be adopted, they must be nonthreatening. New living patterns tend to filter down from the values and actions of a relatively small number of pacesetters in the society. With the exception of Village Homes in Davis, California, today's 'solar villages' or village-scale experiments are mostly intentional communities, drawing to them people who already have a value system that includes an ecological awareness and a desire to live by consuming less and sharing more. Such examples are important, and while we would expect to attract a significant number of buyers who practice 'volun-

tary simplicity,' the design of Solar Village should not exclude the large number of potential residents with more traditional values. Living in Solar Village should be an experience in ecological awareness and the conservation ethic that grows on you.

4. **The plan can be carried out without government subsidy.** Solar Village is not 'experimental' or 'futuristic.' Indeed, it emphasizes the use of simple, proven approaches and techniques for enhancing sustainability and reducing fossil fuel dependency. If we employed various capital-intensive technologies, the energy and food balance in Solar Village could be made to appear more favorable. However, these more experimental systems would require special subsidies. Our plan increases energy efficiency by 100 percent; however, the consumption of imported fuels is still great. A conclusion that can be drawn is that attaining higher levels of ecological balance or energy sustainability within the Village requires either life-style changes or a planning boundary that balances on-site density with a broader resource base in the region.

## Context

The site presents both special opportunities and some particular problems. While directly adjacent to Highway 101 and residential neighborhoods to the north and south, the site has a feeling of remoteness from the surrounding sprawl, and spaciousness is enhanced by the broad views across the Bay and the marshes to the east and north. Access to the community is only from the east. This reinforces the integrity of the site and the concept of a village where workplace, convenience shopping, recreation, schools, and services are within walking or shuttle distance, thus reducing the need to constantly use one's car for short trips and commuting. Other important features of the plan include its aquatic location, rolling oak-studded uplands, and many fine existing buildings. All of these features are integrated into the plan. Existing streambeds restored, and a new pond is created as a site for homes, recreation, and an aquatic ecology. Most of the rolling hills are left in their natural state, traversed by two 'running walls' of solar homes and pedestrian spaces reminiscent of Italian hill towns. Temporary and substandard buildings are removed, but the existing fine complex of sound, red-tiled administrative buildings is transformed into a village center: shops, stores, and professional offices with apartments on their upper floors. Other low-lying areas unsuitable for building are used for community recreation, gardens, and on-site agriculture, contributing to the open feeling of the plan.

Novato, in the north end of Marin County, is the fastest-growing area of the county, and the area where much of Marin County's future growth is expected to take place. In the last several decades, most of

An earlier version of the plan returned 640 acres of diked lowland areas — including the runways — to managed aquaculture.

Gordon Ashby

the new, moderately priced housing has been built there. While the growth rate is slowing and Novato may adopt a growth management plan, it will continue to be the focus of new residential growth in the county. A key county policy calls for the creation of new jobs, particularly in the northern sector. The location of new light industry, and corporate administrative and research facilities will not only balance the county's tax base but will serve to provide an alternative to the heavy 101 commute, which is creating severe rush-hour traffic problems on this primary north/south artery. Major corporations, including Fireman's Fund, McGraw-Hill, Fairchild Semiconductor, and Digital Telephone have located in north Marin in recent years. Thus, the Solar Village concept, balancing new, moderately priced housing and new employment, is wholly compatible with the city and county's objectives.

No plan can succeed unless it is economically feasible and offers secure and attractive long-term investment opportunities. The plan rejects the simplistic notion of 'highest and best use' in favor of more strategic land-use planning that emphasizes the creation of long-term value by strategies such as enhancing the site's natural amenities, clustering residential development for the most economical construction and servicing, a phased development plan, and plan pre-approval by local jurisdiction.

Energy planning at the community scale is a key objective of the plan and the initial reason Solar Village came into being. A number of different and mutually supportive cost-effective strategies are used. They include:

• Conservation and solar retrofit of existing buildings.

- Passive solar design of all new buildings reducing space heating and cooling demand by 80 percent.
- Solar water heating.
- On-site production of gas from biomass resources.
- On-site electrical co-generation to reduce peak demand.
- On-site production of fresh fruits and vegetables.
- Convenient alternatives to auto use through pedestrian ways, bike paths, and an internal minibus loop to local employment, schools, and services.
- Recycling of water and wastes to agriculture and tree crops.
- Health maintenance through the extensive recreational complex and jogging paths.
- Community stability through integral neighborhood design.

All of these features add up to *sustainability*: less dependence on fuels and resources whose future supply and price are uncertain, coupled with designing for greater community self-reliance and use of local resources to sustain a high quality of life.

## Site Plan

The plan envisions approximately 1,900 dwellings built over a ten-year period in five distinct neighborhoods. The types of units include a variety of attached homes and apartments. All dwellings are south-facing and have private gardens or terraces. The gross density is approximately four units per acre.

There are no through streets in any neighborhood. Each neighborhood is bounded by a loop road. Cars are parked under buildings or in peripheral surface lots. No home is more than 300 feet from the car. Neighborhoods are connected by pedestrian and bicycle lanes that are also accessible to special service vehicles. Grades are generally flat.

At least 770,000 square feet of existing space is rehabilitated for light industrial and commercial use and housing. 800,000 square feet of new office and light industrial space will be constructed.

Most of the site is open space, including over fifty acres in agriculture and energy production, and forty-two acres in community parks and recreational use.

Services include on-site sewage treatment using the Solar Aquacell system that discharges no waste water into the Bay, and on-site disposal of solid wastes with methane recovery. There is a small on-site co-generation facility to minimize peak power demand, reusing heat in structures. An internal minibus circles the entire village at fifteen-minute intervals with major stops at employment centers, the Village Center, the transit center, and schools. Water runoff is carried on a surface system and stored in ponds for summer reuse for irrigation.

If the community is built according to the prototype plan, overall

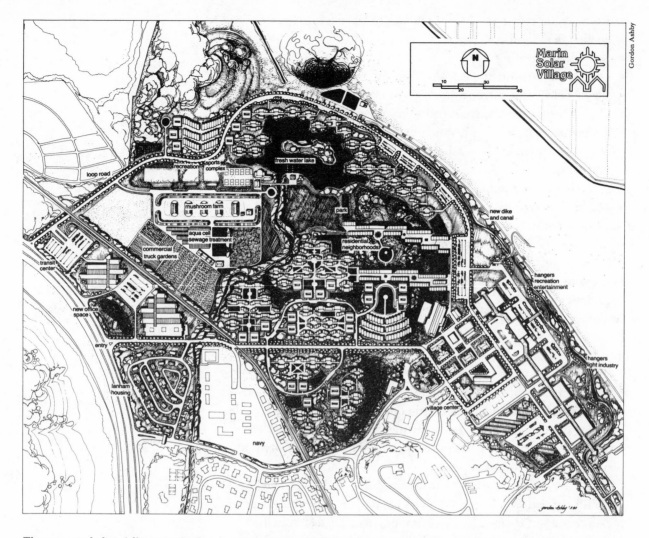

Gordon Ashby

The conceptual plan. Adjacent to the freeway at left is the corporate center. Adjacent to it is the agricultural area and biological waste treatment facility. 1900 attached housing unit occupy the center of the site with a rehabilitated town center and industrial area occupying existing buildings on the right.

energy use in buildings, transportation, services, and food systems will be reduced 45 percent from today's levels. These functions typically account for over 90 percent of the direct energy use in Marin today. Our savings are achieved without any major changes in life-styles or any significant cost premium. In considering technologies, we have been conservative, selecting only those that are proven and cost-effective today. These energy savings replace depletable fuels, primarily petroleum and natural gas, in a variety of ways.

The biggest energy consumer, transportation, which consumes over 50 percent of Marin's total energy budget, is reduced 40 percent, primarily by bringing jobs closer to people's homes, thereby reducing the commuting population by at least 25 percent. In addition, while the personal auto is no more than 400 feet from one's dwelling, incentives are created for walking or cycling to work, village stores, and other activities. Besides an extensive network of pedestrian ways and bicycle trails, electric minibus service loops each neighborhood every fifteen minutes, connecting homes, business, shopping, schools, and a transit center with connecting buses to other locations.

Buildings following the usual development pattern consume about 32 percent of Marin's energy budget. Extensive computer analysis that simulated and compared the energy use for heating and cooling Solar Village housing prototypes to similar nonsolar multifamily housing built to current State energy standards indicates a savings of better than 80 percent. A fraction of the fuel for backup heating can be supplied by wood harvested from reforested areas of the site, while 50 percent of the backup hot water heating and cooking gas needs is supplied by natural gas derived from processing organic wastes produced in the village.

The outlook for generating any of the village's electrical needs using on-site energy resources is not favorable. Climate, cost, and space requirements rule out solar thermal electric as well as wind. There are insufficient organic materials and space on site to justify investment in a facility to convert wastes to electricity; however, provisions for on-site electrical co-generation using conventional fuels to reduce peak demand may be feasible. State-of-the-art conservation measures reduce consumption 26 percent, while peak load (which determines the need for new utility generating capacity to meet increased demand) is reduced 40 percent through co-generation and other peak-load management. Additionally, detailed study may further reduce electrical demand. We have not calculated energy savings that result from more efficient sewage treatment and reduced water-pumping costs.

Another important set of resource and energy savings occurs from capturing winter runoff for later use in landscape irrigation; recycling water and nutrients by means of innovative sewage treatment; and allocating some site area for commercial truck gardens and orchards, as well as community and backyard gardens. We estimate that 30 percent of the fruits and vegetables consumed by the community can be grown by the on-site commercial truck farm. Additional home production can increase this figure significantly.

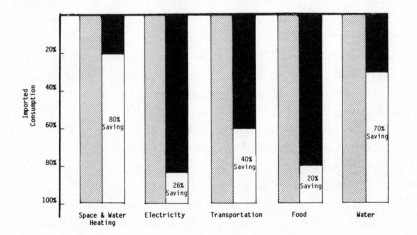

The graph indicates projected energy and resource savings produced by the plan as compared to standard development of the same density. In absolute terms, the biggest energy savings are realized by living close to the workplace and by energy efficient residential design measures.

67

An electric minivan provides internal transit for residents.

## Access and Circulation

The maximum distance between any two points within Solar Village is approximately one mile. It is possible to walk or bike to any place in the Village completely free of major intersections. The circulation system is designed to discourage the use of automobiles for intravillage short trips. (This type of trip in the standard residential community accounts for over half of the automobile fuel consumption.) However, one's home in Solar Village is never more than 400 feet from the parking space, a short block at most. Except for the hill neighborhood, gradients are flat, not exceeding 3-5 percent. All ground-floor residences and all commercial and institutional facilities are fully accessible to handicapped persons. To further encourage efficient transportation, the Village is served by a small electric thirty-passenger minibus connecting neighborhood residences to Village Center, employment centers, schools, adjacent military housing, and a transit center where residents can connect to the greater Marin bus system. The shuttle bus system is designed to operate on a fifteen-minute interval. Carpools, vanpools, and flex-time arrangements will all contribute to an efficient and convenient movement system.

## Residential Neighborhoods

Solar Village comprises five distinct residential neighborhoods, phased to be constructed over a five- to ten-year build-out period.

There are no single-family detached homes in Solar Village, but there are a variety of townhouses, apartments, and other forms of attached residences. These housing types yield a gross density of fifteen units per acre, resulting in more efficient land planning, lower construction costs and sales prices, and reduced energy consumption and waste. Each residence type and neighborhood is designed to enhance privacy as well as community. With one exception, the maximum dwelling height is three stories, and the entrance to any unit is not more than two stories off grade. All dwellings have a private garden or outdoor terrace. Buildings are located for maximum solar access so that no south wall is ever in shade. Dwellings within the neighborhood are grouped around common outdoor spaces so that each component of each neighborhood has a distinct and unique spatial character.

The North Reservoir Hill neighborhood is perhaps the most dramatic: a double band of three- and four-story townhouses climbing San Francisco-like up and over the hill. Between the bands is a street and a series of small plazas that give this neighborhood an Italian hill town flavor. The wooded knolls and steep ravines of the hill are left in their natural state as places for solitude and contemplation.

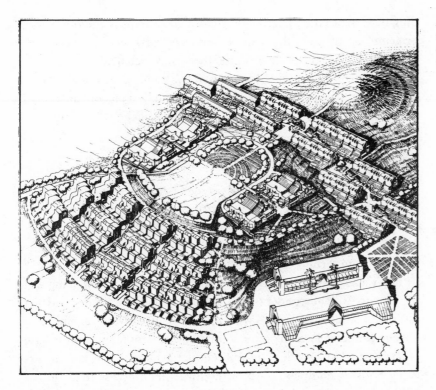

An overview of hilltop housing. The unit orientation recognizes that solar access has an importance as great as topography.

From the hill dwellings, residents will have an unparalleled view across San Pablo Bay and to San Francisco. On the south slopes of the hill lie three crescents of terrace housing opening onto the tree-lined boulevard. North Reservoir Hill is the most urban of Solar Village's neighborhoods. One can walk a short distance to the Village Center with its shops, cafes, and community center.

The South Reservoir Hill neighborhood is bounded on the north by the entrance boulevard, on the east by the railroad right-of-way, and below by the south entrance road. The westerly rim of this neighborhood overlooks the charming red-tile roofs of the chapel and the existing main administration building, which will become the community center. It is a compact neighborhood, highly accessible but out of the way; a place of great natural variety.

The Meadow area lies in the center of the Solar Village. Its townhouses are configured in a variety of clusters. On the easterly edge, they border the restored Pacheco Creek, lined with alders and other native plantings. On the north, they open onto the spacious 20-acre Village park with its clubhouses and lake frontage. Townhouse clusters are separated by generous courts, community gardens, and neighborhood play areas. Cars, except for those of guests, are not visible, yet they are close at hand in the covered parking areas underneath the Atrium apartments.

To the north lie the Rock Hill and Lakeside neighborhoods. Terrace homes nestle on the protected south slopes of the hill. The surrounding bare slopes have been reforested with eucalyptus and other fast-growing, hardy trees that can be harvested for firewood and power generation. Cluster homes surround the lake, which holds runoff water from the surrounding hills. A small island is home to the many aquatic birds native to brackish marshes. To the north lie a lagoon and marsh that are used in the final stages of purifying Village waste water.

## Village Center

A 'village' is different from a suburb or 'bedroom community' in that it brings together homeplace, workplace, and necessary services and amenities into a well-balanced, complete community. Thus, the integration of employment centers and convenience shopping and services is an important aspect of the solar village plan.

The Village Center is designed to provide convenience shopping and services to Village residents, the adjacent neighborhoods, and the estimated 3,800 people who will come in daily to work on site. The Village Center is located on the southeast corner of the site at the base of Reservoir Hill and directly adjacent to the hangar area and the existing housing complex. Two of the three main access roads in the Village converge on the center. This area was formerly the base administrative center and includes a number of fine, sound buildings that are converted to commercial and other uses. The area contains approximately 500,000 square feet of space.

Stores and eating places occupy the ground level of these buildings. Professional offices and apartments occupy the top two floors. The existing base headquarters at the hub of the center, a gracious Spanish-style building, is the community center and 'city hall.' A large wooden trussed warehouse building is converted into the community market

The conversion and infill of the existing base administration buildings provides for a compact village center.

and fronts onto a small village plaza providing a pleasant place to meet friends. New one-story structures fill in some of the gaps to give the center coherence and vitality. The walks are lined with mature trees. Every fifteen minutes the electric bus glides by, having made its loop around the neighborhoods and employment centers. On the eastern edge of the center lies a small amphitheater for community events and a permanent exhibition with models and displays that tell the full story of Solar Village to visitors. One hangar has been converted into an indoor recreational center with ball courts. Surface parking for visitors and others using automobiles to reach the Village Center is located at its edges.

## Employment Centers

There are two major employment centers within Solar Village. The first occupies twenty-four acres adjacent to the freeway and the Transportation Center. Our design shows two three-story office buildings. This space will be leased to one or more tenants who require

A rendering of typical office block.

office or light industrial space. The buildings are designed for energy efficiency, including extensive use of daylighting and passive solar heating and cooling. The location of these facilities directly on the transit corridor is designed to minimize the need for wasteful auto use and, although adequate parking is provided, employees living off site will be encouraged to use buses, carpools, and vanpools. A major amenity and a savings of energy are made possible by matching employment and new housing within the Village. A major corporate tenant

71

relocating employees from another area could negotiate for a block of new housing to meet its employees' requirements. Lack of housing is becoming a major deterrent to corporate expansion in the Bay Area; thus, a strategy of matching jobs and housing is an important asset of the plan.

The second major employment center is the Solar Technology Center located in the refurbished hangar complex adjacent to the Village Center. The hangars are structurally sound and in good condition. They offer relatively inexpensive space for light manufacturing, assembly, warehousing, and research activities. An added mezzanine level creates extra space for offices and lofts, while the space below serves as workshops, storage rooms, and service spaces. A second-story covered walkway connects the mezzanine level. The name we have given to this complex signifies the desire to create a center that provides affordable space for small and medium-sized businesses that are engaged in research, manufacture and sales in the emerging area of solar and renewable energy technology and self sufficiency. Examples of businesses include manufacturers, distributors, and installers of solar collector panels; research, development, and manufacture of wind electric systems, electric vehicles, sailboats, and nonmotorized recreational vehicles; home garden systems and supplies; natural food distribution; holistic health-related technology; and communication and design service organizations related to sustainability.

A closer view of corporate center in the model. The adjacency of information oriented industry and intensive agriculture provides a visible reminder that high information technology and healthy local agriculture are two compatible aspects of sustainability.

Peter Xiques

72

In addition to these two major employment centers, Solar Village will provide other opportunities for full-time and part-time work for residents and others in the county. The commercial farming operation and horticulture at Solar Village will employ approximately fifty people. Local services, including Village transit, recreation, shops, and maintenance activities will provide additional employment opportunities. Many of these jobs may be shared or part-time.

## Open Space, Recreation, Ecological Restoration

Over one hundred acres of Solar Village are dedicated to community-use open space. In addition, another one hundred acres are devoted to on-site food and energy production. The Solar Village open space network is varied and diverse for a community of its size.

Peter Xiques

Intelligent site planning increases amenity and sustainability. Although its density exceeds that of most suburbs, the Solar Village plan provides a greater measure of useful and useable open space.

Much of the hill area is left in its natural state with its live oaks and seasonal grasses. The once barren Rock Hill area is reforested to provide firewood for the residents. It is a place for quiet contemplation offering a measure of solitude and wonderful views toward the East Bay. In the lowlands area at the approximate center of the site, there is a grassy twenty-acre park. On the north, it fronts a sixteen-acre lake that is fed with winter runoff and recycled water. This lake accommodates small rowboats and fishing. At its center there is a small natural marshy island, providing habitat for native birds and small native animals. The park is bisected by a small restored stream lined with alder and other riparian trees. An area for active recreation and organized sports is located on the east side of Pacheco Creek. Here we find a Village clubhouse with an Olympic-sized pool, game rooms, lockers, and other facilities. There is a soccer field with bleachers, two baseball diamonds,

Gordon Ashby

A view of the refurbished hangars. Lofts in these buildings offer the opportunity to create low cost live-work spaces.

and ten tennis courts. Other tennis courts and ball courts are located in each neighborhood. The clubhouse and active games area are accessible from the loop road. A jogging path and par course border the recreation area, running along the stream and neighborhoods. It is possible to jog, walk, or bicycle the entire circumference of Solar Village without crossing major loop roads.

In addition to these major open spaces, each cluster and each neighborhood has its own open spaces, serving a variety of community uses. We have not attempted to design each of these, as their particular character and use should be determined with the participation of residents, as has been done successfully by Mike and Judy Corbett, developers of Village Homes in Davis, California. People may want to use some spaces for community gardens, others for tot lots, active sports, or quieter areas. Each space has been designed so that it is connected to and becomes part of distinct dwelling clusters and neighborhoods.

## Food and Energy Production, Waste and Water

Reducing today's wasteful and inefficient consumption of fossil fuels through careful, conserving community and building design is only half of the equation to be considered in planning a sustainable community. The other half involves producing some part of the essential food, fuels, and other resources that are needed to sustain the community's daily life. In approaching this problem, our goal has not been to design a 'self-sufficient community' — or closed system walled off from its surroundings. Solar Village is one cell in a vast and complex urban and bioregional whole. Its life and economy are only possible through a constant and rich exchange of energy, materials, and information. As part of an extensive urban corridor, its economic values, land uses, and human values preclude anything approaching total self-sufficiency in food, energy, or other resources. However, we believe the concept of integrating these essential forms of production into the life of suburban and urban communities not only reduces dependency on increasingly uncertain and uncontrollable sources of supply but enhances the health, beauty, and viability of the community. Most people today, regardless of income or status, do not have direct access to, nor the ability to control, the essentials they need to survive. They are powerless, fragmented consumers of the products of vast centralized resource systems and unseen networks. By bringing some measure of production into the design of the Solar Village, residents achieve a connection to the vital roots of existence in today's denatured technological world.

Approximately forty acres of the Solar Village are given over to agricultural production of vegetables and soft fruits and to related facilities. It is estimated that in commercial production this area can supply approximately 30 percent of the Village population's requirements for fresh fruits and vegetables. In addition to commercial agriculture, space has been provided within each neighborhood for community gardens, backyard gardens, and terrace planting. Home garden production by residences could significantly increase the amount of the total food requirement that can be grown on site. Climate data and experience in the region suggest that the Hamilton site is an excellent one for diverse production of vegetables and fruits.

The former ordnance storage area has been redesigned for mushroom production, using the existing facility. It is estimated that this activity can gross approximately $1.3 million a year and employ forty people. The entire water need for agriculture can be supplied by recycled wastewater held in a reservoir. In addition to the agricultural component designed into the plan, commercial horticulture and a tree nursery appear to be good uses of the south end of the hangar complex. The agricultural plant will be developed as part of the Solar Village infrastructure cost and leased to commercial operators for a percentage of the gross.

Water for the Solar Village will be supplied by the Marin Municipal Water District. Residential water requirements exclusive of landscape irrigation are estimated at 265 acre-feet per year. Runoff water on site will be collected in the lake. The Village is designed for water conservation through the use of drought-resistant and native plantings and through the reuse of purified wastewater for agricultural use. Low

Commercial greenhouses provide for economical year round production of high quality fresh produce for local consumption.

A cutaway of the Solar Aquacultural
system for biological treatment of waste
water. The design incorporates a
polycultural mix of plants and
micromarine life.

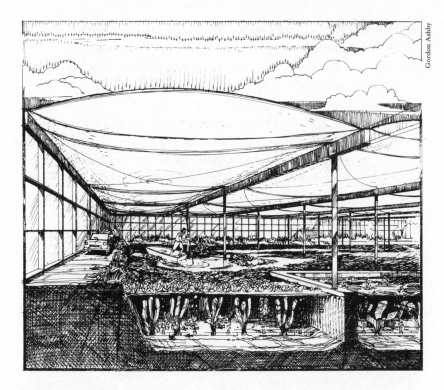

Gordon Ashby

water-using fixtures (such as the IFO Cascade Toilet which uses only
one or two quarts to flush) are standard in the project.

The wastewater treatment facility is directly adjacent to the
agricultural zone. The system follows the design of an innovative
wastewater facility developed by Solar Aquasystems, San Diego.
Wastewater is purified in closed greenhouses using a variety of
biological techniques that create special habitats for facultative bacteria
and microorganisms that absorb nutrients from the waste stream. During the dry season from May to November, no effluent is discharged
into the Bay, but it is used for crop irrigation.

Energy production on site will take several forms. Solar energy will
provide 80 percent of the space and water heating demand that is con-
ventionally supplied by natural gas or electricity. Wood grown on site
will provide backup heating needs for dwellings that are equipped with
energy-efficient airtight wood- burning stoves. All organic solid wastes,
including paper, will be buried in a landfill on the far southern edge
of the site at the end of the runway area. A network of pipes will capture the methane gas naurally produced through the fermentation of
garbage and other wastes. The methane gas generated from on- site
wastes will be sufficient to supply energy for residential cooking and
some water heating.

A number of different options for generating electricity on site were
analyzed including wind power, solar thermal generation, photovoltaic
cells, and biomass combustion. Site cost constraints as well as the
relatively small scale of the project have ruled out the present use of

any of these technologies to generate a significant portion of the required four megawatts of required peak capacity. Structures have been designed so that photovoltaic cells can be added to buildings when they become competitive with centrally — produced utility power. Peak elecrical demand in the Village is estimated to be 60 percent of present per capita Marin use. Peak load management through computerized management of the Village system is expected to make a significant contribution to reducing additional load on the existing utility grid.

## Housing Plans and Prototypes

The housing design for Hamilton is, in a sense, the pivotal point of the village plan. All aspects of the community design are interdependent with the housing: transit modes, quantity of retail space, quantity and type of employment, land use, total energy demand, food production, recreation, and economics. No fixed housing program, in terms of quantity, type, and income was mandated; the goal was to generate a balance rather than assume the housing levels as *a priori*.

Several qualitative design guidelines developed from a range of social, economic, and energy criteria. Briefly, the first guideline identified attached dwellings rather than single-family dwellings as a high priority. There have been many studies demonstrating the energy and economic efficiency of townhouse-type construction. Reductions in heating and cooling demands of 50 percent result from party wall construction. Similarly, both building construction costs and site costs are reduced by these denser forms of housing. The spatial arrangements of the various attached housing forms have some implications for the feasibility of mass transit and a more pedestrian-oriented environment. Housing density is not the only variable in this complex question of circulation and cannot in itself reduce transit consumption. Denser housing patterns free land for recreation, farming, and open space.

A brief comparison of a typical Hamilton neighborhood and a neighborhood of detached houses on typical lot sizes highlights some of the differences. In terms of land areas, the Solar Village neighborhood consumes 66 percent less while providing a rich variety of open spaces. Rather than just private yards, the plan provides a range of open spaces and uses: private yards for each unit, cluster courtyards for small children to play in under close supervision, larger squares and greens for games, barbeques, and neighborhood functions ringed with fruit trees, and community gardening space for household vegetable gardens.

By our use of a more compact housing form, the auto is eliminated from circulation within the neighborhood while still remaining accessible. The centralization of parking, under the Atrium apartments, vastly reduces the amount of paved surfaces and their inherent con-

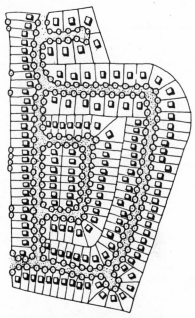

— DETACHED SINGLE FAMILY —

— MAXIMUM SOLAR DENSITY —

A comparison of land requirements for typical suburban scale development and the proposed solar village units. Density need not reduce the potential for access to the sun.

— HAMILTON SOLAR VILLAGE —

struction costs and storm drainage. The pedestrian quality of the neighborhoods should enhance social integration and discourage use of the auto within the village.

The average energy and hot water consumption of detached single-family homes in the Novato area is 1,350 therms, while for a nonsolar townhouse it is 764. Because the townhouse is naturally more energy-efficient, its solar heating system is smaller and less expensive.

The townhouse building type reduces construction costs as well as energy loads. The construction costs listed in **Construction Systems Costs** show a $7 per square foot cost difference between the detached and the low-rise attached housing types. These reduced construction costs are matched by reductions in site development costs. The smaller land areas, reduced roadways, and shorter utility lines all contribute to the overall reduction in costs. The reductions in construction materials used — asphalt, concrete, pipe, lumber, etc. — represent, in a larger sense, energy and resource savings.

On the whole, the denser housing types are a more efficient and ecological form. Historically, societies have tended toward compact settlements for a variety of reasons: defense, social interaction, shared resources and facilities, transportation, and tradition. The current awareness of resource limits may cause a return to these traditions. Party walls, plazas, and pedestrians may replace fences, yards, and cars. The result would be a less gluttonous environment and, perhaps, healthier communities.

The second major design guideline concerned the scale, orientation, and solar access of the housing units. A direct connection to the ground and private entry were desired for as many units as possible. Qualitative goals were set to maximize the size and quantity of private yards. Geometric criteria of solar access are dependent on building sections, time of year, and percent of building shaded. Simple, direct, passive solar space-heating systems were assumed, so solar access for each floor

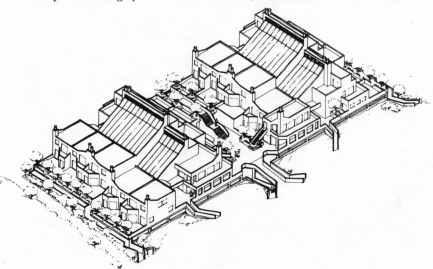

A view of atrium apartments combined with village parking underneath.

78

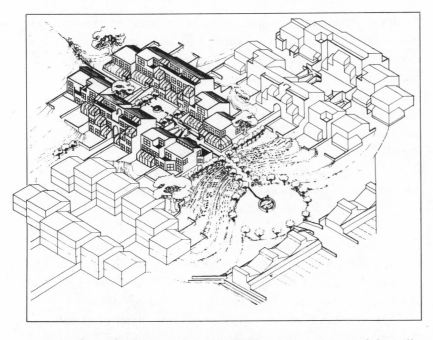

A cluster of twelve attached homes each with private yard space grouped around a common courtyard.

was required. Deviations of up to 30 degrees from due south have little effect on passive solar heating efficiency. However, shading and the
resulting cooling loads for nonsouth orientations directed the design
toward a primary due-south orientation.

The final design guideline concerned the social issues of economics
and life-style. The economic guidelines indicated that the total project
would need a minimum of 1,000 units and would improve, from the

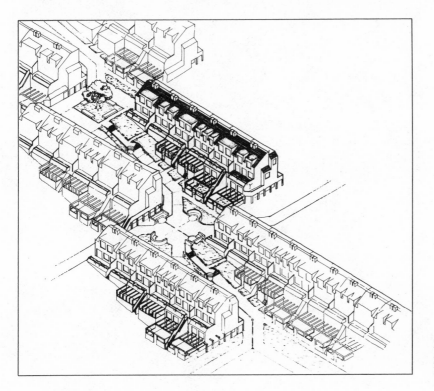

Row houses stepping up a hill recall a
pattern indigenous to the San Francisco
Bay area.

developers' standpoint, by increasing this number. Market-rate and entry-level housing costs were desirable from a philosophical perspective as well as from the clear need to create a balanced community. Differing employment types would necessitate a variety of housing costs. Life-style and demographic character of the Village were assumed to be extremely diverse. Recent studies have shown, for example, that the nuclear family will no longer be the dominant housing unit by 1990. The size and features of the housing types therefore remain flexible. Within the basic building types and massing, a great variety of living patterns could be accommodated, from 12,000 square-foot shared living clusters, through single-family townhouses, to small studio and apartment residences.

From these various assumptions and guidelines of density, orientation, solar access, and social character, a familiar pattern has emerged. Accommodating the special considerations of solar access and orientation, the plan employs a low-rise, high-density mix of townhouses, row houses, and apartments. The planning concepts emphasize social groupings of differing scales. Clusters, streets, and neighborhoods provide the basic structure. Shared open spaces, such as neighborhood greens, squares, community gardens and open fields, provide social gathering points and identity for the cluster, neighborhoods, and the Village at large. Planning to reduce the presence of the private auto and to encourage pedestrians, bikes, and small buses was a high priority.

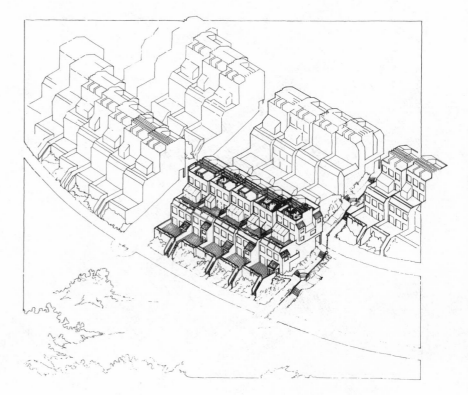

The attached housing type integrates privacy and community in a compact and efficient urban pattern.

## Solar Access and Density

Abstract, two-dimensional studies of solar access and density were conducted to provide guidelines for schematic design. A morphology of patterns was developed for typical residential building sections of various heights and setbacks. The two-dimensional section is a simplification of the solar envelope concept, essentially disregarding direct solar access to the east, west, or north as a criterion. The shading angle chosen, 25°, is the profile angle at 10:00 A.M. and 2:00 P.M., December 21, at 38° latitude. The building section is assumed to be 30 feet deep, as thicker sections create problems for passive solar systems. The first diagram represents schematically the high-rise versus low-rise options. In **Architectur**, published in 1934, Walter Gropius presented a similar study which demonstrated, as this does, that high-rise buildings with identical solar access to low-rise buildings achieve higher densities and therefore more efficient land use. By increasing the number of stories, he claimed, the exposure improved for any given land size and housing quantity. Although the total land in shade is identical for the high- or low- rise option, the total area of the building's footprint increases with low-rise. This effect of 'saving' the land the building occupies accounts for the increased efficiency of the high-rise. However, the additional roof area in the low-rise option has valuable solar access. This area can be profitably used as roof apertures for passive solar gain, for ventilation, and for active collectors. If the roof solar access is credited as a south wall projection, there is no theoretical difference between high- and low-rise options in terms of total exposure.

Leaving other planning issues aside, such as scale, open space definition, and quality of use, maximized south wall solar access and density, with no roof credit, favor the high-rise. However, the efficiency is not continuous. This figure graphs density versus number of floors for the given solar access angle of 25°. It is clear that after four to six floors, the curve flattens out. The diminishing effect of additional stories must be noted when generalizing design guidelines. Ultimately, a theoretical limit to density exists for any given profile angle. In this case, the curve will approach but never exceed 40.62 units per net acre.

The formula for net density, not including roads, open space, or recreation other than shaded land, is:

$$\text{Density (units/acre)} = \frac{c}{1/\text{Tan } \theta + \frac{w}{x}}$$

As x (total height) approaches infinity, the density approaches a limit dependent on the assumed unit dimensions and the sun angle:

$$\text{Density} = \frac{43560}{HD} \times \text{Tan } \theta$$

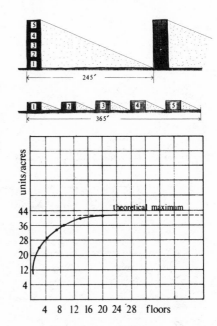

From the 1934 Gropius study.

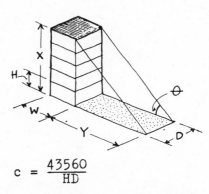

$$c = \frac{43560}{HD}$$

all dimensions in feet

81

| UNITS/ACRE | S.F./UNIT | YARD AREA | SETBACK | PER CENT SOLAR ACCESS | TYPE | BUILDING SPACING | BUILDING WIDTH |
|---|---|---|---|---|---|---|---|
| 21 | 1500' | 1175' | 15' | 100% | Town-house | 62' | 20' |
| 22 | 1500' | 875' | 15' | 100% | Town-house | 42' | 30' |
| 23 | 1500' | 750' | 0' | 100% | Town-house | 42' | 30' |
| 28 | 1500' | 437' | 0' | 75% | Town-house | 20' | 30' |
| 32 | 2-1500'<br>1- 750' | 600' | 15' | 100% | Stacked Town-house | 42' | 30' |
| 38 | 2-1500'<br>2- 750' | 562' | 15' | 100% | Stacked Town-house | 62' | 30' |
| 42 | 2-1500'<br>2-1200'<br>2- 750' | 250' | 15' | 100% | Apart-ment | 30' | 80' |

The table indicates that a variety of low rise forms and configurations are possible while maintaining full access to the sun.

The factor H.D. is simply the area of the south wall, indicating that as the south wall area per unit increases, the density decreases; and as $\theta$ increases, the density increases.

The importance of this limit is that many low-rise high-density housing patterns can achieve similar densities. These densities are based on a 25-foot dimension party wall to party wall and a secondary easement of 30 feet for two units. They do not include primary feeder streets and open space recreation areas, and therefore represent net maximums. Once attached units with east and west party walls are assumed, densities in the low 20s are possible with a variety of schemes. The two-story townhouse form, with a ground floor entry and a private yard, has a maximum density of around twenty-eight units per acre if one-quarter of the total south facades is shaded. Stacked units of various configurations range from thirty-eight to forty-two units per acre. A mix of townhouse and stacked units providing 66 percent ground floor entry will produce a density of thirty-two. Finally, the centralized collector space of the Atrium apartments essentially removes the solar access criteria from the south facades. This allows even higher densities.

In plan, the configuration of these two-dimensional studies has assumed an abstract parallel block configuration. Although this is a fairly classical row house configuration, lining streets in an urban context, it does not offer a desirable amount of variety and differentiation of space. Staggering blocks of townhouses, varying their height and the dependent spacing, stepping each unit, and varying the orientation are all techniques that can relieve the monotony of strict solar access.

To conclude, passive solar access places a limit to density well below many urban environments. Within these limits, many low-rise two- to four-story options can match densities achieved with high-rise. Given that the maximum density of approximately forty units per acre is not desirable in many cases, a rich variety of attached townhouses, stacked flats, and apartments is available.

# Case Study 2 — Golden, Colorado

## Context

The project envisions infilling a large tract of vacant land — in this case, 400 acres — that lies within the path of present suburbanization, and that, left to the normal development process, would be converted into more of the same suburban fabric; hence, the opportunity to plan at a scale that is similar to but less isolated than 'New Town,' and more physically, socially, and ecologically coherent than today's suburb.

The plan is a program diagram of a community based on integrated systems. The central concept is to reintegrate a diverse base of human activities, presenting a village scale miniaturization of the activities normally segregated throughout a region. This mix produces an economic, psychological, and biological vitality generally missing from our single-use residential subdivisions and urban cores. Combining the house, workplace, recreation, services, food production, and entertainment in an environment tuned to the pedestrian reduces auto dependence and promotes community. Integrating solar- based energy systems reduces infrastructure costs and resource consumption. The coincidence of the social activities and ecological strategies produces a new model for development in the Sun Belt: a sustainable and human environment.

The specific site is located nine miles west of Denver between the towns of Golden and Lakewood. It is bordered by a major freeway (Interstate-70) leading from the mountains to Denver and is traversed by a major commercial strip road, Colfax Avenue. The site is one of a few left between the press of Denver's urban sprawl and the once isolated community of Golden. Surrounded by development, it represents an infill site rather than a 'hopscotch' development. The four hundred acres are held by a single owner, who has already developed the northern part into an office park (currently occupied partially by the Solar Energy Research Institute) and is in the pro-

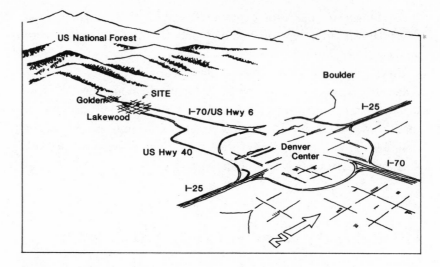

cess of developing the sections across I-70 into more office space. The
design site concerns the remaining two hundred acres of this holding.

Scattered, low-density urban sprawl has become a dominant feature
of the regional landscape and is expected to characterize future
growth. By the year 2000, Denver's population is projected to grow
by only 14 percent, while Lakewood is expected to grow by 64 percent, and Golden by 132 percent. Unincorporated areas of Jefferson
County, including those adjacent to the site, are expected to show
large population increases.

The private automobile is the metropolitan Denver area's major
means of transit. The area sprawls over 200 square miles with home-
to-work trips averaging 15-25 miles (round trip) per capita. Most trips
involve one person per car. The average car size is dramatically down,
however, in the past five years, and car-pooling is slowly catching on.
Mass transit currently consists of bus service only.

The site is directly affected by three major employment centers
beyond the Denver West Office Park: the Denver Federal Center,
employing up to 20,000 people and located two miles from the site;
the Adolph Coors Brewing Company within approximately three
miles; and the new SERI Building within a mile and projected to
employ up to 2,000 people.

As in many Sun Belt areas, the local economy is expected to remain
strong, and most areas will continue to exhibit above-average incomes. Economic activity, including housing and commercial construction, is expected to remain at the present high level in Jefferson
County. This should prove particularly true in the area surrounding
South Table Mountain as easy access and large-scale developments
like Denver West continue to attract new tenants.

The site is bordered on the north by I-70 and the Denver West Office Park and by existing single-family residential housing to the south
and east. Further west is a cliff and plateau formation called a

84

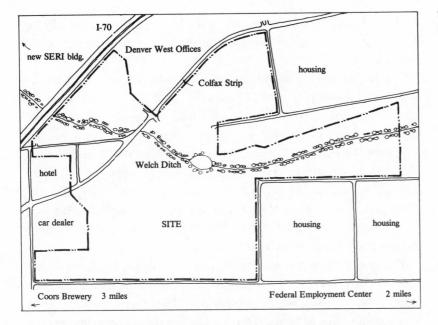

The proposed site — a large infill area in a fast growing suburban crazy quilt.

hogback, which is the future location of SERI's new office/lab complex. Topographically the site is flat with its major area under 7 percent slope. It is drained by an irrigation canal that has been serving various agricultural operations to the east for eight years. This canal is a dominant feature in the landscape, supporting cottonwood and willow trees along its bank. It represents a significant public right-of-way through the surrounding neighborhoods. The rest of the site is covered with buffalo and grama grasses. The location is considered arid, with 15 inches of rainfall per year and little more than one foot of topsoil over clay. The general area of the east Rockies is considered a marginal agricultural zone confined to grazing and dry-land hay production.

## Climate Description

The Denver metropolitan area climate is classified as semi-arid. The area is typified by sparse rainfall, low relative humidity, clear skies, and large diurnal and seasonal temperature variations. Periods of extremely warm or extremely cold weather are generally short, due to the modifying effect of the Rocky Mountains. The annual heating degree day is 6,016.

Temperatures in the summer rarely exceed 100 degrees Fahrenheit (38 degrees Centigrade), but maximum temperatures above 90 degrees Fahrenheit (32 degrees Centigrade) occur about seventeen times per year. During the winter months, the mean maximum temperature is always above freezing, but rapid cooling at night is common, with an average minimum temperature for January at 18 degrees Fahrenheit (-8 degrees Centigrade). Daily temperature swings in all seasons tend to be large, with daily highs and lows generally 30 degrees apart. A diurnal swing of less than 20 degrees Fahrenheit is extremely rare.

The site enjoys an abundance of solar radiation on a year-round basis. May, June, July, and August show the lowest monthly averages of incident radiation on a vertical surface. September, October, February, and March all show averages exceeding 415 langleys per day, with November, December, and January not significantly lower. Heating-season sunshine is abundant in an average year, with very infrequent periods of extended cloudiness. The usual pattern is one of frequent snows of brief duration followed by quick clearing and bright sunshine. Given the high altitude (5,600 feet) and low humidity, sunshine is particularly intense.

The general precipitation pattern is one of rain in the summer, snow in the winter, with a mix (mostly snow) in the spring and fall. June, July, and August are the only months showing no snow in an average year. The annual average of 15-16 inches of rain classifies the site as semi-arid. Long periods of either rain or snow, however, are very infrequent. Summer rains are generally in the form of late afternoon thundershowers.

The site enjoys relatively mild winds most of the year, but, being located just east of the foothills of the Rocky Mountains, it is subject to severe chinook winds blowing from the west during the months of November through March. The chinooks can be prolonged, irritating, and damaging, with periods of as long as a week, a sustained 40-miles-per-hour wind, and gusts of up to 100 miles per hour.

The Golden/Denver metropolitan area has a major air-quality problem, largely fostered by urban sprawl and heavy automobile use rather than industrial sources. The site is at the western edge of the broad basin that traps the pollution. November through March is the worst period, with frequent inversions lasting for three or four days at a time.

Relative humidities are generally very low with extended periods of high humidity virtually unknown. Winter days generally start at 70 percent and drop to 20-30 percent. Summer days start at 30-40 percent and drop to 10-20 percent. There are often two or three summer days per year with humidity reaching the 0-5 percent range.

## Design Goals

Beyond the generic design goals of new growth in a sustainable pattern, this site generated some specific objectives:

- **Identity** — Establish a sense of place that is not an island in a single-family sprawl but will in effect provide a focus for the surrounding neighborhoods.

- **Community** — Establish a balance of people, jobs, and services to create a coherent place.
- **Employment** — Provide work spaces for small-scale production and services to balance the local large scale employers.
- **Services** — Provide commercial and civic services at various scales for the region, community, and neighborhoods.
- **Transportation** — Walking/bicycling should be encouraged and internal auto use discouraged. Link the site by mass transit to the major employment centers.
- **Water** — Careful use/control of water needs for vegetation, drainage, and household use.
- **Wilderness** — Respect and enhance natural conditions of the site such as trees, riparian corridors, and natural grasses.
- **Food Production** — Commercial, community, and private production should be encouraged and accommodated.
- **Energy** — Base supplies on solar, climate, on site recycling, and regional renewable resources.
- **Housing** — A rare infill site in an area with great growth pressures; housing density should be maximized without sacrificing any of the other goals or amenities of owners.

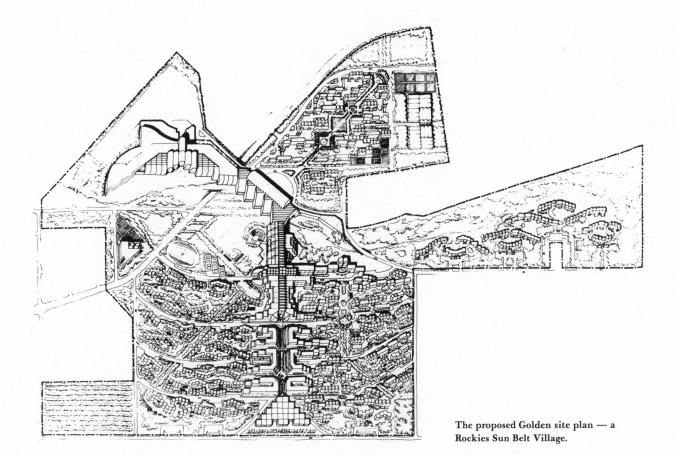

The proposed Golden site plan — a Rockies Sun Belt Village.

## Site Plan

The central concept of the site plan is to focus activity along a pedestrian spine while providing clearly defined domains for smaller neighborhoods and housing cluster groupings. The northern and eastern edges of the site are buffered from the freeway by regional commercial stores and a large orchard. The southern and eastern edges open to the existing housing neighborhoods, maintaining continuity and providing access to the village center for the larger community.

The irrigation canal traversing the site is a dominant feature as a linkage to other areas, as a source of water, and as a unique part of the landscape feature. As the ditch represents a non-auto right-of-way to the neighborhood school, the office park location, and beyond, it is developed as a pedestrian/bike path. Such right-of-ways potentially can offer pleasing bike paths in many communities.

A 40-acre site in close proximity to the existing office park is isolated by Colfax Avenue and bordered on the north by I-70. This truncated area serves as a regional shopping center, located near the freeway for visibility with parking placed as a buffer. This area is tied to the rest of the development by a sheltered pedestrian spine that draws the housing, neighborhood services, school, and civic functions together. The irrigation channel runs inside the covered street to reinforce the coincidence of the different systems. The housing branches out from this central collector, encountering an orchard buffer to the west and commercial greenhouses to the south, and running parallel to Welsh Ditch to merge with the housing on the west. In the low northern corner of the site an area is designated for solid waste composting and biological sewage treatment. On an island of land north of Colfax

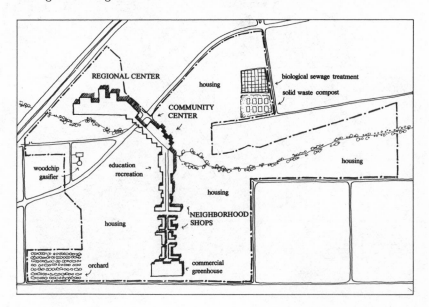

The suburban strip and shopping mall redesigned into a new configuration: an enclosed pedestrian spine.

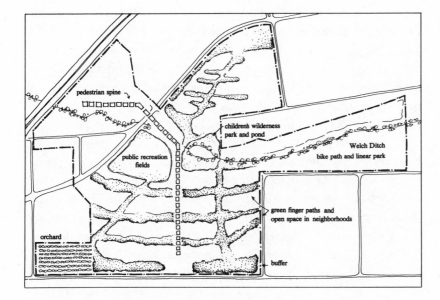

The open space pattern consists of branchlike fingers of green converging on the pedestrian spine.

Avenue, a woodchip gasifier plant is located to receive imports of wood from the mountains and produce natural gas.

A variety of open spaces is integrated throughout the site. A large playing field/park is south of the covered street on which the school and community services are located. This space acts both as a public open space and as a recreation area for the school. As the irrigation channel emerges from the street, a smaller park for children is developed with a pond. Along the tree- lined ditch is a bike path, linking the village center to the elementary school just off the site. The housing is configured to provide fingers of neighborhood greens and smaller play areas associated with individual housing clusters.

## Main Street as Bioshelter

The central collector street, which unifies the site, is in some sense a version of the classical 'Main Street, U.S.A.' with some significant modifications. As with traditional main streets, the public and commercial activities of the community line its edges. Its linear quality allows many neighborhoods to tie into it at various points and allows a progression from regional- to community- to neighborhood-scaled activities.

By covering certain sections of the street with south-facing greenhouses, the meaning and function of the street are intensified and transformed. First of all, it protects the pedestrian year-round in the severe climate. Functioning like the continuous arcades in many pre-auto European cities, it symbolizes a commitment to pedestrians by providing an alternative to the shelter of their car. As a year-round accessible public space, it can become the focus of community activities and identity for the new development and surrounding areas.

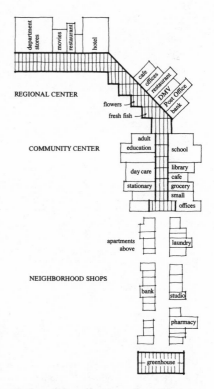

A plan of the pedestrian spine with suggested uses.

Beyond the energy implications of reduced auto dependency within the site, the glazed street will reduce the heating demands of the adjacent buildings. The street acts as a passive thermal buffer zone that will not experience the temperature extremes of the outside environment. Like a solar greenhouse on a residence, the covered street will provide both heat and useful space.

The site is poorly suited for open field food production. Thus, parts of the solar arcade street are zoned for greenhouse production and commercial propagation of ornamentals and other high-cash-return crops that could be sold along the street. The potential for some areas to be used for intensive fish farming in tanks was also investigated. In both cases, the temperature ranges of the solar street would support such activities; the waste heat from the buildings and the configuration of the glass roof provide the temperature required for the biological processes. Integrating such productive activities near the center of the community becomes important psychologically and symbolically.

The activities along the street range from the most public — a regional shopping area — to a residential neighborhood. At the northwest end, the regional shopping area starts the street. By drawing from the regional scale, many services that cannot be economically sup-

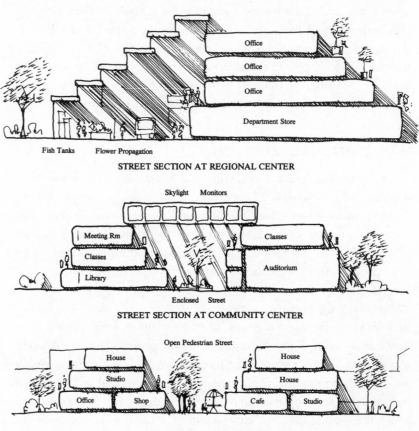

Sections through the pedestrian spine. Top view shows "bioshelter", middle view a typical top lit mall; at bottom the open mall.

90

ported by one community become available to this high-density pedestrian village. Simultaneously, the village and its spine will serve the larger community by providing a focus and center to a sprawling bedroom community. Two levels of retail are mixed with office space in this section.

As the street bridges Colfax Avenue, its character changes: local stores, branch government services, and a multi-use school occupy this diagonal section. The area is adjacent to the primary open spaces intended to become a noncommercial public focus. The school straddles the street, with students using the public way as a corridor between classes, integrating education with the life of the community. The school facilities are multifunctional, housing the public library, meeting rooms, recreational areas, day-care areas, adult education services, and theaters for the whole village. This will not only conserve public funds and building material resources, but will reintegrate education into the mainstream of public life.

As the street turns again to run south, it opens to a pond and a park/path along the irrigation canal and the playing fields. This southern leg of the street is partially covered, becoming more neighborhood and residential in character. A need was identified for small workplace/home combinations. These mixed-use spaces comprise this final section of the street. They are not dependent on high public exposure, but are flexible enough to serve the nonresidential needs of many self-employed individuals or to provide space for more neighborhood services. The street terminates in a large commercial greenhouse.

The purpose of this forceful, monumental street configuration is to focus and intensify the presently scattered public life of a community. Such covered spaces are quite common both to shopping areas and office complexes. The designs for many adjacent energy-efficient office buildings testify to the energy savings of similar atriums. In this case, the intent is multifold: the shelter works socially as well as thermally and biologically. This social dimension, creating common ground and strong identity, is intended to knit the community together culturally and psychologically as well as physically.

## Housing Plan

The residential design is intended to provide high-density, low-cost, efficient housing without sacrificing the needs of individuals or compromising the site. The desire for density is twofold: first, to create the context and intensity for a pedestrian community; and second, to reduce the quantity of land, materials, and money consumed in development.

The two- and three- story townhouse configuration is traditionally

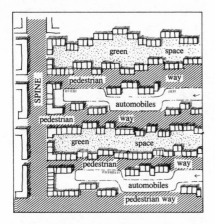

Diagram showing linear pattern of separate autoways, pedestrian paths and open space in the village.

energy- and material-efficient because of its compact form and party walls. At the same time, it doesn't sacrifice the identity of the individual dwelling or the potential for private open space. Oriented correctly, townhouses are excellent passive solar applications because of their reduced loads and cross ventilation potential.

A variety of sizes and configurations are convenient. This plan calls for slender, 20-foot deep configurations in the low-density areas, building to more traditional, 30-foot deep configurations near the main street. In all cases, the individual units have a private south-facing yard and a private entry.

Given this range of solar townhouses as a basic building block, a plan of pedestrian and vehicular fingers interlacing the housing clusters was developed. For each vehicular finger, which terminates just before the main street, there are two pedestrian streets and two green buffer zones. The pedestrian streets widen at each parking area, marking a cluster of homes. Each cluster of ten to twenty dwelling units has its own play area, laundry, vegetable garden space, and electrical co-generator (a Fiat engine 'Totem'). The parking is conveniently located to reinforce the entries off the pedestrian street.

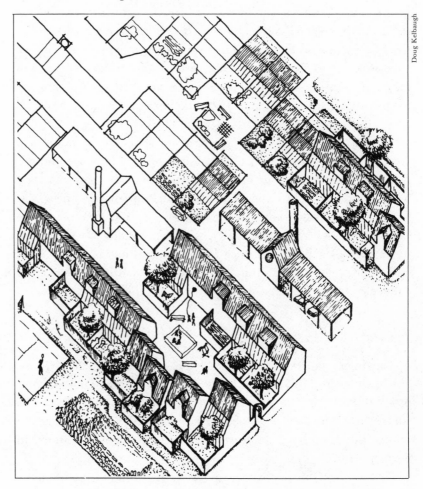

An isometric view of residential cluster.

The smaller clusters combine into neighborhoods that share the east/west pathway and green space. Paths running north/south across the pattern link the open space and scattered play areas. All the fingers converge on the main street, tying the whole community together and providing small corner stores and cafes.

The pattern is comprehensible, but not monotonous. Alternating streets and green areas clearly define a neighborhood's domain, while variations in building materials, surface configuration, and landscaping work to differentiate areas. The buildings are spaced proportionally to their height to allow year-round solar access. A range of passive solar strategies are available to add variety to the units: greenhouses, trombe wall, direct gain, roof aperture, and various combinations of all of these. Cooling loads are accommodated by natural ventilation, evaporative cooling, and night ventilation, taking advantage of the large diurnal temperature swings. These cooling strategies take advantage of the same thermal mass employed in the solar heating systems.

## Energy & Biological Systems

In the Denver metropolitan area, most of the electrical power is locally generated by a series of coal-fired power plants, all quite large. One old gas-fired plant is being phased out to coal. One new nuclear plant, thirty miles to the north, feeds the power grid but is notoriously unreliable and, in its five years of service, has never run at 100 percent capacity. House heating generally employs natural gas with few cases of air conditioning present.

Beyond the passive solar systems embodied in the covered street and townhouse designs, a strategy for backup heating and cooling and for on-site electrical generation was developed. The system is based on a combination of regional renewable resources, solar energy, and resource recovery as energy sources.

The mountains west of the site have a modest timber industry, but nothing that would, in itself, provide a large supply of waste material. During recent years, however, there has been a serious infestation of bark beetles in the ponderosa stands of the foothills. The State Forest Service is the major control focus of the effort to beat the beetles, but the effort will take no less than fifteen years at best. Long-term beetle control is also dependent on better forest management, which in turn, means constant cutting and thinning to strengthen the remaining stands in the semi-arid, competitive climate. This currently wasted wood resource can be trucked to the site and processed by a wood chip-gasifier. The gas produced is piped to individual 'TOTEMS' (total energy systems) located in each housing cluster by the parking area. These units generate electricity and provide waste heat for the hot water and space heating within the cluster. The electricity would be generated and

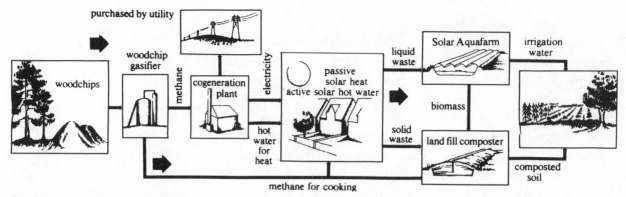

woodchips

woodchip gasifier

methane

cogeneration plant

electricity

passive solar heat
active solar hot water

hot water for heat

liquid waste

solid waste

Solar Aquafarm

biomass

land fill composter

irrigation water

composted soil

methane for cooking

**Possible energy pathways for the Golden site include gassification of woodchips generating electricity, methane, and hot water. Methane is also generated by composting of wastes.**

sold to the local utility company at peak rates. The community would buy electricity on demand and would pay the difference between their production and consumption.

This system is intended to be an interim solution, bridging to the eventual employment of photovoltaics for electrical supply. Approximately 300 square feet of photovoltaic surface would be required for each household. Heat-pump heat recovery from the photovoltaic collectors provides for water and space heat backup. The 'TOTEM' hardware can be replaced by photovoltaics as it wears out and the cost of photovoltaics comes down.

These electrical and heating energy strategies are integrated with and supported by the waste and nutrient cycle systems. These cycles convert liquid and solid household wastes into useful biomass for energy, fertilizer, and feed. The process is managed by small private businesses operating at the community scale, representing local employment and revenues.

The liquid wastes are processed by a system developed by Solar Aquafarms. The sewage is retained in a series of ponds in a solar greenhouse with inflated plastic roofs. Water hyacinths grow in the solar-heated ponds along with a variety of living organisms. These plants and organic forms extract the nutrients to produce quantities of biomass (plant matter, algae, sludge), fish products (shrimp), and

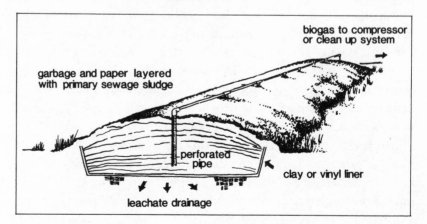

biogas to compressor or clean up system

garbage and paper layered with primary sewage sludge

perforated pipe

clay or vinyl liner

leachate drainage

**A diagram of landfill method of generating methane gas from garbage and sewage sludge.**

irrigation water. The biomass is combined with the solid wastes to produce methane or is processed into food and fertilizer.

The solid waste system starts with source separation in the household. Valuable metals and glass are separately collected from the house and recycled, providing more local employment. The carbon-based waste material is processed by a landfill biogas treatment process. This landfill composter consists of several 1,000-square-foot underground piles made of layers of primary sludge from the sewage system, garbage, and paper. As the pile decomposes, a pipe draws off the biogas to a compressor and is linked back to the co-generators at the housing clusters or is used for cooking. After the pile has completed its decomposition, it provides valuable topsoil material for sale or for use on the lawns, orchards, and landscaping within the project.

## Agriculture and Aquaculture Systems

Various agricultural activities are proposed for the site to complement the other life-support systems. As with waste recycling and energy, these systems are economically viable as small businesses.

Foremost are the greenhouse propagation and nursery activities. Housed in a large glass house at the end of the spine, a nursery for ornamentals and tree propagation would provide a locally desirable product and be extremely profitable. The orchard planned for the lower southwest corner of the site provides a buffer for the site, visual open space, and more land-based business.

At a private scale, space for community vegetable gardens and backyard gardens is an integral part of the site plan. The green spaces between housing 'fingers' provide community garden space and help define the various neighborhoods. Those green buffer areas also include recreational facilities for the neighborhoods. The private south-facing yards associated with each townhouse provide additional space for home food-production. It has been demonstrated that one-sixth to one-half an acre (depending on the climate), intensively gardened, can produce all the fruits and vegetables required by an average family. The site's open spaces will be landscaped with a combination of native ornamentals, low-maintenance fruit trees, and drought-resistant plants.

In addition to the solar greenhouse nursery and the waste recycling center, various forms of solar aquaculture are feasible. Fish production in solar-heated tanks utilizing mixed biological environments is proving to be much more productive than traditional fish farming. These solar tanks could operate in some portions of the southernmost greenhouses or even in zoned sections of the glazed spine. In the latter position, they would provide another level of integration: a visual link between people and production; and the thermal mass, in the form of water needed to modify the temperature swings in the space.

# Case Study 3 — Chino Hills

## Context

The Chino Hills comprises a largely undeveloped upslope area of some 18,000 acres southeast of Los Angeles, separating the eastern edge of the Los Angeles basin from the largely agricultural Chino Valley. In 1981, the San Bernardino Board of Supervisors proposed that in order to check the conversion of prime valley agricultural lands into suburban sprawl, the county, in cooperation with Chino Hills land-owners, develop a Specific Plan to channel the region's explosive growth into the agriculturally less desirable hill area. Van der Ryn, Calthorpe and Partners was retained to develop energy efficient planning and design options for this specific plan. The major features of the plan developed by the county's consultants did not assume any radical departure from existing life-styles and growth patterns in the area. It was assumed that most new residents preferred a suburban way of life and would commute long distances to work. Thus our proposal did not challenge these basic assumptions, but instead concentrated on measures that could fine-tune the standard model of suburban sprawl toward energy savings, particularly in transportation, which is responsible for 60 percent of California's energy budget. These measures were largely directed at defining the form and characteristics of village centers that would serve as the hub around which more standard development would occur.

The intent of the Chino Hills Specific Plan initiated by San Bernardino County is to provide a comprehensive framework for the development of largely undeveloped land in the Chino Hills area. This general

**Chino lies on the east side of the coastal hills in the rapidly expanding Los Angeles basin.**

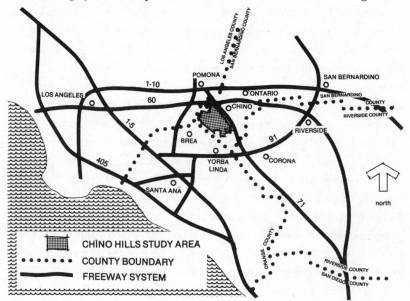

96

area should experience rapid growth in the '80s because of the demand for new housing in the Greater Los Angeles area. The initiation of the Specific Plan process has created a unique opportunity to direct anticipated development in a new way: a way that avoids the waste and inefficiency of piecemeal development; a way that anticipates problems of resource depletion, rapidly escalating energy costs, and the degradation of the environment through the pollution of air, land, and water; a way that responds positively to the need for affordable housing and livable communities.

Aerial view of typical pad grading in the Chino Hills.

Every eight weeks, the equivalent of another new city of 400,000 people gets built in the United States: new homes, factories, shopping centers, freeways, schools, and sewage plants. For the most part, piecemeal development only adds to the problems of waste, inefficiency, resource depletion, and environmental degradation. In Chino Hills, where up to 100,000 people may live within a generation, the specific plan process sets the stage to produce a new community in which public purpose in partnership with private interest create a community where environment, energy, and economic and human interests all converge to produce a significantly better model for living in the '80s.

The purpose of the study has been to develop and analyze energy-efficient design options that can be incorporated into the Specific Plan.

97

These options occur at three levels: (l) area-wide land-use planning and transportation; (2) site planning and infrastructure; and (3) building design. Those areas of energy and resource use which are most within the scope and control of the plan include:

1. **Minimizing the length and number of resident auto trips to local services**. This can be done by concentrating residential development in close proximity to village centers and by carefully specifying the size, location and mix of services available at the village centers. Increasing residential densities near trips out of the area. Our estimates show that the improved design of village centers can reduce total energy use for transportation per household by 25 percent or 100,000 BTU per day through reduced auto use. This is the equivalent of two hundred gallons of gasoline per family saved each year.

2. **Reducing the first cost and annual operating and maintenance costs (in energy as well as dollars) of infrastructure and services by compact energy-conserving design**. Again, this can be achieved through a more compact design that limits development in steep and inaccessible areas, thus reducing the cost of building, providing services, and maintaining an unstable landscape with its problems of erosion, landslides, and runoff. The **Cost of Sprawl** study estimates that more compact design can remit 50 percent first-cost savings in utilities, streets, and roads, and a 13 percent savings in operating and maintenance costs.

3. **Reducing the first cost and the annual operating costs (in energy as well as dollars) of building through the implementation of site-planning and building-development standards**.

## Planning Strategy

The main planning strategy is to provide compactness through the creation of workable, livable, village centers. The salient feature of Chino Hills is its topography, with its steep, inaccessible slopes, narrow canyons, valleys, and natural drainages. Low-density development, spread throughout the entire area, will destroy its present character and produce expensive, long-term problems of maintenance and servicing, resulting in wasteful energy use. The same total density of development can be achieved by concentrating more development in and around village centers that are located in the valleys. Thus, the village center becomes a way to save land and energy, while enhancing livability and community.

The costs and environmental impacts of compact (as opposed to more spread-out development are carefully documented in **The Cost of Sprawl**, a study prepared in 1981 by the Real Estate Research Corporation for the U.S. Government. This study estimates that compact development patterns produce 30 percent less sedimentation and 20

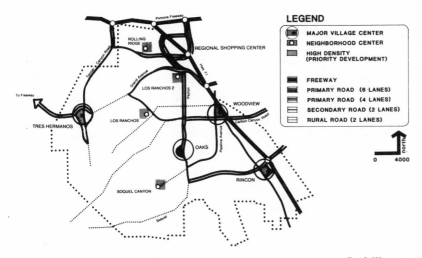

The legend on the diagram reads:

LEGEND
- MAJOR VILLAGE CENTER
- NEIGHBORHOOD CENTER
- HIGH DENSITY (PRIORITY DEVELOPMENT)
- FREEWAY
- PRIMARY ROAD (6 LANES)
- PRIMARY ROAD (4 LANES)
- SECONDARY ROAD (2 LANES)
- RURAL ROAD (2 LANES)

percent less storm runoff than spread-out developments. In hilly terrain such as Chino Hills, the difference is apt to be far greater. The study estimated 30 percent less water use, based on less area to irrigate. The application of our recommended Landscape Development Standards will reduce this figure still further once plant materals are well established.

The study also analyzed savings in roads and utilities both in the first cost and the operating and maintenance costs for two contrasting types of development. They show a potential 50 percent savings in the first cost for streets and utilities, and an annual operating and maintenance savings of 13 percent for higher-density developments.

The greatest potential for energy-efficient design within the context of the Specific Plan can occur through land-use design measures that reduce the number and length of local auto trips to stores and other services. The recommended strategy calls for the development of four major village centers in relatively flat valley areas, each serving 15,000 to 20,000 residents, integrating a complete mix of services and moderate-density housing. Approximately 28 percent of the total, or 1,940 dwelling units are within a quarter-mile radius of the commercial and public service core. The estimated impact of this strategy will be a 23 percent reduction in energy use within the transportation sector.

Concentrating the bulk of development around village centers reduces the need to build extensive infrastructure in steeper, less accessible portions of Chino Hills. A more compact development strategy results in the preservation of steep and inaccessible natural areas and ridges within Chino Hills and vastly reduced infrastructure costs associated with the construction and operation of grading, roads, erosion control, drainage, water, sewer, and utilities.

Climate-responsive building design is another major area in which energy-efficient design goals can be realized. In Chino Hills, this means reducing air conditioning electrical loads and summer peak time electrical demand through building design. Because cooling is the main issue, site-planning measures to ensure southern exposures for solar space-heating are not critical to achieving the goal, although landscape and road profiles can affect building and outdoor comfort levels.

It is possible to make a quantitative estimate of the savings arising from these concepts as compared to a standard suburban plan. Energy costs to the homeowner are reduced by 30 percent, an average savings of $200-$300 per home at 1980 prices. Savings in gasoline due to more accessible services raise this total energy savings to $1,000. For a Chino Hills population of 44,000 households, this amounts to over $25 million a year in energy savings to residents in 1981 dollars. An important environmental benefit is that air quality degradation is significantly lessened through lowered auto use and less burning of natural gas for home heating.

The figure gives a graphic comparison of the estimated consumption of energy in a typical household in the Draft Specific Plan as compared to a typical household in the Energy Efficient Plan option.

Transportation is the biggest use of energy. Work trips are reduced through car-pooling and transit incentives which become feasible with the residential concentration of the village design. Village trips are reduced because those trips made by car are closer, and short walking trips are feasible for residents within the quarter-mile pedestrian zone. Density and road standards encourage smaller, more fuel efficient cars. Overall energy use in the transportation sector is estimated to result in a 23 percent savings, for a project completed in 1980. We estimate that within twenty years these savings may total 55 percent because the plan, if implemented, is highly compatible with projected

Estimated energy requirements for transportation, buildings and support services for "standard plan" (bar on left) and the "energy efficient plan" (bar on right).

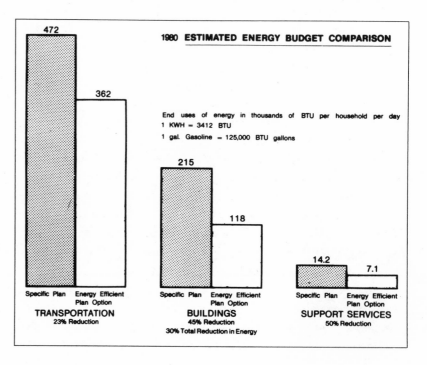

fuel-efficiency vehicle improvement and mass transit opportunities.

In the building sector, savings of almost 50 percent are realized through the implementation of a simplified version of California Energy Commission Residential Building Standards. These measures are designed to reduce summer cooling loads through passive design, such as orientation, shading, and thermal mass, and through the use of a performance energy budget.

The major energy use in support services is the electrical energy used to supply water and treat wastes. The adoption of recommended conservation measures in landscape design can reduce water use and resultant energy consumption by half.

## Village Centers

The concept of Village Center developed for the Chino Hills project is an important innovation towards the restructuring of suburban cores. Key aspects of the concept are: a full mix of shops and services frequently used by residents; clustering attached housing around the core, and a transportation and infrastructure design that makes walking an attractive alternative to exclusive use of the automobile.

The figure shows the three main aspects of the concept, and their

An illustration of a key concept of the plan: the Village Center.

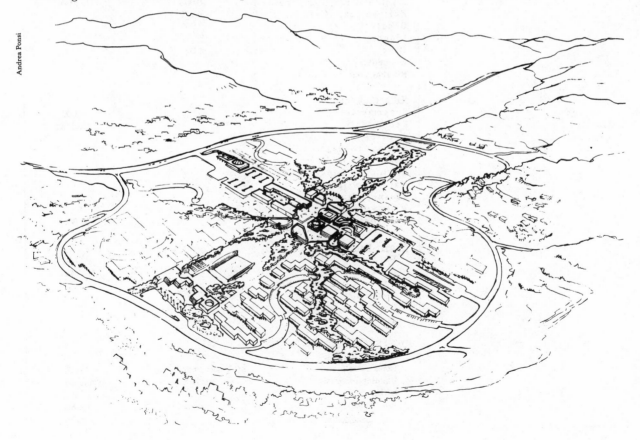

Andrea Ponsi

101

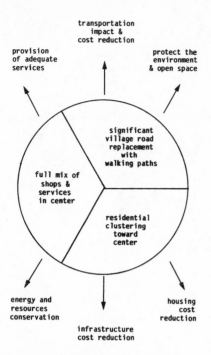

transportation
impact &
cost reduction

provision
of adequate
services

protect the
environment
& open space

significant
village road
replacement
with
walking paths

full mix of
shops &
services
in center

residential
clustering
toward
center

energy and
resources
conservation

housing
cost
reduction

infrastructure
cost reduction

The circle encloses the three key principles in village center design. Arrows point to energy and cost benefits of these principles.

relation to achieving the overall plan objectives. The most important part of the concept is planning a sufficiently large concentration and mix of shops and services so that residents can meet everyday needs through "one stop shopping" rather than the common suburban pattern of traveling by car to a variety of shopping centers and locations. This approach reduces the number and length of trips to satisfy everyday needs. Moreover, by locating some twenty percent of total housing within walking distance of the core, we can project that a great deal of auto travel can be wholly eliminated for these residents.

The Development Standard specifies uses and their maximum square footages for the Village Core and Neighborhood Centers. Bonus uses are those whose presence further strengthen the attraction of the Village Center. The concept also requires the use of minimum densities in order to insure an overall compact design

Neighborhood Center = 80,000 sq feet minimum total floor area
Village Center = 200,000 square feet minimum total floor area

| REQUIRED USES | Maximum Square Footage per Use | |
|---|---|---|
| Neighborhood and Major Village Centers people) | Neighborhood Center (Serves 8.000 people) | Village Center (Serves 20.000 |
| | | |
| Small Market/Specialty Foods | 10,000 | No Max. |
| Refreshments/Cafe | 4,000 | " |
| Beauty/Barber | 3,000 | " |
| Liquor | 3,000 | " |
| Drug | 4,000 | " |
| Elementary School | | " |
| Recreational Facility | | " |
| | | |
| Village Center | | |
| Supermarkets | | 25,000 |
| Restaurants | | No Max. |
| Apparel | | " |
| Sewing/Yardage | | " |
| Insurance/Real Estate Tax Offices | | " |
| Stationary/Book/Art | | " |
| Hardware/Garden | | " |
| Cleaner/Laundry | | " |
| Variety/General Merchandise | | " |
| Religious | | 30,000 |
| | | |
| Bonus Uses | | |
| Furniture | | 30,000 |
| Bank | | No Max. |
| Library/Civic Building | | " |
| Electronic Service | | " |
| Florists/Garden | | " |
| Toys/Crafts | | " |
| | | |
| USES EXCLUDED OR LIMITED IN SIZE | | |
| Department Store | excluded | 20,000 |
| Building Materials | excluded | excluded |
| Office | 1,000 | 10,000 |
| Auto Sales, Service | excluded | 10,000 |

in which a walking radius no greater than a quarter mile to the center of the core makes it possible for 5500 people living within the Village Center to walk. The Table accompanying the Development Standard indicates the percentage of household trips to various services. Data in the first column is from the 1977 National Personal Transportation Study. Column Two has been corrected to eliminate non-service trips. The table indicates that a Village Center with the specified mix of uses will capture ninety three percent of all household trips to services.

The next figure indicates the relationship between dwelling density and walking distance to the Village Center. Within the quarter mile radius of the Village Center, residential density is established between 25 and 30 units to the acre, while at a distance of greater than one mile, density falls to a more typical suburban density of five units per acre.

| Activity/ Trip Attraction | Percent of ALL HH Trips | Percent of POPULATION-SERV'G. Trips |
|---|---|---|
| Small Markets | 6.8% | 12.4% |
| Gas Station | 2.9 | 4.9 |
| Small Cafe | 2.1 | 3.8 |
| Bars | 1.6 | 3.0 |
| Refreshments | 1.5 | 2.7 |
| Beauty shop | 2.3 | 4.2 |
| Liquor store | .9 | 1.6 |
| Supermarket | 3.4 | 6.2 |
| Drug Store | 2.2 | 4.1 |
| Barber shop | 1.2 | 2.2 |
| Large Restaurant | 1.0 | 1.9 |
| Apparel, Women's | .6 | 1.0 |
| Auto Services | 2.9 | 1.1 |
| School | 4.3 | 7.9 |
| SUB TOTAL, NEIGHBORHOOD | 33.7 | 57.0 |
| Sewing/Yardage | .4 | .7 |
| Insur/R.E./Tax/Ofcs. | 1.8 | 3.3 |
| Bakery/Meat/etc | 2.8 | 5.2 |
| Stationary/Book | 1.6 | 3.0 |
| Hardware/Garden | .5 | .9 |
| Cleaners/Laundry | 1.4 | 2.6 |
| Gifts/Novelty | .3 | .6 |
| Radio/TV, Photog. | .4 | .8 |
| Variety | .4 | .8 |
| Apparel Men's | .3 | .5 |
| Bank | 1.2 | 2.2 |
| Savings/Loans | 1.1 | 2.0 |
| Furniture/Appl. | .2 | .4 |
| Recreation Ctr. | 2.6 | 4.8 |
| Movie/Entertainment | 2.5 | 4.6 |
| Dental/Medical | 1.4 | 2.6 |
| Church/Temple | 1.0 | 1.8 |
| SUB TOTAL, VILLAGE | 53.6 | 93.8 |
| Civic buildings | 1.8 | 3.3 |
| Sporting Goods | .3 | .5 |
| Acces'y, Women's | .1 | .2 |
| Dept. Store | .1 | .1 |

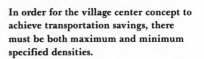

In order for the village center concept to achieve transportation savings, there must be both maximum and minimum specified densities.

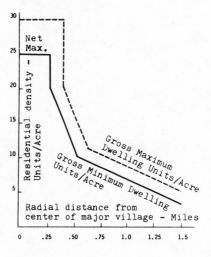

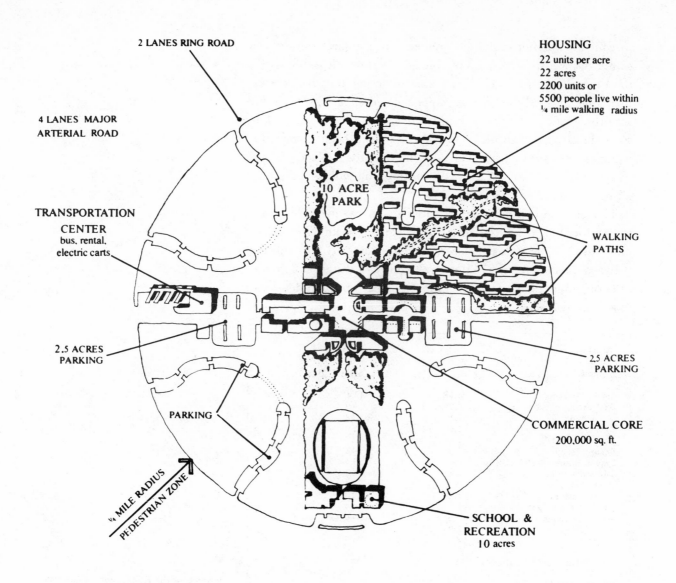

2 LANES RING ROAD

4 LANES MAJOR
ARTERIAL ROAD

HOUSING
22 units per acre
22 acres
2200 units or
5500 people live within
¼ mile walking radius

10 ACRE
PARK

TRANSPORTATION
CENTER
bus, rental,
electric carts

WALKING
PATHS

2.5 ACRES
PARKING

2.5 ACRES
PARKING

PARKING

COMMERCIAL CORE
200,000 sq. ft.

¼ MILE RADIUS
PEDESTRIAN ZONE

SCHOOL &
RECREATION
10 acres

**Diagram of the conceptual Village Center.**

Illustrated is a schematic plan which integrates the design principles inherent in the Village Center concept. The specific configuration and arrangement will change according to the requirements of a specific site. Note that the Center is not bisected by any roads which would discourage pedestrian use. However the Center is accessed from a ring road which provides five acres of parking directly adjacent to the Core Area. The commercial core comprises 200,000 square feet of space. This has been integrated with a park and school and recreation zones. The integration of commercial and other public uses seems a logical extension of the growth of shopping malls which have become the de facto community centers in today's suburbs.

The surrounding housing areas are serviced by cul de sac auto roads and parking. These are interspersed with walking paths leading to the core area. The elimination of traffic hazards is a key to providing incentives for pedestrians, particularly the elderly, handicapped, and children.

It is an interesting commentary on the design of today's culture that the single strategy which produces the greatest impact on reducing energy consumption in this modified suburban design is the reduction of shopping trips accounting for almost half of all auto use in our auto oriented society. Indeed, the Village Center proposal is a direct descendant of the "neighborhood school planning" dogma which dominated suburban planning a generation ago. Then, the key concept was to locate neighborhoods around a half mile walking radius of the elementary school. Today, education and other key consumer services may form the core for new pedestrian oriented energy efficient communities.

# Part Two: The Context for Sustainable Design

# The Mass and Information Economy

*Paul Hawken*

Most people view the growing economic crisis as evidence of something gone wrong. Depending on one's economic philosophy, one can put the blame on various groups and institutions. Conservatives point to the government, monetarists blame the Federal Reserve Bank, Marxists blame the capitalist system, politicians blame their predecessors, consumers blame big business and OPEC, and big business has blamed consumers, OPEC, and government. Like a losing team, we see only our failure, and as a result, we have turned on one another. Economic opinion has diverged because the economic events of the past decade do not fit into any economic theory. We are bewildered by an economy in which some suffer while others grow rich, in which some towns are worse off than they were during the Depression while others are booming. The economy defies not only prognostication but categorization. Some things are working, while others clearly are not. In 1981 and 1982, more businesses started up than at any other time in history. In 1982, more businesses failed than at any time since the Depression.

There is another way to look at present economic events. We have entered a period beween economies, or, to be more precise, between economic structures, and the troubled economy reflects the passage from one structure to the next. Current economic problems are no more a sign of failure than adolescence is the failure of childhood. While coming of age may not be the most apt metaphor for our crisis, it at least expresses the trauma that can accompany rapid change when proper understanding is lacking.

The reason it is difficult to step back and see an underlying pattern is that many things *are* wrong. We have gone from double-digit inflation and recession under President Carter to double-digit unemployment and recession under President Reagan. Unquestionably, we are witnessing the relative decline of what I call the mass economy, the economy of the industrial age, a period during which nations amassed enormous manufacturing capabilities that depended on the large-scale extraction of resources, particularly fossil fuels. The mass economy was a *formative* economy in which virtually all of the work that human beings once did by hand or with the assistance of animals became mechanized through the use of machinery, technology, and energy. This mechanization included the development of the automobile, steel, rubber, chemical, electrical, heavy equipment, and machine tool industries, as well as the thousands of businesses required to support them. Infusing the mass economy was what economist Robert Heilbroner calls the 'thrusting, restive search of the participants...for their material advancement.'

The success of the mass economy in producing a profligate amount of goods has in turn changed the formula for success. Energy, the resource that accomplishes most of the work in an industrial economy, is more expensive than it was ten, twenty, even one hundred years ago. Because it costs more to get things done, industrial countries face a choice. They can consume more energy and drive its price higher, making goods more expensive and causing inflation and declining wages; or they can make the economy more informative by developing methods of production and patterns of consumption that use less energy and capital resources and more knowledge. Inevitably, we have chosen and will choose the latter. It is this transition from a mass economy to an informative economy that is causing world economic crisis.

The crisis of the developed nations is concentrated at the top of the economy, not at the bottom. Historian Fernand Braudel divides the economy of capitalist nations into three distinct segments, the top one of which encompasses the large governing institutions of international banks, multinationals, and centralized political administration. Under this segment is the market economy, the making and selling of goods: businesses, stores, shops, and farms. Submerged further, but just as important, is what Braudel calls 'material life,' the constant and undefined activity of sharing and barter, the giving and taking and making of objects and services between people in local areas. This most basic level — a 'rich zone, like a layer covering the earth' — and the market economy above it have changed dramatically in the past decade in response to higher prices for energy, higher costs for capital, and declining wages. We are changing our behavior, and as we do, the top of the economy, whose existence depends on its ability to control and manipulate the lower levels, is in crisis. Big businesses are threatened, banks face insolvency, and governments are rapidly turned over as successive economic failures destroy the confidence of voters. While governments and politicians debate their course of action, consumers, householders, and businessmen are already adapting.

Adaptation to the rising cost of energy is creating the informative economy. Industry is inventing more efficient manufacturing processes and redesigning products so that they use lighter, more durable materials and require smaller amounts of capital investment as well as less energy to produce. American cars weigh 30 percent less than they did a decade ago, last longer, and are more fuel-efficient. New housing is smaller, uses fewer building materials, and needs less heating and cooling. Consumers wanting to preserve their standard of living are choosing those products that conform to this adaptation while shunning those that ignore it. The result is less consumption of materials and energy (mass).

One way to reduce consumption is through microelectronics. The industrial age mechanized manual labor; now semiconductors and microprocessors are bringing technology to the mind: analysis, communication, design, and decision-making. The microprocessor imparts to manufacturing processes, products, and services much of the power of the human nervous system. Automobile engineers have discarded the bulky carburetor for electronic fuel-injection in order to reduce waste and increase efficiency. The Boeing 767, part of the new generation of fuel-efficient aircraft, could not have been designed without computers. Such repetitive service occupations as bank teller and telephone operator are being replaced by silicon-chip microprocessors. This is how information is replacing mass — by revolutionizing the design, creation, and function of goods and services. Whether in satellites or subcompact cars, toasters or tractors, semiconductor technology is reducing the size, cost, and energy requirements of products while making them more sophisticated, intelligent, and useful.

Whether the conservation of mass is accomplished through the new techniques of computer technology or the old virtues of workmanship and design, the informative economy comprises those individuals, companies, and institutions that understand that every unit of physical resource, regardless of whether it is a gallon of oil, a ton of steel, or a stand of timber, will need greatly increased intelligence (informed activity) to transform raw material into the components of truly economic goods or the instruments of effective services. The ratio between mass and information is changing, and it must continue to change. Our prosperity depends on it.

There is no better example of the shift from a mass ecomomy to an informative one than energy conservation. To conserve means to reduce the amount of mass — in this case, energy, in the form of oil, coal, and gas — used by industry, transportation, and housing. To do so requires information — new technologies, improved designs, and better maintenance. Pacific Gas and Electric, the nation's largest utility, has realized that it is less expensive for them to offer no-interest loans to homeowners for insulation and weatherstripping than it is to borrow capital and build new power plants. By applying new ideas and techniques in an effort to decrease existing energy consumption, the economy can produce as much as it had formerly, reducing costs and lowering the ratio of mass to information. The Mellon Institute estimates that the United States can reduce the amount of energy used in producing a GNP dollar from the 55,000 BTUs required in 1973 to 27,000 BTUs by the year 2000.

It was the philosophy of the mass economy that conservation was a negligible factor in the ability of the United States to achieve energy independence. All administrations since 1973 have concentrated on new energy production. President Reagan, asked about conservation in his energy policy, described it as 'being hot in the summer and cold in the winter.' Despite such government attitudes, the U.S. economy is moving rapidly toward energy conservation, promising to make it one of the biggest industries of the informative economy. It is estimated that by 1990 the energy conservation industry could total between $50 billion and $70 billion. The largest segment would be residential conservation, totaling some $31 billion. Other major areas would be co-generation systems, in which steam wasted in generating electricity would be recaptured to produce heat; more efficient electric motors that could save the United States 10 percent of all the electricity it consumes; energy management systems in large and small buildings; and industrial heat recovery. Further, the U.S. auto industry will be producing cars whose fleet mileage will average 40 miles per gallon — almost triple the 1974 average of 14 miles per gallon.

Reagan's attitudes reflect the commonly held belief that energy conservation is not economic growth whereas energy exploration and development are. If our view of healthy economic growth is synonymous with more, what do we call an economy that consumes less and preserves more? For example, suppose a person who used to buy a new car every three years finds a mechanic who makes this proposition: he will maintain the new car from the outset for a period of twelve years for a flat fee of $1,000 per year plus parts. The contract, although expensive at first, shifts the advantage, as time goes on, to the owner, who has not had to replace his vehicle in the fourth, seventh, and tenth years. The mechanic will only benefit if he does an excellent job of maintenance. If he does a bad job, the car will break down, and his income per hour will drop. In this situation, society has received the benefit of a car — transportation — for less cost than it would have if it replaced the car; less materials have been used and more labor has been used per year than would have been employed making a new car every three years. The problem is that productivity has gone down and the economy has shrunk, as has the auto industry. Such a practice would be reminiscent of the ancient Chinese method of paying the physician a retainer as long as the patient is healthy; when the patient gets sick, the retainer is dropped until the patient recovers. The incentive on the doctor's side is to keep the patient healthy, as no benefit is derived from pathology. Since the GNP currently grows as someone gets ill, is an economy in which the GNP goes up when cars last and people are healthy conceivable? Imagining such an economy requires an entirely different comprehension of growth.

Just what is growing in our economy? Do we necessarily want all that grows? If we use fewer drugs or X rays or spare parts in our bodies, are we a failing economy? We do not bemoan the fact that when our sons and daughters come of age they cease to grow taller. At adulthood, we entirely redefine the concept of growth. Can we not define the economy similarly? The 'unremitting cultivation of goods,' as George Gilder, author of **Wealth and Poverty**, describes a capitalist economy, is but mere incessancy. We now require a new definition of growth — a type of growth that will allow us to use our resources more conservatively. If you take what is grown and make it more complex, self-aware, accurate, and effective but do not expand its boundaries or external scope, it will be internally differentiated. What exists will become more refined — more specific to task, function, and need. This requires labor, materials, energy, capital, communication, and virtually all the other components that go into an economy, but the proportion of the components used will be altered.

The informative economy will not replace the mass economy; it will absorb and include the mass economy in the course of its evolution. We will need steel, rubber, airplanes, pulp mills, and trucks for centuries. The industrial age was not a failure but an unmitigated success. If we refuse to change and try to extend the industrial age beyond its useful life, we will change success into failure by not recognizing our maturation.

The shift of the mass economy to the informative economy can be compared with 'product life-cycle' theory. When a successful product is introduced, demand for it grows quickly, and emphasis is placed on the rate of production. As demand begins to be satisfied, variations of the new product are introduced. Again, economic emphasis is on the rate of production to satisfy demand. Eventually, the market approaches saturation, and resources that were formerly directed toward increasing the rate of production are channeled into improving the quality of the product — in production, performance, and cost. While this phenomenon has long been observed in certain product cycles, the theory has not been applied to the macroeconomy as a whole.

In the case of the economy, the underlying reasons for the shift from mass to information are different from those leading to an improved product. In product life-cycle theory, the shift in emphasis from the rate of production to the quality of production is caused by decline in demand. The shift from the mass economy to the informative economy is being caused by a decline in the supply of resources rather than a decline in the demand for goods. In this respect, the economy, during its present period of transition, resembles a species adapting to a changing environment.

The mass economy carried with it a sense of unlimited horizons and resources that was confirmed by the falling prices of most raw materials since 1870. That resources in fact are limited is not important, because the economy, if we may ascribe animatedness to it, has acted as though resources were unlimited. Because of this, the 100-year period between 1870 and 1970 was dominated by a high rate of growth and replication. There was no attention given to the maximum carrying capacity of the environment with respect to economic activity because very few obstacles to growth were perceived. This sort of activity is referred to as asymptotic growth and can be symbolized on a chart by a **J** curve, because it starts out as a curving line and eventually becomes closer to a straight line of growth perpendicular to the base of the chart or graph. In nature, when J-curve growth occurs among fauna, such growth is rewarded with a 'bust,' because species growth soon outstrips the environment's food supply. At that point, population growth halts and contracts to a point where the environment can support this new lower level of population. This pattern of boom and bust applies whether we are talking about starfish on a reef or deer in a forest.

There is another type of adaptation to rapid population growth seen in nature, and this is represented by a sigmoid, or **S**, curve. In both J and S growth, the population, whether birds, bushes, or bacteria, expands as much as the supply of food or nutrients allows. Since there seem to be no limits at first, growth starts as an exponential curve. But in S-curve growth, the species begins to detect limits to expansion. These limits are the capacity of the environment to provide food at the same rate as the rate of population expansion. In S-curve growth, feedback results that causes the species to limit the rate of reproduction, producing the reversal from an exponential curve to a sigmoid curve. What is often observed is not a smooth, perfect S, but the beginning of an S curve, followed by rapid oscillations of growth and contraction, amounting to no overall growth. A species

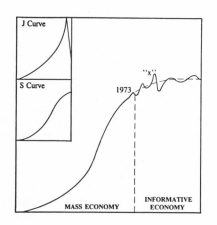

long accustomed to growth cannot immediately adjust its rate of reproduction to the end-capacity of the environment.

Using growth curves seen in animal population expansion as an analogy for economic behavior, we can see in the figure that the informative economy is not different from the mass economy, but, rather, that it describes a more mature stage of economic development, a stage that at first will be volatile, turbulent, and chaotic. As I have drawn the chart representing the economy, my guess is that we are on the point marked with an **X**. We have experienced nine years of slow growth — a tapering off of the rate of expansion of our gross national product.

What becomes obvious when one uses such a chart to depict economic transition is that strategies appropriate during the rapid growth of the mass economy are inappropriate to its mature phase, the informative economy. Those strategies are worth repeating here as a group in order to contrast them with strategies appropriate to the informative economy.

---

## Qualities and Strategies

### MASS ECONOMY

**Expansive:** Everything grew in scale. An idea became a shop, a shop became a chain, a chain became an industry — for example, McDonald's. Cheaper resources favored centralized manufacturing and therefore large-scale factories' distribution and marketing. Expansion was a rising sea that lifted much before it but left many smaller business submerged.

**Replicative:** Large-scale production required product uniformity and long runs to achieve maximum efficiency. Styles were homogenized; the United States became a poor copy of itself.

### INFORMATIVE ECONOMY

**Contractive:** In an environment of unlimited resources, expansion is the key to survival in business. When resources are no longer limitless or inexpensive, contraction can be the key to survival. Witness how many corporations have divested assets, subsidiaries, and property. Contraction makes consumers smarter and business leaner.

**Differentiative:** Contraction causes mass markets to break up. Production must become more flexible to meet specific needs of smaller groups. Production efficiency is not as important as consumption utility: "Does the product really work for me?"

*(continued next page)*

As the mass economy moves toward the informative economy, there will initially be disorder, because the activity of all economic components must change behavior, movement, and pattern. Products must change. Energy-intensive, marketing, consumption, and consumer habits must also change. Each component of the mass economy must either adapt or perish, but it will take time to understand what part each plays (or no longer plays) in what will be the new economy. This loosening, or untightening, of the economy is a necessary stage in the creation of another system. The new informative system will be characterized in part by the merging of the old science of economics with the new science of ecology. Economic laws, theories, and observations, such as Gresham's Law and the theory of the marginal efficiency of capital, are still valid, but they must be applied to a new context.

---

## Qualities and Strategies *(continued)*

| MASS ECONOMY | INFORMATIVE ECONOMY |
|---|---|
| **Accretive:** Wealth and power were achieved by gathering and amassing resources or by cornering and dominating markets. | **Mutual:** Instead of accretion, society benefits from mutuality of interests in order to maintain living standards. Adversary regulation and rule are too expensive; power accrues to those who can bring groups together. |
| **Affluent:** Expansion, replication, and resource exploitation created large outflow of goods. | **Influent:** Fewer overall goods means benefits of goods are achieved by widespread use rather than single ownership. |
| **Consumptive:** The stress on production prior to industrialization changed to a stress on consumption during industrialization as energy-intensive manufacturing and production-liberated workers raised wages and in turn required a high demand for goods and services. | **Conservative:** An overconsumptive ethic threatens the well-being of society because it reduces what is available for all, and thus causes shift to a conservative ethic. |
| **Intermediative:** Rapid growth and expansion required the constant introduction of new goods and services to "mediate" the distance between economic components. | **Disintermediative:** Contraction and increasing population stability will mean less need for intermediaries, and will instead promote "disintermediation": more efficient economic path- |

Ecology is the study of the relationship between organisms and their environments. Since our wealth, economic health, and real growth now depend intimately on our understanding of our environment, any business or economist without an ecological sensitivity runs the risk of not adapting. For decades, ecological science could be ignored by businesses and economists because the environment was forgiving of demands placed on it. The planet was large enough and the population small enough to allow us to ignore the limits of resources and the expense of waste. Now we must pay attention to what the environment tells us.

Gently but firmly, the environment is telling us that we are outstripping its capacity to fill our current demands. According to Lester Brown, author of **Building a Sustainable Society**, the world reached a major watershed in 1960 that we have yet to acknowledge. During

---

| MASS ECONOMY | INFORMATIVE ECONOMY |
|---|---|
| | ways created to conserve energy, resources, and unnecessary labor. |
| **Entropic:** High consumption of resources and energy produced high levels of waste, pollution, and toxicity. | **Information-Rich:** Instead of an excess of expended resources causing entropic decay, there can be an excess of information causing overload and stress to systems. |
| **High Wages:** The high rate of resource extraction and energy consumptions meant high income for workers. | **Lower Wages:** Resource consumption is conserved by the substitution of people for energy; wages slowly fall and stabilize at a new level. |
| **Specialization:** Expansion required a narrow set of skills. | **Broad Skills:** In the mass economy, rewards were for specialization and consumption. In the informative society, people need to have general skills, be more self-sufficient (disintermediative) and less reliant on specialists. The higher ratio of information to mass demands more knowledge by each participant in management and business. |

that year, the world's population reached 3 billion, and for the first time 'the yields of three basic biological systems [forests, seas, and grasslands] expanded less rapidly than population.' Since that time, the margin between total demand and total output has narrowed and even become negative, so that today we are eating into past reserves. Many items, such as fish, wool, and meat, have steadily dropped in both per capita and absolute production since the early 1970s. Part of this biological shortfall was met by such an intensive use of petroleum-based fertilizers and mechanization that fertilizer usage increased 600 percent between 1950 and 1980. During that time, population and production did not increase 600 percent. This means that reliance on oil increased faster than the rate of population growth and the increase in basic foodstuffs. There is no end in sight to this disproportionate growth.

The mass economy has met food demand through the industrialization of agriculture. Large equipment operating on large farms has changed farming from labor-intensive to capital- and energy-intensive. The problem with increased U.S. food production has been that intensive methods of cultivation and fertilization are rapidly reducing the amount of topsoil and topsoil fertility. In other words, we have turned our farms into mines, and what we are extracting with our food is long-term fertility or, at the very least, the ability of the land to produce food without increasingly expensive applications of fertilizer and pesticides.

The industrialization of agriculture was made possible by the low cost of energy. We could afford to use more energy per unit of output, reducing our labor costs during a period when labor was leaving the farm for higher-paying jobs. It is estimated that the United States expends ten calories for every calorie of food taken off the field, while the Chinese spend one. In order to achieve yields at one-tenth the energy cost of ours, China uses more labor. While the United States does not want to go back to a labor-intensive agriculture to save energy, U.S. farmers are faced with the prospect of continually higher operating costs and dwindling profits. However, the world is making more people, not more land. Our only hope of supplying sufficient amounts of food for ourselves and others is to have more people on the land working ever more productively.

Having more people work the land flies in the face of conventional wisdom about the benefits of increasing mechanization, but conforms closely to the idea of an informative economy. For food production to increase and the land to regain its fertility, there will have to be a shift in the ratio of mass to information. Mass is represented by land and energy; information by intelligence, technique, and people. Smaller, more intensively worked farms are considered a romantic notion. It was Secretary of Agriculture Earl Butz, under President

Nixon, who advised American farmers to 'get big or get out.' But during the past three years, many of the farmers who got big got out, bankrupted by the high cost of capital, while conservative farmers who stayed small and kept their debts low survived. More important, the cost of oil in the form of diesel fuel, pesticides, herbicides, and nitrogenous fertilizers has skyrocketed since 1973. With the ongoing decontrol of natural gas, which is the main component of anhydrous ammonia, the cost of fertilizers is expected to triple within the next five years.

What made American farmers the most productive in the world is now threatening to put them out of business: abundant energy. From a labor-intensive livelihood, farming has become a capital- and energy-intensive industry that requires the investment of large amounts of capital and energy into the land and obtains high yields in return. But, like big industry, farmers have been fooled. By putting so much capital into energy-intensive machinery and technologies, they are being driven into insolvency. In 1982, farmers earned $19 billion in income — about the same amount as they did in 1932 when the earlier figure is adjusted for inflation. But this income will not even service their $200 billion in land, equipment, and farm debt. Land prices have skyrocketed since World War II, primarily because such large yields could be obtained. New farmers who try to start out by purchasing their own land are locked into trying to obtain the very highest yields in order to make their land payments. This means intensive cultivation and fertilization. Because farmers have been successful in producing fence-to-fence, there is too much food, which has resulted in depressed crop prices. These conditions in turn have forced farmers to try to produce themselves out of their financial difficulties. Thus, in 1982, we had record yields of wheat, corn, and soybeans — and the greatest number of farm bankruptcies since the Depression.

The shift from a mass to an informative economy reverses the polarities of what is and isn't economical. It was romantic to think of farming a small amount of land in the past few decades, because the economies of scale prevented a person from making a living unless he were growing specialty crops like wine grapes or tobacco. The $50,000 combine and the $40,000 tractor didn't pay for themselves on the 100-acre farm. And for many years, small equipment didn't pay either, as land prices rose and crop prices fell. Equally romantic now may be the large farm, or, at the very least, starting a large farm and having it serve its debt or give even a moderate return on equity. But whether a farm is large or small, the means to make it pay for itself are the same. The farm must produce more income relative to expenses. Since U.S. farms, in general, have pushed yields to the upper limits of the soil's capacity, the answer must involve lower costs.

And the way one lowers the cost of fertilizers, equipment, fuel, pesticides, and herbicides is to use less or to use none at all. So-called biological farming techniques, once considered frivolous or idealistic, were recommended for serious consideration by Bob Bergland, Secretary of Agriculture during the Carter administration. Bergland said that organic farming could rebuild soil fertility while lowering the costs of production. The way to farm with a minimum of fossil fuels and chemicals is to farm more intelligently: to know the land, the crops, the pests, and the cycles, and to develop a farming technique that uses nature instead of fighting it. That kind of knowledge cannot be applied mechanically; it must be derived from experience.

As long as farmers could replace labor with machinery and fertility with fertilizers, the green revolution could proceed apace. Farming could make the huge productivity gains it has during the past fifty years. With the peaking of the mass economy, much of what the farmer learned is no longer useful in adapting to a time of rising resource prices. The knowledge that is required now is not how to wring more out of the soil but how to obtain suitable yields with less. If you are using pesticides, you want to know what will kill aphids or whiteflies. If you wish to eliminate pesticide expense, you have to know how to attract ladybugs. Learning to use fewer resources per acre will require large farms either to add more trained personnel or to begin a gradual reduction in farm size in order to be worked intelligently. Farms will slowly become smaller because it will be easier for a smaller farmer to make money than a giant farmer. And as this happens, a vast new field of agricultural technology will open up.

In countries where geography or demographics prohibit large holdings, there is already a demand for such technology. In the United States, the need for downsized machinery will be slow in building, since land ownership patterns can only change gradually over decades. Nevertheless, American companies are feeling the impact of this changing demand, particularly in their export sales. While International Harvester staggers toward a possible bankruptcy, Kubota of Japan is flourishing overseas and in the U.S. market. Kubota has aggressively pursued the small and intermediate-size tractor business, a market American manufacturers largely ignored while concentrating on air-conditioned, cab-over rigs equipped with televisions, lasers, and telephones.

The conclusion that small farms work better than large farms has recently been confirmed by the Department of Agriculture. In a 1981 study, it found that in the Corn Belt the most efficient farms were those of 640 acres, but that over 90 percent efficiency could be attained by farms of 300 acres. On wheat farms, the most efficient were found to be ones with 1,476 acres, but, again, 90 percent efficiency could be accomplished on 232-acre farms. By contrast, in some developing countries, the most efficient farms have between 2 and 5 acres. In both cases, the most efficient farm size is one that can be worked by a family that owns its land, or at least receives the fruits of its work and production. Whereas the U.S. farmer can afford the machinery to work 640 acres, the farmer in India must cultivate largely by hand. Each case reflects a different ratio of mass to information, but a proper one for the land and economy in question.

There is also a social ecology to adhere to in an informative economy. This is the way people relate to their greater environment, what philosopher James Ogilvy refers to as our 'neo-nature,' the human-made environment around us comprised of cities, institutions, employers, neighborhoods, and laws. Our relationship to that environment must also change. For example, as the economy begins to contract, there already has been a marked change in the relationship between unions and business. During the expansionary stages of the mass economy, growth required a 'who gets what?' bargaining strategy. Unions and big business were fighting over the spoils by using each other's withdrawal from participation — strikes or lockouts — as bargaining chips. Now that real contraction has set in, both business and unions recognize that their survival depends on the other. Recent union settlements, for the most part, have been characterized by a 'who gives what?' approach, whereby each side is making concessions to the other in order to get what both need: jobs, profits, and survival.

For example, Uniroyal has created a council composed of workers and management that will engage in an ongoing discussion of the company's finances, marketing, and corporate planning. Unions also have been granted the right to make presentations to Uniroyal's board of directors, in return for which they gave up cost-of-living allowances for three years, which would have increased salaries by $25 million.

Timken, the ball-bearing manufacturer, has agreed not to relocate to a new plant in the Sun Belt, in exchange for an eleven-year no-strike clause in the new union contract. Colt Industries, McLouth Steel, Pan American Airways, Continental Airlines, United Airlines, and Western Airlines have agreed to open their books to unions in return for pay freezes or cuts.

To cope with rapid economic change and the need for workers and management alike to keep abreast of new developments, Japanese management rotates employees through different jobs, avoiding the overspecialization so common to U.S. business. The advantages of rotating personnel through a corporation are threefold: first, a worker does not solely identify with one part of the company but sees himself or herself as part of an integrated whole; second, cross-fertilization of staff develops better channels of communication among departments, eliminating battles over turf; third, people who feel they can move through and about an organization will be more likely to stay with that company, which eliminates costly turnover while building employee experience, flexibility, and loyalty. Rotating people so that they accumulate generalist skills provides them with a sense of learning and development and maintains for them an atmosphere of being in an information-rich environment where one is constantly challenged by new ideas.

For an informative economy to succeed, we must inform each other about what we do and how we work. In a booming and expansive economy, there may be complex interrelationships between individuals as entities in an economy, but there is no real dependence because economic growth provides an abundance of new wealth. When an economy stabilizes or contracts, our individual condition and standard of living come to rely much more heavily on the actions and decisions of others. This is the kind of behavior seen in a flood or natural disaster: hardship brings all together under a common purpose that supersedes the petty differences that may have formerly existed. We are not undergoing economic disaster, but instead are experiencing a slow but inexorable change in our national wealth, a shift from mass to information. To be informed is to learn. It is no accident that the world's leading technology company, IBM, spends $500 million per year in training, educating, and reeducating its employees. In the informative economy, learning will be essential for all healthy economic activity. This learning results from paying attention to the feedback provided by the environment to the economy. By ignoring it, we risk a bust, both personally and nationally. By paying attention, we can adapt.

# Design as if People Mattered

*Clare Cooper-Marcus*

I left the profession of planning many years ago because I was concerned about the enormous gap between the scale at which people draw plans, make models, and think a place is going to work, and the real experience of place, which is at the scale of the front porch, where the children play, and can be seen from the window by their parents. Few people experience the environment on the scale of the grand plan or the birds-eye view model.

So my first plea in terms of design as if people mattered would be: make lots of little, if not micro-scale, plans. Project yourself into your drawings, and ask repeatedly: 'How would it really be to move from A to B, or to sit at C?' Beautifully rendered drawings are not enough.

Once the question of scale is accepted, it is important to remember who we are designing for. This may seem patently obvious; yet, when we look around at new housing, most is still being built for the traditional nuclear family: Mom, Dad, two kids, a dog, and a station wagon. This, despite the fact that we're seeing an increasing number of small and single-person households because of divorce, people marrying later, having fewer children, etc. We're also getting more and more unconventional households: two men sharing with occasional visiting children; a divorced woman plus children renting rooms to students to keep up the mortgage payments; etc. And yet, we see very little housing currently produced for anything other than the nuclear family. So I would make a plea to provide housing for a much greater range of family types. I mean by *family* anything that considers itself a family — be it two adults, or four adults, or any particular grouping that chooses permanently or temporarily to live together.

## Working Women

There are more and more women working. In fact, it's predicted that by 1990 eighty percent of all preschool children will be in day care, which means not only more provision of day care, but more work opportunities in or close to residential neighborhoods for both men and women, more possibilities of part-time and flex-time work, and greater accessibility to public transport. Although there has been much discussion about the latter in terms of energy conservation, a recent study showed that of all those people who don't have access to a car and who want it, 70 percent are women. Women are more penalized by not having a car and will be better served if we have better public transport.

## Children

More working parents and single-parent households means consciously thinking of neighborhood design in terms of the safety of children who may increasingly spend time alone between the end of school and their parents' return from work. That's a very difficult time, between 2:00 and 6:00 P.M. Do you let your children come home with a key, do you let them wander in the neighborhood, or do you come home from work early yourself? The Swedes have really dealt with this marvelously in the suburbs around Stockholm. Neighborhoods are designed first and foremost for the pedestrian and the child, and second for the commuting adult in the car. The whole neighborhood is safe for the child to move from school to home, from day-care center to shops, from home to playground. Until we start seeing the needs of children and child-rearing as a high priority in the design of residential neighborhoods, we will be selling short the next generation — our most precious resource.

## Shared Facilities

I think we're going to see a greater demand for opportunitites to do collectively what people have previously done in isolation and in separate dwellings. Perhaps we're going to see some examples built into new neighborhoods in this country, based on the models in Sweden and Germany of collective kitchens and dining rooms. A very successful, medium-density housing model in Sweden since the 1930s includes in it a restaurant/kitchen/dining room for residents. You can come home from work, pick up your kids, go and have a meal or take a meal up to your apartment, and not have to worry about cooking or shopping.

A recently approved proposal for kibbutz-style housing in Fairfax, California, has each cluster of 4-6 apartments sharing a cooking and dining space. Of course, this is not everyone's choice of how to live. But to the single people, single parents, and elderly people applying to live in this scheme, it clearly offers something preferable to standard dwellings. When proposing the joint use of interior space, we must be careful that sharing does not lead to potential tension or conflict. A shared entry stair used by 4-6 households can work; a similar space used by 10-12 households may lead to conflict over noise or cleaning responsibilities. The shared kitchens in Fairfax are likely to work because residents have chosen this option; shared kitchens in housing for the elderly in Sydney, Australia (St. John's, Glebe) did not, and costly modifications had to be made.

In a fascinating paper entitled 'What Would a Non-Sexist City Be Like: Speculations on Housing, Urban Design and Human Work,' Dolores Hayden presents an example of how to redesign the typical suburban block, which has been planned on the assumption of a stay-at-home housewife who maintains the house and runs around as a taxi driver. Fewer and fewer women are prepared to do this, and Hayden proposes a redevelopment where, for example, the front gardens, which are currently useless pieces of space, would be fenced as proper private gardens; the back gardens would be amalgamated into communal open space in which there might be community gardens, a children's play area, etc.; some of the larger homes might be subdivided into smaller, more flexible units; there might be a dial-a-ride taxi service, which would eliminate some people's needs for cars; certain unused garages could be converted into workshops and day-care facilities; and there might be a collective kitchen and dining room. These proposals would densify the block, make it more acceptable to working men and women with children, and also create local employment. One block in Berkeley, California, in fact did something similar. One owner acquired all the houses on the block and took out the backyard fences. All the residents had a little piece of private yard outside their back door; this opened onto a shared outdoor space used for play, barbecuing, gardens, etc. A University of California thesis about this block compared it with a neighboring block where the private gardens were 'intact.' A much greater rate of satisfaction was found on the shared block, higher rates of neighboring, of knowing people, of outdoor play, and of people feeling secure.

## Nature and the Child

Not only are crime and traffic in our cities causing the home range of children to be more and more restricted, but fewer and fewer children in the city and in the suburbs have any access to true wild nature. How can we expect the next generation to care about the conservancy of nature if they don't have access to it now? Many don't.

Clare Cooper-Marcus

Is this how we want our children to experience the environment? Some asphalt between two sets of chairs labeled, "play area"?

I often do an exercise with my students in Berkeley in which I ask them to write their own environmental autobiographies. It's quite a revealing exercise. It helps you to understand how your current unconscious and conscious biases toward the environment often come from the past; not just from your childhood but from a whole lifetime of environmental experiences. When I ask students to describe a favorite childhood place, it is amazing how many — I would say a good 80-90 percent — recall a wild or leftover place, a place that was never specifically 'designed.' Very rarely does anyone recall a park or a playground. If they grew up in a developing suburb, they remember the one lot at the end of the street that wasn't yet built on, where they constructed camps and dug tunnels and lit fires; or the little place at the end of the lot where they weren't supposed to go, but went anyway. Those growing up in cities tend to remember urban equivalents: a vacant lot, a back alley, the shared space in a housing project. Almost always, the valued space was outdoors and away from the normal domain of adults. If these are the most poignant memories of students thinking back a good many years, they must have been important places; yet, it is just those wild leftover or unassigned spaces that we tend to plan out of existence.

There is a hopeful innovation in Holland called 'wilderness landscaping.' Recognizing that children growing up in neat and tidy housing projects were not playing on the neat and clean lawns or in the playgrounds, landscape architects began deliberately turning part of the site into a wild landscape where the grass is never mown, and where fast-growing forest trees and shrubs are planted. Sometimes ten years before they know they're going to build housing, a forest is planted so

Children, and their parents, like to have a play space within sight and calling distance of home.

124

it's in good shape to withstand use when the housing is built. The spaces are highly used by children.

When I discussed this approach with landscape architects in this country, I found them skeptical and fearful of crime in such areas. True, we must protect our children from the potential of crime or accident, but if our response is unimaginative asphalt and grass deserts, what have they gained? Our feelings of anxiety have been reduced, but what of children's needs to explore, build forts, find bugs, or just hide? The success of the Washington Environmental Yard in Berkeley is proof enough that, given the choice, many children prefer the hidden excitement of an urban forest to the glaring boredom of an urban desert.

## Adaptable Housing

Another obvious socioeconomic trend is that a decreasing percentage of the population can afford new housing as it is currently built. The need is for cheaper housing, smaller and more flexible units, more shared facilities, densified surburbs, and more human-scale inner-city development. All of the above suggests clustered, medium-density housing, which is not only economically and in energy-conserving terms the most suitable, but also in terms of children's needs and the needs of parents. Certainly, for many households, it's a better solution than single-family homes in suburbia. When we're considering such housing, the two crucial issues are the twin and often-opposing issues of privacy and community. If we're building at a higher density, we have to be very careful of protecting people's privacy, both aural and visual, because you can never have the development of a sense of community until you have first provided for people's privacy needs. We have to figure out what it is in terms of architecture and site planning that helps to facilitate a sense of community — of seeing ourselves all living on this planet — and at the level of the actual place or locality.

Looking back at models from the recent past of how architects feel we should build in the city and create more livable and sociable environments, the most striking example is the Towers-in-a-Park approach. It looked so nice in Corbusier's persuasive drawings and writing, but housing families with children in such buildings proved to be socially disastrous. The open space at the base of the building, which Corbusier saw everybody rushing down to use after work, is at best an occasional soccer pitch for teenage boys and at worst a crime-prone, windswept, vandalized no-man's-land. Women with small children in the upper levels have been driven half crazy from the lack of easy access to the outdoors for play. Clearly, Corbusier never had to raise children in one of his buildings.

The other model is the so-called Radburn layout, dating from a scheme in suburban New Jersey in the 1920s. Attached houses are ap-

Sensitively designed medium-density
housing; pre-school children can play
safely in the court shared by 6 families.
The older children can play beyond the
fence and gate.

proached via cul-de-sacs; each house has a small backyard, and the rest
of the site is devoted to communal open space with lawns, trees,
playgrounds, footpaths, and, sometimes, recreational facilities such as
swimming pools or tennis courts. Though successful at the time, and
repeated in the New Deal New Towns and in European New Towns
after World War II, it was only in the 1970s that this form of layout
became commmonly acceptable. Known in various parts of the
English-speaking world as low-rise high-density (U.K., U.S.A.), mid-
density (Canada), or medium-density (Australia), the basic notion of
attached dwellings (apartments, townhouses, or row houses), reduced
private open space, but compensatory increased communal open space,
seems to fulfill the needs of a lot of newly emerging urban households.

The most successful clustered housing schemes have been those
where the psychological, social, and aesthetic importance of the communal outdoor space has been recognized from the beginning. This
is not some little piece of luxury green space to be fitted in after building
location, parking, fire access, and so on have been determined. If done
sensitively, the shared outdoor space can be the heart and soul of the
community — where children play safely, where adults meet and stop
for a chat, where people exchange ideas over adjacent garden plots,
where an oasis-identity can be forged in a desert of look-alike
homogeneous streets.

Many people in cities and suburbs alike are lonely. Sharing a common pedestrian space of modest dimensions enhances the potential for
neighborly social contact and children's play. The key words here are
*modest dimensions*. Somehow, as designers, we're compelled to put large

green patches on our plans because it looks good and we can say, 'Look at all that open space!' But when it gets built, it's often too big. Not only is this a waste of space, but people are actually intimidated by it, especially on a windy day, and especially children.

Another mistake that was commonly made in clustered housing of the Fifties and Sixties was to allow the communal open space to come directly up to the dwelling, creating a lot of conflict about invasions of privacy, and a lot of ambiguity as to whose that space was and who was responsible for it. In many of the current redevelopment schemes for older public housing, the first thing that's done to improve the environment is to give everyone a small garden, which creates a privacy buffer from the common space. People not only take care of their private space, but they begin to care about and use the adjacent communal space, because the ambiguity is eliminated as to what is private and what is common.

An excellent example of well-planned clustered housing is St. Francis Square in San Francisco, where three hundred dwellings are arranged in three-story buildings around three courtyards. The reason that this scheme works so well is partially that it is a co-op, which is very important, but also because its site planning enhances the social and community life of the residents. The site plan is such that when you're walking down an adjacent street, you're not likely to misinterpret the communal courtyards as public parks. People at St. Francis Square come out and use these spaces, because they're on the natural routes from home to car or laundry or garbage area, and because of the at-

Shared landscaped space creates a possibility for casual neighborhood meetings, or even a strong sense of identity.

Smaller backyards can be a boon to some, but only if they are private and receive plenty of sun.

127

A successful inner-city housing co-op in which 6 families share each stairway, and 100 families share each of 3 landscaped courtyards.

Clare Cooper-Marcus

tractive planting, benches, and pathways. People meet each other and look out for each other. This scheme is in a moderately high-crime district. It's right next to an eight-lane highway, and yet, inside, it's a very beautiful, well-maintained green oasis in the city. There is literally a 200-300 person waiting list to move in.

So there are many, many people who still want to live downtown if we can create green and pleasant and quiet places for them. When I interviewed residents of St. Francis Square, I found that most were happy to live in what are fairly ordinary apartments in return for the total milieu of a green oasis that is pleasant to look at, pleasant to walk through, and safe for their kids. I asked people who had fairly minimally-sized kitchens whether they would rather have a larger kitchen and fewer trees, and 75 percent said they would rather have the trees and make do with the small kitchen.

A systematic study of the use of the outdoor spaces at St. Francis Square illustrates what is true for nearly all medium-density housing: that the predominant use is by children. The site is mostly grass, trees, and pathways, and every bit of it is usable.

Because it's a co-op, the residents have been able, over the years, to change the physical design of the outdoor spaces. They've rebuilt every play area, they've changed the position of pathways, they've taken out trees and put in trees. They've voted to put in solar panels, and additional lighting, and fencing. I'm convinced that a very necessary part of a satisfactory living situation is having control: having power over changes in the environment as needs change through time. However well we design for year 1, children are going to change from preschoolers to teenagers, and will need different things. And there has to be something built into one's role relationship with the environment to allow everyone to be involved in those changes who wants to be.

Turning our backs on the city and creating a green oasis is not, however, the only solution. Sometimes it can be the wrong solution. Some years ago in inner-city Baltimore, the planners ripped out the fences around junky and unused backyards and put in a park-playground in the center of the block. It seemed like a good idea — but nobody used it. The planners had failed to realize that people socialized in this neighborhood at the front — on the stoops and on the sidewalk. Not even a park for their children was going to change that. In the next round of planning, the streets were redeveloped as street-parks, partially closed to traffic, and the results were much more successful.

Another successful form of street 'reclamation' is the Dutch 'woonerf.' A journalist whose child had been killed by a car got together with other bereaved parents and started an organization lobbying for safer cities. It was called 'Stop the Child Murders.' The result was a form of redevelopment of streets which is now very successful in Holland, and which has spread to other West European countries. In a woonerf, cars and people are allowed to mix, but on a very controlled basis. The whole street is essentially pedestrian; cars may enter and park, but due to surfacing, planters, and right-angled turns, they must do so very slowly and carefully. In some British new towns and suburban subdivisions, a comparable new form of street access is used, known as 'mixer court.' In place of the classic, round-ended cul-de-sac, paving and planting create a pleasing pedestrian environment. Cars are allowed in, but must drive circuitously to the garage, and give the right-of-way to pedestrians. Clearly, and happily, the Car-is-King syndrome is being reversed.

Whether we're planning our neighborhoods around street-parks, woonerfs, mixer-courts, or communal landscaped spaces, there are clearly common issues with regard to sustainable design. Houses must be separated enough to allow solar access. In those crucial spaces-in-between, we can introduce edible landscaping, community gardens, bikeways to shops or school, walking or jogging routes, communal laundries or swimming pools, shared compost areas and orchards, adventure playgrounds, tot lots, and picnic places. What is critical to their success is to look at these spaces not as 'what's left over when the buildings are built,' but as the positive heart of a community, just as the commons or the green was to a Medieval village or a New England country town. What is doubly heartening is that the kind of space we're proposing to enhance sustainable and solar design is just the kind of space that is best for the healthy development of children.

As we plan, design, and redesign our cities, we should be constantly asking ourselves: 'Who is best served by this plan — and who is most penalized?' As mentioned above, many Berkeley students recall most fondly from childhood wild or leftover spaces, while Third World students tend to produce very rich drawings of a great variety of urban spaces and activities. I recall one student, however, raised in a typical California suburb, who drew a bare grid pattern of streets, with a house at one end of the drawing and a school at the other. She wrote about her childhood in three sentences, which said in essence: 'I walked from my house to school. I walked back again. And sometimes on Sundays, Dad drove us around in a sports car.' And that's all she could write about. In personality she was shy and uninquisitive.

Now, I'm not suggesting that this environment caused this kind of personality. But this example might give us pause to consider: when we plan predominantly for the commuting adult, who is being penalized?

When cities are built for cars — who is being penalized?

# Local Self Reliance

*A Response to the Changing Rules of the Game — **David Morris***

We live on the cusp of a new era. The price of crude oil rose 1,500 percent between 1973 and 1980. Never has a society experienced such a rapid change in the price of so important a commodity. This basic change in resource economics literally made much of American society obsolete overnight. Yet, institutions, technologies, laws, and habits do not change so quickly. Thus, we find ourselves caught in a time warp. One foot is in the past. One foot is in the future. We continue to do things that no longer make sense because it takes time for a society to adjust.

However, the future need not be bleak. At the same time that we exponentially deplete our raw material base, we exponentially expand our knowledge base. We are learning about the world around us at a geometrically increasing rate. That knowledge can be put to good use in refashioning a society compatible with resource constraints. Indeed, one can see harbingers of the new era throughout the society. The task will not be an easy one. We must overcome a century of development based on the assumptions of infinitely available cheap energy.

Between 1880 and 1980 American development was characterized by two factors: bigness and fragmentation. Our production systems grew larger as they moved further from their markets. We separated work from play, and business from the home. This separation occurred throughout the society. But it is perhaps best illustrated in the energy sector.

In 1900, more than half of the nation's electricity was generated on-site. Each business had its own power plant. Most of the nation was still using wood, or else manufactured gas from nearby areas. But as power plants increased their size, it became economical for the independents to relinquish their generating capacity. In 1903, the largest power plant in the nation served 3,000 households. This relatively small size allowed utilities to be regulated by cities. By 1925, power plants had outgrown the cities' jurisdictions, so states established oversight regulatory commissions.

By the Depression, more than a quarter of the nation's natural gas and electricity crossed state boundaries. The development of giant utility holding companies forced the federal government to assume a regulatory role. With the advent of nuclear power, the shift in oversight functions became more pronounced. In the early 1970s Minnesota tried to implement radiation emission standards for nuclear plants located within its jurisdiction which were more restrictive than those the Atomic Energy Commission had promulgated. The Supreme Court ruled that the state did not have this power. The largest power plant constructed in the mid-1970s served two million households.

Local, neighborhood power plants had become regional, and then national, grid systems. Harold Young tells the story of how interrelated the country had become by citing the example of a utility in Ohio which suffered a service interruption. The impulses set up by the failure were felt at progressively greater distances, as there seemed to be no idle capacity to take up the slack. The first plant to respond was in Arkansas, where a hydroelectric facility was idling. The plant was automatically controlled, and when the demand came, the plant started up. Coincidentally, the opening of the gates released a large volume of water below the plant. A fisherman had come too close to the plant for his own safety. The sudden rush of water capsized the boat, and the fisherman lost his life. So closely knit had the utility companies' operations become that an outage in Ohio could result in a fatal accident in Arkansas.

The nuclear power plant may be an excellent symbol of this era, because its product, electricity, has been replacing all other forms of energy. In 1930, ten percent of the nation's energy was used to generate electricity. In 1960, twenty percent was used in this manner. In 1980, more than thirty percent of our primary energy was used to generate electricity. Many experts predict that by the next century more than half our total energy will be used in electric power plants. The all-electric home has taken its place next to the automobile as a symbol of America.

The energy sector is not out-of-step with the rest of society. States like Massachusetts and Vermont, which were food self-sufficient in the nineteenth century, will have become totally dependent on imported food by the end of the twentieth century. We are proud to grow tomatoes in California and eat them in Boston.

Industries have moved out of communities. In 1910, there were some four hundred local breweries. By 1970, only a few dozen remained, and experts predicted that by the end of the century only a handful would survive.

At the turn of the century every neighborhood had a bakery. By the mid-1960's, the baking industry announced that it was about to construct facilities that would serve customers five hundred miles away. Perhaps the best illustration is the Twinkies plant on the East Coast, which has only three workers and packages tens of thousands of Twinkies each day, to be sent to retail stores all over the region.

The energy crisis may change all of this. As it changes the calculus of energy, it forces us to rethink such basic issues as scale, the relationship of the individual to the community, and the concept of separation as a basis for social planning.

Very large power plants take about ten years to come on-line. In order for utility planners to efficiently bring on such large plants, they must be able to accurately predict demand far into the future. Between 1910 and 1970, electric demand increased 7 percent annually, doubling every decade. But after the oil embargo, electric demand actually decreased. By the late 1970s, it had begun to increase again, but only by 1-2 percent per year. Utilities are burdened by power plants they do not need. This is an extremely expensive situation. Utilities have begun to respond by looking to smaller power plants. These can come on-line more rapidly, and can therefore be more easily matched to changes in customer demand.

Rising energy prices have revived the practice of co-generation. For every 100 BTUs of energy we consume in our power plants, only 30 BTUs actually enter our businesses or homes as electricity. Seventy percent goes off as waste heat. That heat can be recovered, but as power plants grew larger, they moved away from population centers and it became increasingly uneconomical to recover the waste heat. Smaller power plants can be located in our communities.

As power plants decrease in size, ownership patterns may change. One automobile manufacturer sells a modified auto engine as a household energy plant. It can run on gasoline, methane, or natural gas. It can supply most of the heat and electricity needs of several households, and costs about the same as an automobile. Household power plants are now in the marketplace.

The 1,500 percent increase in crude oil prices has been accompanied by rapid price decreases in renewable based energy generation. In some cases, the price reductions have been a result of technological maturity. In other cases, they result from politically motivated tax incentives. In 1978, for example, it cost about $2 to produce a gallon of alcohol fuel. Gasoline cost 50 cents a gallon. In 1980, alcohol prices had dropped to about $1 per gallon for 190 proof alcohol. Gasoline prices are now

$1.25 per gallon. In eighteen months, the economics of renewable liquid fuels has turned upside down.

Electricity generated from photovoltaics costs 2 percent of what it did in 1973. In the same period that crude oil prices increased fifteen times, solar electric prices decreased by 98 percent!

Oil, natural gas, coal, and uranium are located in concentrated deposits unequally around the world. They lend themselves to ownership by national governments or large corporations. Sunlight, wind, plant matter, and water power can be found everywhere, although in significant variation. Solar energy is a diffuse energy source. It lends itself to decentralized collection, and therefore, potentially, to decentralized ownership.

As the price of conventional energy increases, the issue of scale becomes relevant for solar energy. In the 1950s, for example, a hydroelectric facility could compete with an oil-driven power plant only if it harnessed the power of the nation's major rivers. The hydroelectric facility had to generate enough power to serve several hundred thousand homes. In the mid-1970s, the rising price of conventional energy made it economical to revive the small-scale hydroelectric systems that had been the basis for the foundation of many New England and Midwestern towns. These facilities serve about 10,000 homes, an order of magnitude less than their older counterparts. In the late 1970s, and in the 1980s, we have begun to hear of new technologies, called micro-hydro. These power plants require no dam. They generate power for a dozen homes. There are even hydroelectric plants that now serve only one or two households. Maybe a good name for them, given what has gone before, is infinitesimal hydro!

We have also discovered that the principle of co-generation can apply to solar as well as to conventional technologies. A photovoltaic device, for example, has an efficiency of less than 20 percent. That means that 80 percent of the sunlight striking the surface of the collector goes off as waste heat, an inefficiency comparable to that of a conventional power plant (although, in the case of solar, the fuel is renewable). At least one manufacturer now sells solar units that generate heat as well as electricity. These can convert up to 75 percent of the sunlight striking the collector, and repay themselves in less than ten years in northern climates.

In 1978, the federal government recognized the new energy reality by enacting the Public Utility Regulatory Policy Act. PURPA strips electric utilities of their monopoly status. They must now purchase power from small-scale power plants that use co-generation or solar energy. The utilities must pay a very high price for this electricity. They must provide backup power at low rates. They must permit a qualifying facility to send electricity across their grid system to another utility if the independent power plant can get a better price there. PURPA exempts many qualifying facilities from state and federal regulations that apply to electric utilities.

Public service commissions and publicly owned utilities are now developing the guidelines for implementing PURPA. In 1980, there were about 5,500 power plants in this nation. By 1985, there may be 50,000, mainly commercial and industrial power plants using cogeneration. By 1990, there may be a million plants, mainly hydroelectric, wind turbines, and photovoltaics. By 2000, there may be twenty million such plants. From 5,500 to twenty million in twenty years! That is a revolution without precedent. How do we develop a new energy system that can integrate so many producers? It is a fascinating question.

To date, most solar advocates view the household as a self-enclosed unit. The objective is to decrease household demand, either through conservation or the use of passive or active solar energy. With the new federal legislation, and with the maturation of solar electric technologies (as well as district heating systems), the household could become an income producer. What is the trade-off between self-sufficiency and interdependence?

The first computer simulations of household photovoltaic systems may provide a clue. These reveal that a typical single-family detached dwelling can generate sufficient energy on an annual basis to provide not only all that is necessary to operate an energy-efficient household, but enough remaining to power the family electic vehicle. However, this energy is not produced at exactly the time it is needed. One could be self-sufficient, but one would have to pay the price of an oversized system and a storage system, with a backup on-site. From a social standpoint, this would be highly inefficient. It appears than an optimal configuration in Boston, Phoenix, or Seattle would be for the household to export 50 percent of its electricity to the grid, and to import about 50 percent of what it needs from the grid. This development of a symbiotic relationship, in which we all become partial producers — or 'prosumers' to quote Alvin Toffler — may become the new symbol of society.

The changed calculus of energy prices also makes us aware of how fragmented our systems are and what the benefits would be of integration. The household that installs a greenhouse for space heating quickly discovers that it is an excellent place to raise food. When we raise food, we discover that organic and human wastes make good fertilizer. We begin, as the ecologists might say, to 'close the loop,' using the wastes of one system as the raw materials of another. One of the best examples of this way of thinking is in the sewage treatment plant at Hercules, California. It uses water hyacinths to treat the water, it generates methane and fertilizer, and it is beginning to raise food and fish. Thus, a plant which five years ago was perceived as a 'waste treatment facility' is now seen as a farm, a fish hatchery, a fertilizer plant, and a power plant.

We can step back from the household or community level to see how rising resource prices might affect the society as a whole. This is a more difficult area for prognosis. But some things appear likely. We will begin to use more recycled materials. When this occurs, we will look to our cities as the largest repositories of post-consumer scrap. A city with more than 100,000 residents 'generates' each year more paper than a good-sized timber stand, more copper than a medium-sized copper mine, and more aluminum than a small commercial bauxite mine. Since factories tend to locate near their raw materials, industries that use recycled materials will locate near cities. Factories that rely on recycled material use less energy, sometimes 90 percent less energy, as is the case with aluminum. They use less water and they pollute less. They can also be built much smaller than those that use virgin ores. Since they are smaller, they can serve local markets.

In the broadest sense, we appear to be moving away from a society based on iron ore and fossil fuels to one based on sand, plant matter, and sunlight. Sand, the basis for our electronics industry , solar collectors, and solar cells, is the only commodity produced in every state in the nation. Plant matter can provide the feedstock for the same materials now made from petroleum. Sunlight, in its direct and indirect forms, will be the basis for our energy system.

Finally, the industries of the future may well be, in John Blair's words, 'knowledge-intensive,' rather than energy-, materials-, or capital-intensive. Blair coined the term 'centrifugal technologies' to indicate the post-World War II developments of the materials sciences, the biological sciences, and electronics, which rely more on professional expertise than on energy or raw materials.

If scale does indeed become a major issue, it may become the basis for policy. That is, we can develop production systems that emphasize the use of local resources. If this is done, we owe a debt to the late Ernst Schumacher, the father of the Intermediate Technology Development Group in England, and the author of the best-selling **Small Is Beautiful**. ITDG is a consulting group, working primarily with the developing nations. Developing countries found themselves importing Western technologies incompatible with their own needs. These technologies required large internal markets, a great deal of scientific expertise, and a lot of capital. Yet, the Third World is characterized by small markets, relatively little scientific expertise, and an abundance of labor, not capital. ITDG was invited to design technologies better suited to local resource patterns.

Schumacher tells the story of being invited to Chile in the late 1960s to solve a problem. The Chileans told him: 'We grow strawberries, but send them to Britain, where they are processed and bottled, and sent back to Chile as strawberry jam.' They wanted to know if Chile could make its own jars. Schumacher's group discovered that although wood ash was not available in Chile, seaweed was. If seaweed were used in glassmaking, the product would be green-tinted. If arsenic, a trace element that is very expensive and must be imported, were eliminated the glass would have little bubbles. If locally available clay was used to build a refractory furnace, the furnace would have to be replaced every year, but would work as well as a steel furnace that would last 7-10 years. Thus, ITDG concluded that Chile could have a native jar-making factory if it were willing to replace the furnace every year.

When I heard the story, I had to smile. I have a farm on the edge of Appalachia. In the summer, the roadside stands sell antique bottles. They are green, with little bubbles in them. If we build new production facilities on the concept of local resource utilization, we should take into account the trade-offs involved.

If a renewable based, energy-efficient society is our goal, and if we are accurately assessing the dynamics of modern technology, the role of local government will become increasingly central to any integrated planning.

We are witnessing a national revolt against government at all levels. Tax limitations have severely eroded the tax base of local governments. Cities are faced with severely restricted budgets. However, if we look back over the past two decades, we can trace an extraordinary expansion in local governmental authority. One of these areas concerns local government's ability to interfere with the flow of commerce through its borders. We should remember that in large degree the American Constitution took the place of the Articles of Confederation specifically in order to impose a common market, a free-trade zone, in the United States.

Cities have been upheld by the courts when they enacted bottle bills. These ordinances effectively banned the sale of certain products within municipal limits because they imposed an environmental burden on the city. Courts have also upheld cities in other interesting areas. Several cities require municipal employees to live within city limits. (California cities were prohibited from doing this by a constitutional referendum in the early 1970s.) Courts have upheld these ordinances for two reasons. Judges felt that employees who lived within the city would be more responsive to their work. Moreover, the judges believed the city had the right to try to retain public money within its borders. Thus, the city is no longer being viewed as a completely open economy. It has the right, albeit a minor one at this time, to try to change its balance of payments by reducing the outflow of local dollars. The next step may be for cities to begin to discriminate in favor of local businesses. This is starting to happen. Several cities allow local contractors to bid higher than those outside the city and still be awarded the contract. In at least one state, school boards can pay slightly more for food raised in-state.

Cities have always had the capacity to go into debt. As we move toward local self-reliance, the city might be involved in mobilizing the huge amounts of capital necessary to rebuild society. Cities traditionally float bonds for this purpose. They are tax-exempt bonds. Underwriting firms in the major regional money markets buy these bonds and sell them to rich investors in blocks of $10,000 or more. But recently cities have begun to experiment with so-called 'mini-bonds.' These are issued in small enough denominations (say, $100 or $500) that they can be sold to local residents. Thus, the local residents reap the tax benefits and interest return of these bonds. The money is raised locally, and the benefits of the tax-exempt bonds remain local. It is the principle of local self-reliance extended to the economic system.

As we move toward an economy based on the principles of local self-reliance, we may see a significant reduction in the trade of products or raw materials, accompanied by a rapid expansion in the trade of information, knowledge, entertainment, and culture. As we move toward a steady-state society with respect to raw material consumption, we may begin to redefine the nature of labor itself.

In the nineteenth century, there lived a man named Josiah Warren. Unlike the schemes of most other Utopians, every project he directed was successful. He was an inventor who lived in the New Harmony community of Robert Owens. He saw that community fail, and analyzed the reasons. He believed that it failed in large part because the people were too collectivistic, too communitarian. There was no individual equity. He developed a method of exchange based on labor.

In Cincinnati, he opened the first time store. Everything in it was priced according to the time it took to make it. (Of course, that was an era when people still had actual skills. Robert Heilbroner accurately describes the fundamental transformation in the last century from a nation of farmers, with their broad skills, to a nation of clerks, with their overall lack of skills.) Warren gave people chits that could be redeemed in labor. The store was so successful that other stores in the neighborhood were forced to copy it. Warren closed the store after four years, and later opened another one, which was equally successful.

It probably takes no more of a doctor's time in 1980 to diagnose and prescribe for an illness than it did in 1900. But it may be one hundred times more expensive. This incredible difference between the labor involved in tasks and the money required to get these tasks performed may be driving the society to copy some of Warren's ideas. In 1978, the city of Hartford, Connecticut, established a system for the poor to work off their city taxes. More than half the population of the city of Hartford is under the poverty level. As inflation hit, property taxes rose. The elderly were faced with the default of their homes. The city was faced with the probability of vastly reduced budgets for the services that the elderly and poor required. Hartford now allows citizens to perform necessary tasks, at more than the minimum wage, to be credited against their city tax obligations.

The end result of this might be for a city or community to estimate the amount of labor hours required for its maintenance, and to divide up the tasks among people within the community. It would be so much more directly related to people's needs than is a taxing system that takes money from the population and sends it to the federal government, which sends a portion back to the city, which spends it in ways completely unrelated to the community's needs or desires.

This has been a wide ranging discussion — from energy to local self-reliance, to the role of local government, to a labor-based economy. Yet, there is a thread running through these apparently disparate subjects. The rules of the game have changed. Resource economics now forces us to reexamine the way we do things. It can mean the beginning of an era of symbiosis as well as synergy, when we become producers of wealth as well as consumers of goods, when we trade knowledge rather than raw materials, and when the concept of local self-reliance becomes the basis for reconstruction.

# Architecture and Biology

*A Necessary Synthesis — **John Todd***

I should like to discuss three stories or themes: science, New Alchemy and my work, and a conference that was held in April 1979. The conference, entitled 'Village as Solar Ecology,' was dedicated to the memory of Margaret Mead.

Science impinges on all aspects of our lives and frames the horizons of the designer's art. It provides the world-view of this predominantly secular society. What is interesting to me is that science is beginning to undergo a revolution. It is in the process of attaining a dimension, or potential, to express itself in sacred terms. It is in a period of synthesis.

For the last two centuries, science has grown exponentially; but in the process, it has split itself into increasing numbers of separate disciplines. The unity of hermetic Renaissance science did not endure when the fragmentation, which continues to the present, shattered it. There have been notable examples of reintegration, the theory of evolution being perhaps the most significant. Overall, the trend has been toward learning more and more about less and less; and as the bits of knowledge get tinier, they tend to fly apart, seeming unrelated. Like the expanding universe, science moves toward a penultimate black hole in which humans know an infinite amount about nothing.

The story won't end this way because opposite and integrative forces are at work. At the moment of fragmentation, mechanistic secular science spirals toward a higher plane where a new unity begins.

Fragmentation and reunification are an ongoing process whose heartbeat is measured in centuries. It is difficult to describe the change in science, as it is comprised of many mutually supporting currents and

139

elements. Instead, I shall illustrate a few of the unifying elements. All of them are concerned with the nature of nature in nonlinear terms.

The theory of systems and cybernetics grew out of attempts to understand homeostasis and control. They led to descriptions of phenomena in which patterns, relationships, and varying velocities 'dance' together. The 'dance' was expressed in a mathematical language. Ironically, our early understanding came from weapons research.

More important is the young science of ecology. By ecology I don't mean just the mathematical formulation of some of its subdisciplines, but, in its broadest context, a science of relationships among living things and between them and the physical and chemical elements with which they interact. It is a science which, in its totality, helps us to comprehend how the world works. Ecology has a multifaceted lens that allows us, as Gregory Bateson has said, to discover the patterns that connect. There are many, many levels to this.

An ecological sensibility has already added a new dimension to current thought. Out of it has developed a theory of the earth as a being, an entity that is itself whole with its own kind of 'awareness.' It is called the GAIA theory and is the brainchild of Lynn Margulis and James Lovelock. Their theory came from the discovery that the ordinary rules of chemical equilibria were not being obeyed by our planet's atmosphere, whereas the lifeless planets, like Mars, showed predictable conditions on their surfaces. From this they deduced that life on earth was not the result of conditions here. Quite the opposite, life in the aggregate actually created a livable world. Earth is organizing the chemical conditions necessary for its own survival. In doing so, it behaves, like ourselves, as an organism. It is ironic that the quest for life in space is teaching us something extremely important about Earth, and in the end about ourselves.

On a practical level, ecology can be the basis for a design science. As a design science, it provides the framework for fascinating linkages in science and technology that can be applied to human settlements. Polymer physicists begin to invent materials that function like our skin, or like the terrestrial atmosphere. Electronic, computer, and informational networks couple to food-producing ecosystems and provide a memory and a story of biological phenomena that in turn influence design and architecture. Buildings become 'organisms.' Villages and cities can be developed within this context. Architecture is in a position to express profound sociological concepts and anthropological and historical insights. The polymer physicist communicates through time with culture in a biological language that in turn extends the physics. Gregory Bateson's patterns connect, and the disciplines communicate.

This is leading us to a unity of knowing and the feeling is sacred. I don't mean an all-knowing or a still-point. I mean a dynamic unity which ecological design, at its best, can express. Nature speaks through patterns, structures, and interrelationships, and these are becoming more accessible.

At this point, I should like to explain how I work, because it might clarify the above abstractions. I often will sit and look at a forest, and ask it questions like, 'What are you doing?' and 'How do you do it?' and even 'What are the structural forms and instructions that have allowed you, a forest, to grow from a meadow, which was here twenty-five years ago?'

Framed in this way, there are answers. It is possible to go further. I recently began designing a model farm for small acreages in New England. It was based on the forest and its instructions because that is what the land hereabouts wants to be.

The integrity of nature can guide us, for in the broadest, truest sense, nature is the only thing that has proven adaptive and successful in the long run. Some of its elements have become extinct and been replaced by others, but its structure and information have become enriched through time. I wonder if it would not be prudent to design human enterprises on blueprints from nature.

Relationships between energy, architecture, structure, spacing, and transport, as well as agriculture and manufacturing, may be expressed in more adaptive ways. For example, might powering human settlements with renewable and pulsing forms of energy (as happens within ecosystems) create — within the village or town — forms of energy that makes it flexible and changeable as exterior conditions are altered? I think so, particularly if there is a simultaneous effort to replace capital-intensive machinery and hardware with information. Information will be expressed as good design, sophisticated use of materials, and support ecosystems that substitute for energy- and capital-intensive processes. There has been enough progress by the New Alchemy Institute and a number of other people and organizations in substituting information for hardware over the last decade to give me confidence that it is a strategy worth further exploring.

My confidence is based on experience with trying to rethink agriculture on the small, sometimes fogbound sand spit of Cape Cod. In our enthusiasm and naivete, we wanted to take on energy, architecture, and even settlements and transportation. But we started first with growing food.

We also started with a premise — namely, that our food must be grown in such a way that more food calories are produced than the energy calories used in production. Petroleum-addicted modern agriculture does just the opposite, putting one food calorie on the table for up to ten to fifteen calories expended in growing, processing, and delivery.

I approached the problem by asking myself what, in my experience, works best. The answer was Earth, so we took it for our model of design. We started to design a miniature 'Earth' made up of ecosystems with as many of the components as possible having useful-to-people foods in them.

I pondered how the Earth works and then applied its overall methods to my model. The Earth is inhabitable for life because of its atmospheric blanket which traps solar energy, including heat. Our 'Earth' had to have an envelope that was a heat trap and was transparent to light. This led us immediately into structures and architecture. The closest architectural analogues to the atmosphere that we knew of were R. Buckminster Fuller's geodesic domes. Their shapes were inspired by the great circle arcs of the planet. As solar traps, the multifaceted triangular surface of the domes turned out to be superb. No matter where the sun is in the sky, the domes have facets or surfaces that directly intercept its light.

But a dome on the ground's surface is no environment for growing things. It behaves like a desert, sizzling at noon and freezing at night. Planet Earth solved the problem of climatic stability by having 70 percent of its surface, made up of water in the form of the oceans, absorb and slowly release solar heat. So, in our miniature 'Earth,' we set aside 70 percent of the interior for water in the form of a pond. It worked, freeing us from heaters, fans, coolers, air exchangers, and, most important, fossil fuels. In a 30-foot-diameter, twin-skinned geodesic dome containing a pond, we had a year-round growing environment on Cape Cod.

The pond became the vessel for photosynthetically- or plankton-driven food chains, the end products of which were fishes and aquatic food plants. We had in fact built an ocean in micro, although the pond was fresh, not salty. The principal fish species, the African perch or Tilapia, comparable to herring and anchovies in the sea, feed by swimming and filtering microscopic plants. The then food editor of the **New York Times**, tasting them fresh from our pond, called them, in a feature article, the finest-tasting farm-raised fish. The Tilapia, in their turn, activated detritus food chains; and on these, catfish and Chinese carps did well.

Oceans are productive, in part, because of upwellings or stirrings where nutrients are brought to the surface. To simulate this water movement, we introduced a fish with powerful tail muscles that churned up the bottom and sent the nutrients rising to the light. This fish was the delicious Mirror carp from Israel. Rivers serve oceans by supplying them with a constant renewal of nutrients washed off the land. In our pond, we simulated this process with a mechanical component and a biological strategy. The mechanical component was a small electric pump that circulates water through an adjacent 'river.' Subsequently, we began to use windmills to power our 'rivers.' The biological strategy was a fish that eats terrestrial plants, especially garden weeds and water hyacinths. Its long, convoluted intestine breaks down plants delivering 'upstream' or outside nutrients to the pond. The fish we used was a hearty vegetarian from China called the White Amur. What the Mississippi is to the Gulf of Mexico, our White Amur is to our pond.

This story of assembling a miniature world is somewhat more complicated than I have described it here. Some of the same kinds of thinking went into assembling the terrestrial food-growing ring that encircled the pond in the dome with its deep soils, linkages with the pond and essential micro-control ecosystems that protected the fruits and vegetables. The figs grown there are close to pure ambrosia.

Many of the design strategies, and in some cases the actual organisms, were a result of my travels as a biological explorer, particularly in the tropics. Where and when nature seemed particularly clever, I tried to understand those places so that what they 'knew' could be applied to design.

In one instance on Cape Cod, we simulated a particularly productive part of a tropical stream by using an assemblage of components that included a water-pumping windmill, three terraced ponds connected to form a serpentine recycling loop, and a solar greenhouse over the lowest and largest pond. Our tropical, wind-powered and solar-heated recycling 'stream,' with its segregated purification and production components, turned out to be a first-class little fish farm, one we still operate. Except for the windmill, which needs furling prior to high winds, the whole system generally takes care of itself.

Designing the tropical 'river' taught me a lot about natural pulses and their importance. Light, tides, winds, clouds, temperatures, and humidity all pulse or vary in nature, functioning to tune and stabilize ecosystems. Most architecture or design attempts to flatten natural pulsing and provide, on the supply side, steady inputs that require a heavy use of energy. In recent years, this has become an addictive dependency on continuous and heavy infusions of fossil fuel-based sources of power. Living systems take a different tack and employ many strategies to cope and thrive on pulses and interruptions in supply. Some of these are elegant, and we can employ them to serve our own needs. Systems that thrive on pulsing have loops and storage elements designed into their structure. Storage 'batteries' in ecosystems are diverse and varied; the list is almost endless. Sometimes such batteries are mass, others are chemical, and still others are biological. Some are all three. In all cases, they are integral to the functioning of the whole: A good passive solar house with an attached bioshelter begins to approach the kind of design I envision, but only as a start, as yet by no means sophisticated.

There are other kinds of models less global in scope, but as important as the miniature farm or the tropical river analogue I described. Some models are derived from what is around us. In New England, if a piece of open space is left alone, it will transform itself into a young forest in a decade or two. Our climate dictates that this be so. Farmers spend much of their time fighting this natural, successional process. Current traditional agriculture is stopping the forest.

At New Alchemy, we have recently begun to ask the question, 'Can a farm be forest-like?' In other words, is it possible to mimic ecological succession and design a farm in the image of our local forests? The image of the farm then changes. First of all, it is no longer static. It must mature and change to remain viable. Secondly, it cannot be a monocrop (say a corn or soybean) farm; it has to have many interrelated components. Thirdly, it shifts from the flat two dimensions of the field to the three dimensions of the forest. It has many zones layered one above the other, all of which produce crops. The canopy or upper zone is comprised of economic trees that produce fruits, nuts, fodder, and medicines. On twelve acres at New Alchemy, we have over one hundred varieties of trees from climates comparable to ours around the world. We are trying to assemble a genetic base for intentional agricultural forests.

The next, lower zone is occupied by vine crops and shade-tolerant trees and shrubs that provide the biological products. Below this is the ground-level, livestock zone, dominated in the early phases by poultry, including geese, and by sheep, and, at later stages, by cattle and pigs. The soil surface zone, on which livestock depend, is comprised of shrubs, legumes, and soil-building plants that feed the livestock and are fertilized by them. Below ground level is a zone made up of aquaculture ponds that store water for crops, irrigation, and fertilization, and provide some livestock feeds in the form of aquatic plants.

In such a multistory landscape, the farmer substitutes rich ecological and agricultural information and a forest model in lieu of fuel-demanding machinery used in tillage, spraying and harvesting. He or she still uses machines, but the calories of work consumed by the machines are less. The crop base is diversified and all our preliminary evidence indicates that it will be far more productive per acre. Forest-model farms can be small and still pay their way. I predict that they will reestablish agriculture on New England's thin and rocky soils.

We are only beginning to understand what working with the sun means and what the benefits are. A few years ago, I tried to conceive of fish farms that would be suitable for cities, urban areas, and arid regions where water and/or space is scarce and precious. I wanted to avoid the capital-intensive and fuel-demanding equipment which was the backbone of closed-system aquaculture. I turned to the sun for inspiration and designed translucent-walled, above-ground tanks or silos for holding water and capturing the sun's energy. In the tanks, I placed an aquatic ecosystem comprised of organisms from over a dozen wild ponds, and then 'asked' the ecosystem to support the intensive culture of fishes with the minimum number of backup components.

It worked. The fish grew with about half of the energy requirements of orthodox pond aquaculture. The tanks were also productive, on a per unit volume basis that was some ten times greater than that of other still-water fish cultures. But that wasn't all. I found that buildings could be heated with the same tanks. Placed inside a 2,000-square-foot New Alchemy greenhouse-like structure, thirteen of these 750-gallon low-temperature tanks (or 'furnaces') made it entirely independent of additional heating. Thirty-two of them provided a climate base for a 6,500-square-foot building in Maritime Canada, which is not exactly a solar climate. My own house, a passive solar Cape-Cod-style retrofit/addition, has in it ten column-shaped solar fish tanks that help to free us from a heavy fuel-dependency. In our climate, the tanks, prior to a tax credit, pay for themselves in about three years through their heating ability alone. The fish are a bonus.

The greenhouse-like structures I have mentioned are more than greenhouses. They represent a synthesis of solar, wind, biology, electronics, and architecture for raising food and living. We have given such buildings the generic name 'bioshelters' to convey the relationship between biology and architecture. Food production and solar dependency are characteristic of all of them. Fishes, shellfish, vegetables, fruits, flowers, and seedlings are produced — in some instances, on a commercial scale. In my own house, and for a time in the bioshelter on Prince Edward Island, housing (as well as gardening and farming), was an integral element.

In a solar age, bioshelters will become what barns were to nineteenth-century, pre-petroleum agriculture. They will be at the heart of the various agricultural cycles and an elegant expression of overcoming the special constraints of winter. Barns stored grains and hay and housed livestock until the spring. Bioshelters allow agricultural cycles to be maintained and help us to side-step the heating and food constraints of winter.

Through microfarming on an ecological model, bioshelters are beginning to shape a new kind of economic enterprise. We have already shown that they are based on a sound energetic footing and are relatively free of the vagaries of fuel prices. We are currently trying to develop a new solar bioshelter that is the outgrowth of a decade of experimentation.

The full expression of the bioshelter is far from being realized. I predict that it will become an integral part of the architecture and design of towns, villages, and city neighborhoods. Streets, alleys, malls, and parks will have bioshelter components. Urban agriculture will be widespread and productive. Sewage will be treated and recycled in bioshelters. Other bioshelter types will have a principal function of heating, cooling, and purifying the air in adjacent buildings. With plants, animals, soil, water, and purifying gases, they will become true workhorses of a solar age.

I mentioned at the outset a seminal design conference held at the New Alchemy Institute two years ago. The story behind it goes back to 1977, when Margaret Mead asked Nancy Jack Todd and me to accompany her to Indonesia. On the Island of Bali, we toured the towns and villages where she and Gregory Bateson had worked in the 1930s. Helped by her explanations, I was struck by the wonderful way the Balinese fused practical, artistic, and religious elements in their villages. Seeing the mundane and the aesthetic so closely linked and interdependent affected my sense of what design could become in our culture.

In one of these villages, Dr. Mead discussed our work with us. Our bioshelters in her view, were significant, especially the thinking behind them and what they were trying to accomplish. But she questioned their scale. As component parts of individual households, farms or buildings, bioshelters then did not address a larger social order. She believed that social change occurs at the level of the village or neighborhood, and she told us in blunt terms that whole villages should be like bioshelters. By this she didn't mean 'inside a building,' she meant that the villages or towns should be designed and assembled using bioshelter concepts. For her they were an epistemology and a way of supporting human communities that could make a difference in the world.

My wife and I met with Dr. Mead again shortly before her death. She asked us what we were doing about this business of villages. Our response was to convene a group of people capable of working together to apply ecological concepts to the design of villages, towns, and even cities. Twenty-one guests and sixteen New Alchemists, whose disciplines ranged from physics to theology, anthropology, community activisim, design, architecture, farming, finance, water purification, cultural history, sociology, urban forestry, and the biological and biotechnical sciences, met at the conference. Our agenda was to determine whether human settlements could be designed as solar ecologies. We began by teaching each other what we knew that would be useful in restructuring communities for a solar and ecological era.

We asked ourselves if it would be possible to design settlements that would be beautiful, enticing, and economically feasible, and would also:

1. Provide their own power and electrical requirements from indigenous sources of energy, particularly the wind and the sun.
2. Provide year-round heating, cooling, and climate from solar-based technologies and design concepts.
3. Purify and recycle wastes, including sewage within the settlements, and reuse the nutrients in agriculture and gas production.
4. Provide a significant internal and adjacent agricultural and aquacultural base with its own economy.
5. Integrate manufacturing, housing, commerce, schools, and

agriculture, and support technologies with each other into mutually reinforcing structural and social relationships. (This reintegration of function is a critical element in ecological design.)

We discussed, argued over, and tried out new design concepts that included these five qualities in new and existing rural and urban communities in coastal Maine, in San Luis Valley, Colorado, in a San Francisco suburb, and in the heart of New York City. The scope ranged from consideration of a whole new village to redesigning a cathedral to transform it into a bioshelter with a religious function.

We parted concluding that it was both possible and desirable to work toward ecologically inspired settlements. Subsequent to the conference, the participants refined their ideas; and a year later, a document entitled **The Village as Solar Ecology** appeared. It is a preliminary expression of the design concepts. Margaret Mead's challenge had borne its first fruit, and many of us reached a new threshold in our own work. Collectively, we realized that there was enough shared knowledge to begin to rethink completely the question of how we live. Margaret Mead's daughter, the anthropologist Mary Catherine Bateson, described it thus: 'We are talking about breathing new life into what we mean when we say we live in a given place.'

# Metropolitan Food Systems and the Sustainable City

*David Katz*

Imagine a New York or Los Angeles, the city a patchwork of fields intermixed with garden-roofed office towers and apartment buildings, bisected by tree-lined corridors. The sun glistens on the varied panes of the greenhouses and growing frames that are part of the buildings and malls of the city.

A business executive, refreshed by the scented, cooling breeze coming from the quilted fields, pauses for a moment beneath a fruit tree before entering her workplace. A farmworker blends well with the early morning bustle as he unloads his freshly cut produce and flowers at one of the city's many small markets.

The farmers working the small, intensively cultivated holdings intertwined with the suburban fringe of the metropolis can catch a glimpse of their children as they walk to neighborhood schools, located in the small woodlands scattered throughout the city.

Down by the tidal flats lie the lagoons storing the reclaimed and purified wastewater of the city. The sheen on the placid surface mimics the smooth finish on the photovoltaic panels that shingle the rooftops of nearby houses. Mirrored on the glass-smooth water are the colors of the wood duck's wing, as it glides in to rest before continuing its journey.

Sounds good, doesn't it? This picture is surely not of any city we know. It's not likely that our metropolitan areas will be so transformed anytime soon. The vision of the ecologically refined city drawn above can only exist in the fertile, optimistic mind of a futuristic thinker. In fact, the images in the myth painted above are all drawn from writings and pictures articulated by various creators and designers working to define the nature of a sustainable city.

We know too well the reality of our current world. There is little room for plants and the natural environment in the modern metropolis. Today's city is isolated from the source of its basic sustenance — food. The by-product of food consumption, sewage, is choking nearby bodies of water or landfills.

Over the last 10 to 15 years, many of us immersed in appropriate technology worked to define, and even design, sustainable urban ecosystems. We were optimistic and excited about the potential uncovered by current experiments and ideas. As we moved forward, the enticing possibilities offered by the myths we had created masked our comprehension of the more practical considerations limiting a sustainable urban ecosystem. Unachievable design goals were formed as a result of our optimism. We skipped over much of the gritty task of changing the current system by focusing on designing a wholly new one. Perhaps what makes these visions of the future into fantasies is the great gap between what is here now and what we seek to attain. I believe that the task before us becomes more feasible if we use more reasonable degrees of self-reliance as our standard in working to redesign our cities for future sustainability. Cities can become more self-sustaining in food and energy, but it is very unlikely that anything close to total self-reliance will be achievable, especially in food. When thinking of urban food self-reliance, we must accept that the structure of our social systems, the nature of the urban built environment, and the economics of our present food system will not be easily changed in big leaps. As we know too well, when urban planners, architects, city officials, and citizens gather to work on problems of the city, ecological concerns are rarely on the agenda. We take for granted the unseen food system that supplies our markets and tables. In fact, creation of jobs and cleaning up urban blight are usually perceived as the primary benefits of urban farming projects when they do come up for consideration.

Speculation on the nature of future urban food systems has, in some cases, contributed to a false optimism that has furthered the acceptance of this unqualified yet appealing picture of a verdant and efficient city. A good example is the imaginative and highly inaccurate information disseminated about the horticultural system called the Biodynamic/French Intensive method.

One of the main proponents of the Biodynamic/French Intensive method expounds the idea of a one-eighth acre minifarm on which the farmer can net between $10,000 and $20,000 a year working a 40-hour week for eight months, with four months off for vacation. To make things even better, this superproductive approach uses no pesticides or chemicals, uses hand labor only, and consumes only a small percentage of the energy used by conventional farms. This image is itself enough to make your hands itch for the handle of a hoe. The credibility of this approach is enhanced for the non-horticulturalist by copious numbers and charts. A closer look reveals a mixture of good home gardening and extravagant extrapolation that relies heavily on an overheated calculator and a misuse of data. My examination of the bulk of published information on the method revealed errors in such things as costs and a simplistic understanding of basic economics and the business of small-scale commercial farming. In fact, the data seems to show that the net yield from the system is no more productive than that now achieved by a good truck farmer using modern methods.

In one report published in California, the author claimed a ten-fold greater yield than the U.S. average for cucumbers and goes on to say that the fertilizer efficiency is nearly five times better. The yield turns out to be two, perhaps three times greater than that found in commercial intensive production in California. When I added up the fertilizer materials prescribed for the French Intensive cucumber operation, I found a cost of $2,949 per acre, as compared to approximately $300 per acre spent by conventional organic farmers. This hardly reflects greater fertilizer efficiency. It is easy to make your facts look good by cleverly choosing exaggerated comparisons or by expressing results using multiples that are meaningless when taken out of context. An unfortunate by-product is that this tends to damage the credibility of all those working with innovative agricultural systems, especially in the eyes of those who control most of the resources allocated for agricultural research.

My intent is not to attack any one approach or to overly dampen our imagination when thinking about a sustainable future, but rather to suggest that the pathway to building new urban food systems is complex and not well served by simple answers that promise great and wondrous changes. The changes will be slow, influenced by a great variety of factors, and often the solutions will be less than perfect. The present relationship between our cities and our food system is both complicated and complex. It is this complexity itself that offers hope and handhold, as it presents many different opportunities to begin to understand and change how we feed ourselves.

If we are to have sustainable, livable cities in our future, it is necessary to create a metropolis that produces much of its food while reweaving the patterns of the natural world back into its infrastructure and byways. The reforming of the metropolis and its relation to nature is a tall order, even if we limit ourselves to the cycles and sustenance of our food systems. Current insight into the future has either articulated a fantasy-like vision, such as the one above, or has maintained that the growth of agribusiness and the use of plenty of high technology will be the direction of the future.

The reforming of the metropolis and its relations to nature is a tall order, even if we limit ourselves to the cycles and substance of our food systems. Insight into the future seems to fall into two broad categories: a variation of the fantasy-like vision I presented at the beginning of this chapter, or the conventional view of business as usual, with giant agribusiness keeping us well supplied using high technology and copious flows of resources

Before moving on to exploring a middle ground that might offer a greener and more self-reliant city, let's take a look at our current food system to see where we stand.

## Modern Agriculture: A Crisis

The U.S. food system seems to be a wonder of modern productivity. Only 3 percent of our nation's people live on farms, yet they grow enough to amply feed us as well as supplying 85 percent of the world's surplus food. A farmer of today, using modern inputs, can produce twenty-five to thirty-five times more crop per hour of work than his predecessor of sixty years ago. Our citizenry enjoy some of the lowest food prices in the world, expending only 13.5 percent of their net income on food.

Exports of U.S. agricultural products amounted to $40.5 billion in 1982 and have played a significant role in paying the oil-import bill for the nation.

Yet all is not well. Agriculture in the United States is in a state of crisis. Massive federal subsidies prop up a farm sector that in 1982 was posting the lowest net income and highest bankruptcy rates since the Great Depression. Agriculture has become increasingly dependent on the use of toxic chemicals to protect its monocultures from pests. The profligate use of these chemicals not only endangers our health but is also poisoning and endangering the natural environment. Perhaps even more critical is the fact that over-use of pesticides has created an agricultural system that lacks biological stability and that is incredibly susceptible to catastrophic collapse through a major pest or disease outbreak.

The soil is the very foundation of our current bountiful productivity, yet every hour about 320 acres of U.S. farmland are converted to shopping centers, housing, reservoirs, roadways, and parks. Unfortunately, one-third of this converted land is prime cropland; the balance is pasture or grazing land. This rate of loss amounts to approximately 2.8 million acres per year.

Government sources show that we are losing an astounding 6.4 billion tons of topsoil per year to erosion. This translates to five bushels of soil lost for each bushel of corn produced nationwide.

People, concentrated in cities, have become wholly dependent on distant food sources. Our cities and the metropolitan areas in which they are embedded now contain over 75 percent of the total population and they depend on 2.6 percent of the population, the farmers, to grow the food they need. By the year 2000, between 80 and 95 percent of all North Americans will be living in or adjacent to metropolitan centers. Outside our borders, the situation is even more severe. Ten of the world's largest cities are in Asia. Current trends show that the shantytowns that house the urban poor are growing two to three times as fast as the cities of which they are a part. By the year 2000, the urban population in the developing world is expected to double. According to researchers such as Isabel Wade, President of Urban Resource Systems, a major hope for food security in the future of the Third World is the development of widespread urban food systems in and around these cities. Her preliminary work indicates that small-scale production in home and community gardens can be a vital component of urban self-reliance if coupled with intensive commercial production on the urban fringe.

Although culture and language may vary, and climate and vegetation zone differ, urbanites of every region have comparable requirements for goods and services, especially food. And the food often comes from afar, handled by many middlepeople, all extracting their due. Vast amounts of energy are used to process, package, and transport food from farm to consumer, adding to the final price with each step.

Unfortunately, the farmer only receives, on the average, 25 to 30 percent of the retail food price, and this percentage is continuing to decline. Of even more concern is the fact that the percentage of food manufacturing assets owned by the fifty largest firms continues to grow. In 1950, these firms owned 35.9 percent; in 1977, 63.7 percent; and the USDA predicts they will control 100 percent by the year 2000.

Will people in our cities be dependent captives of a centrally controlled food system that is operating on an increasingly unstable biological foundation? Or are there other pathways that offer a future in which we can create a food system that will better integrate our lives with the ecosystems that we depend on for our sustenance? The issues are complex, with the development of metropolitan food systems only one element of a potential solution. How can we build a partnership with nature, making our cities more food self-reliant, more livable?

# An Historical Insight: A Look at the Past

The widely held theory of agricultural primacy holds that it was the advent of agriculture that made it possible for cities to appear and grow. Primitive hunter-gatherers learned to cultivate grain and domesticate animals, thus enabling settled and stable villages to emerge, which then grew into cities. And so developed the key social elements that make the city: the complex division of labor, large economic projects, and complicated social organizations.

Jane Jacobs, in her book **The Economy of Cities**, holds the opposite to be the case. She makes a convincing case that cities themselves were the source and site of early agriculture, and it is urban productivity and development that has led to the development of agriculture. She postulates that cities grew as social and trade centers, living off the wild food of their environs. Gradually, animals and plants were domesticated, and were cultured within the cities, and the cities' lifeblood, trade, became the means of spreading the knowledge of agriculture. The city, then, is the first site of farming, which later spread to rural areas and villages that had been subsisting on wild foods.

Less than a century ago, some cities possessed highly productive urban agri-ecosystems that provided a significant portion of their fresh food. One outstanding example is the 'marais' of Paris, which flourished during the second half of the nineteenth century. G. Stanhill's comprehensive research and analysis show that the marais system of cultivation is probably one of the most productive ever documented. The marais system provided a significant portion of the city's fresh food, supplied a valuable export market, and solved the major pollution problem of the time by transforming vast quantities of stable manure into a surplus of highly fertile soil.

The marais cultivation system developed from the walled gardens of medieval Paris, and reached its height during the late 1800s. It involved the year-round production of high-quality salad and vegetable crops, utilizing intercropping and successional cropping to grow as many as six, and seldom less than three, crops per year from each plot of land. Information suggests that there were some 1,400 hectares in cultivation in Paris at that time, with the average holding of 0.7 hectares employing four to five persons. At that time, the area of Paris was approximately 7,800 hectares.

Very heavy dressings of stable manure were an essential feature of the marais system. The manure was composted within specially built hotbeds to provide a heated environment for the culture of crops during the winter months. Reported rates of application of manure ranged between 340 and 1,060 tons per hectare per year, with a mean application rate of 675 tons per hectare per year. This rate of fertilizer application far exceeds that of any modern-day farming system. In fact, it is a good example of the requirement of an intensive food system for very high inputs of nutrients and organic matter needed to achieve high productivity. These fertility levels are practically never economic unless an inexpensive source of material is available nearby. These numbers and the concept become especially relevant when we discuss the application of municipal sewage to urban farms later in the chapter.

The marketable yields achieved in the marais were high by today's standards of crop production. The average yield of 82.1 tons per hectare per year, fresh weight basis, is far above average yields in U.S. farming, and is roughly equivalent to yields reported for modern day intensive farming systems. It should be emphasized that these yields refer to marketable produce and not total yield. Substantial additional income was realized as the heavy dressings of manure each year necessitated the regular disposal of excess soil, mostly from spent hotbeds. This material was used to expand the area of the marais, and its sale helped to offset the cost of purchasing fresh manure.

The availability of plenty of low-paid labor was essential to the success of the marais. This very labor-intensive system was especially dependent on hand labor to operate the relatively unique aspects of the gardens, such as the hotbeds with movable straw-mat insulation.

The efficiency of the marais in energy terms was low, requiring four units of energy input from all sources to produce each unit of food energy output. If the energy output of the excess soil is figured in, then the energy efficiency of the food system is reduced even further.

Many modern food production systems displayed very similar energy efficiencies, utilizing fossil-fuel-derived sources of energy, although most intensive systems are far less efficient. For example, modern production in heated greenhouses in similar climates shows energy inputs as much as twenty to thirty times higher per unit of crop output. The energetic significance of the marais system of crop production is not the actual values found in the ratio of input to output, but rather that the energy input was biological in nature and hence a renewable resource.

The food production by this system, occupying one-sixth of the city, supplied only 1.4 percent of the total food requirements for the population of Paris (estimated at that time to be around 1.5 million). However, the volume of fresh salads, fruits, and vegetables was equal to 50 kilograms per capita, more than the present-day consumption levels of these foods.

While it is impossible to compare the economy of Paris of the 1800s to present-day conditions, it is useful to note that the many additional benefits of the inclusion of agriculture in the city are not included in the usual economic equations. The amenities of open space, fresher air, improved climate, and local food security are good examples. It is these benefits, along with those of fresh, locally produced food, that can make urban agriculture viable now and especially in the future.

## Metropolitan Agriculture

Historically, urban settlements have grown in areas of rich farmland. Together with the ring of counties adjacent to them, metropolitan areas account for 51.7 percent of prime land in the U.S. Many major urban areas have developed around the mouths of rivers or on valley floors where expansion is onto rich farmland. As more and more mega-cities with populations over 10 million emerge and world population bulges, extreme pressure will be put on the world food supply. About 50 percent more food will have to be grown in the year 2000 just to meet present inadequate intake levels. A viable, diverse metropolitan agriculture can meet an important part of our needs.

While probably not the main source of food for cities in the future, metropolitan agriculture can provide an important buffer to cushion the shock of periodic fluctuations or shortages in food supplies, while enhancing local economic and environmental conditions. It is unlikely that metropolitan agriculture will ever displace large segments of rural-based, large-scale agriculture.

The form and location of metropolitan agriculture are as broad and diverse as the cross section of areas included, ranging from densely urban at the center to the almost rural farms at the suburban fringe. They include small-scale home and commercial production woven into the grid of the inner city, as well as the larger and more productive truck farms and fish ponds on the fringe of the city.

The concept of metropolitan agriculture is much more than urban gardening. For the most part, urban garden projects have been located within the urban core of the city, and have been primarily devoted to social goals of cleaning up and beautifying neighborhoods or designed as food-supplement programs for low-income city-dwellers. If we are to meet a more significant portion of our food needs, the scope and scale of urban food-production must be expanded, with careful attention paid to its economic aspects as well as to the social and ecological. If we are to have sustainable, highly productive food-producing systems encircling our cities, we must ensure that urban farming is economically viable for its practitioners. The substantial subsidies enjoyed by conventional agriculture, including low-interest credit, tax incentives, a highly developed extension service, immense amounts of public capital for infrastructure such as water development and a sophisticated research and development system, must be extended to the development of urban food production.

# Sustainable Agriculture

Sustainability in farming relies on far more than good economics and government support. A sustainable agriculture is a system based on the principle that agriculture is, first and foremost, a biological science. As applied biology, it attempts to mimic the natural ecosystem as much as possible, striving to build complexity, cycle nutrients, and maintain the primacy of the sun as the main source of energy driving the system. Complexity and diversity must be built into the farm system at every opportunity. This implies maintenance of a wide range of plant types and habitats on the farm, and the use of a sophisticated understanding of population dynamics in order to manipulate host/pest/predator relationships. Blanket applications of biocides are avoided to prevent disruption of the entire system. Once destabilized, the ecosystem will require the heavy hand of high inputs and drastic measures to avoid collapse.

An important consequence of complexity is that it tends to produce an ecosystemic optimum, usually well below the maximum short-term carrying capacity of the ecosystem. When dealing with agro-ecosystems, the high annual yields that modern economics demand are the expression of this short-term maximum. If long- term sustainability is to become a major criteria for urban farmers, then prices paid to farmers must increase substantially to encourage them to eschew short- term gain for long-term biological stability. This may be attainable to some degree, but high yields will still be crucial. To keep up and still maintain a substantial degree of ecological stability, it will be necessary to employ a rich mix of information and technology.

Modern urban agriculture will not be an exact re-creation of the marais system. The small intensive plots and the year-round activity may be similar, but the intensive hand labor of the marais will have to be partly replaced with small-scale, highly efficient technology, and farmers will adapt to a highly organized information and product distribution system.

Small-scale machinery that uses internal combustion engines will be a key part of the intensive small farm. Following current patterns, these machines will be versatile and highly fuel efficient. A farmer owning one basic tractor will be able to couple to a variety of specialized implements, allowing maximum flexibility at a minimum cost. The design and method of use of the machinery will reflect anawareess of potential ecological impacts, such as soil compaction, so that they can be avoided. Alternate sources of fuel, such as ethanol from waste products or electricity from photovoltaic power sta6tions, will be used to run some farming operations.

Increased production will come from technology that speeds up crop establishment and extends cropping seasons, such as pre-germination of seed, gel-based planting systems, low-shock, mechanized transplanting systems, and the use of all kinds of season extenders that include plastic row covers, innovative mulch materials, and mobile greenhouses.

Sophisticated information management will be crucial to the success of the metropolitan farmer. Computers will be at home here, as they are practically everywhere else. Their use will make application of management and technical inputs more precise and efficient. The intensive monitoring and careful timing critical to the operation of a sustainable farm are made feasible by the appropriate technology of the microprocessor. The extensive technical data base required for rapid, high-quality decision making is affordable through low-cost computer hookups to extensive interactive information centers.

Sustainable metropolitan agriculture involves the management of a matrix of overlapping ecosystems. Some urban ecosystems are greatly disrupted and are incomplete in their resource cycles and must be completely rebuilt, while others offer the opportunity to organize the resources to support a productive agricultural system, while greatly enhancing the livability of the city.

In order for urban areas to develop any real food security, it will be necessary to greatly increase the amount of land used for the culture of plants, both in and around the city. In what will amount to major land reform, cities will have to wrest control of the unused land from speculators and commercial users. The possibility of this occurring and the means required, are questions that I won't attempt to answer. A key side effect of the availability of this land base for intensive food production will be an increase in the ability of the city to utilize and productively dispose of waste, both in its solid and liquid forms. Waste water, including storm drainage and recycled gray water, can be absorbed and used on croplands. Solid waste such as leaves and garbage can be composted and returned to the soil.

Plants and plantings of all sorts, whether for food production or not, are vital to the health and survival of the city. The benefits of creating a biological renaissance in the city are many. Plants help to clean the air, moderate high and low extremes of temperature, and reduce noise. Trees and gardens provide beauty, shade, protection, and comfort for humans and animals. They also provide a sense of scale, and soften the hard edges of the concrete and steel environment. A locale with plants is always valued as a more desirable place to live.

The effect of parks and green space on values of nearby property is well documented. The Federal Housing Administration reports that market values of parcels near green areas are often 15 to 20 percent higher. Other work has shown that the presence of trees on residen-

157

tial lots, or on undeveloped urban land, contributed to 12 to 27 percent of the market value, depending on the number and type of trees present.

### Influence on Climate

Plants can play a major role in modifying the climate in the urban environment. Vegetation ameliorates air temperature by changing and controlling solar radiation. Leaves intercept, reflect, absorb, and transmit solar radiation. Deciduous trees can be very helpful in heat control by intercepting radiation and lowering temperatures. In winter, the loss of their leaves allows the warming rays of the sun to shine in and warm us.

Trees and other vegetation also aid in controlling summer temperatures through evapotranspiration. A single tree transpires as much as eighty-eight gallons of water per day. This has been compared to five average room air conditioners, each with a capacity of 2,500 kilocalories per hour, running twenty hours a day. Expanses of vegetation, such as vegetable plots, would also exert considerable 'natural' air conditioning in the city. Land area covered with vegetation tends to absorb and give off heat more slowly than bare ground or the hard surfaces found in a city. This phenomenon tends to lessen swings in temperature throughout the diurnal cycle.

Trees, planted in rows or groups, can reduce wind velocity and create sheltered zones both leeward and windward. Used as windbreaks, trees can create buffered areas for specialized crops, shelter buildings from heat-robbing wind, or protect streets and pedestrians from irritating winds.

### Air Pollution

The air of our metropolitan areas is practically saturated with pollutants. Automobiles and industry are the primary culprits, and clearly both should be significantly modified to reduce emissions, and/or their use must be curtailed. It is critical that we reduce the air pollution levels of our cities, both to protect the health of the inhabitants and to create an atmosphere in which we can grow food plants without undue contamination or damage.

Some of the more common air pollutants encountered in our cities are: carbon monoxide, fluorides, lead, oxidants such as ozone and proxyacetylinitrate (PAN), oxides of nitrogen, particulates, and sulfur compounds, including sulfur dioxide and hydrogen sulfide. Automobiles are responsible for 60 percent of all urban pollutants. While there is a slight possibility that the use of automobiles will be greatly reduced in metropolitan areas of the future, they will not be eliminated soon. In addition, industry will continue to contribute its share of air pollutants. Therefore, it will be necessary to adopt planting schemes to help protect food crop plantings from airborne pollutants. Until the unlikely time that we have unpolluted urban air, we can use biological media as one tool to capture and reduce air pollutants.

Plants can play a major role in helping to clean up the air of our cities. Plants absorb carbon dioxide ($CO_2$) from the atmosphere and give off oxygen. They replenish our air supply and decrease the amount of polluted air. Trees work in two main ways to filter out particulate matter in the air. Leaves capture dust, holding it until rainfall washes it to the ground. In addition, trees reduce the wind velocity, allowing the dust particles to settle out.

The pattern in which the trees are planted can greatly influence the efficiency of the trees' dust-removing capacity. When planted between a source of air pollution (such as a roadway) and a crop planting, loosely arranged, easily ventilated, alternating strips of trees are more efficient in removing particles than is a dense, compact stand. Landscapers and designers can use the following general guidelines when installing protective plantings:

- Establish plantings perpendicular to the prevailing winds.
- Combine open and permeable plantings with dense barrier stands whenever possible.
- Plant concentrically around a source of pollution.
- Consider carefully the location, construction, and composition of plantings in relation to sources of pollution.

The influence of protective plantings on gaseous pollutants must be considered, since they aren't in the form of large particles like dust and cannot be filtered out by vegetation. There is some evidence that plants take in some air pollutants during their normal gas exchange, but this does not seem to be significant to overall air pollutant loading. One major way that trees can reduce gaseous pollutant concentrations is by increasing the turbulence of air movements, leading to dilution and more rapid dispersement. Studies of New York City showed that the presence of the vegetated expanse of Central Park reduced sulfur dioxide ($SO_2$) levels by as much as 40 percent in the park and immediately adjacent to it.

Both deciduous and coniferous trees can be used in urban areas for pollution reduction. When food-bearing trees are planted along busy streets, the fruit can build up unhealthy levels of certain toxicants, such as lead, on their surfaces. Care must be taken to thoroughly wash such fruit before eating.

## Urban Resources and Agriculture

The relationship of the city to the farm, in the modern view, is limited to the city's role as the market for agricultural production.

The necessary corollary of that role — the generation of sewage, garbage, and other waste resources — is commonly ignored, or at best seen as a nuisance.

If metropolitan agriculture is to succeed, it must complete the cycle of nutrients: from the soil to the consumer as food, and then returning to the soil. Direct benefits of closing this cycle include the realization of the economic value of the wastes used as fertilizers, while defraying the actual costs of disposal that otherwise would be necessary. Also avoided are the external costs that come due when the long-term impacts of offshore dumping become so severe that avoidance no longer is a viable alternative.

Metropolitan agriculture will involve intensive crop-production systems utilizing high crop plant populations and intercropping and successional cropping practices which place heavy demands on the soil. Soil fertility will have to be very high, and the physical characteristics of the soil will have to be carefully maintained. The addition of large amounts of organic fertilizer derived from composting sewage and household garbage would be an optimum approach for providing nutrients and humus to the soil.

According to the sewage data of the Metropolitan Washington Council of Governments, ably documented by Gil Friend, the city of Washington, D.C., with a population of 756,000, produces 309 million gallons per day of raw sewage. This sewage contains enough nutrients to fertilize 13,790 hectares of agricultural land with a balanced fertilizer at levels that would support most crops. If the nutrients contained in the city's garbage are included, 16,230 hectares can be fertilized. If we assume that losses of up to 50 percent may occur in the collection and processing of these organic wastes, we are still left with 8,115 hectares of fertilizer potential. This data points out the tremendous resources inherent in the waste streams of our great metropolitan centers.

Current per capita vegetable consumption can be produced, at average yields, on about 29 square meters per person. Thus, using the Washington example, some 37 percent of the vegetable needs of the population can be met with the nutrients in the waste stream given, only 50 percent recovery and conventional agricultural techniques and yields. As the cheap-energy subsidy is removed from conventional fertilizer production, the value of recoverable nutrients will increase accordingly. Hopefully, this will encourage the development of more conserving and cost-effective means of recovering nutrients that are currently wasted.

Of course, important changes must occur if we are to realize the benefits of using the urban organic waste system as a nutrient source for food growing. Cities must address the problem of sewage contaminated by heavy metals and other toxic products. Attention to this issue has traditionally tended to focus on the determination of 'safe' levels of the substances for waste application to particular crops or soil types. Ultimately, the solution lies in developing strategies to prevent any dumping of these toxins into the waste stream in the first place.

Separation at the source of household refuse and garbage is necessary if composting the organic portion for use on the land is to be economic. Education and strong economic incentives could teach the urban citizenry the value of not mixing glass and plastic into the household garbage. Even a matter such as the evolution of regional transportation systems must become a concern of cities in relation to waste management policy. The movement of raw materials and the distribution of the finished soil amendments will require nearly continuous transport. Reclaimed water derived from sewage treatment and used for crop production will require a separate distribution system from that of potable water supplies.

## Water

Water, long taken for granted, is quickly becoming precious. Most analysts now predict severe shortfalls in water supplies in the near future for both agricultural and urban use. The era of cheap water is over. No longer will immense federal subsidies provide inexpensive water to help keep the price of food low. Water for urban farming will have to be carefully applied, using conserving technology such as drip irrigation. New supplies of water will have to come from recycling and conservation, with little hope for the copious flows of reservoirs of times past. As the price of water rises, urban food producers will be better able to compete with their country cousins.

Aquaculture, using raw sewage as a feedstock, offers a treatment and purification strategy that can yield high protein from plant- or animal-based food products. Experimental systems using sewage to raise aquatic plants that are in turn fed to aquatic animals such as fish or shrimp are operating in areas as diverse as Munich, Germany, and San Diego, California.

On a smaller scale, solar aquaculture, as proposed by a number of workers, promises a system whereby fish and shellfish can be grown in limited spaces, using very little water or supplemental energy. The system uses solar tanks, often translucent cylinders approximately 1.6 meters high and 1.3 meters in diameter, as the basic fish-growing and sewage-treatment facility. In some cases, small ponds not unlike bathing pools serve as the fish-tank and heat-storage units. These tanks can be used almost anywhere, and they double as very effective heat storage units in a solar greenhouse attached to a home or small business.

*Watershed Development*

When cities are built, drastic changes occur in watershed hydrology. The earth is covered with impermeable materials and structures, and precipitation no longer can percolate through the soil into the water table. Natural waterways and drainages are filled or channelized. We spend fortunes for storm drains to carry away the flood of water that quickly occurs during heavy rainfall. If vegetation is to become a significant part of the metropolitan environment, it is vital that the soil reservoir be opened up to natural recharge. This can be accomplished in a variety of ways by using plants and modifying the soil surface. Some general design criteria can be followed by urban planners and builders:

- Compacted lawns and open areas should be perforated to improve water absorption and infiltration.
- Vegetation should be planted on all possible sites.
- Conservation practices should be employed, such as terracing, contour planting, mulching, and sod waterways in yards and gardens.
- There should be temporary mulching of construction sites.
- Permeable drainage channels and cobble drains should be used whenever possible.

The use of permeable surfaces for paths, parking areas, and other open spaces is feasible even if a hard, durable surface is required. Specially shaped pavers and bricks are available which provide an adequate surface to support an automobile while providing openings for the entry of water into the soil.

*Energy*

Americans use about 12 to 16 percent of the massive national energy budget on food production, processing, and preparation. Actual on-farm production of crops and livestock accounts for approximately 20 percent of this total, with direct use of fuel and electricity on the farm accounting for about 40 percent of this total. Energy used to produce machinery for the farm, plus petrochemical inputs, especially fertilizer and pesticides, account for much of the balance of on-farm energy use.

The balance of the energy used in the food sector is for the commerce of food and for its preparation. Processing, packaging, transportation, wholesaling, and retailing represent two-thirds of the cost of food to the consumer. One researcher, in a somewhat ridiculous U.S. Department of Defense study, estimated that the average molecule of processed food in this country travels 1,300 miles before being eaten. In addition to suffering well-traveled food, the average American uses 600 pounds of food packaging material annually. This alone can represent between 10 and 50 percent of final food costs.

When conventional energy resources become scarce and expensive, the impact on our agriculture and food prices will be startling. Close and direct connections between producers and consumers can considerably enhance the possibility of having an adequate supply of high-quality, affordable food. With transportation, processing, and packaging representing major portions of the price of food, metropolitan agricultural systems that can provide fresh food on the urban fringe will have built-in competitive advantages.

## Getting Started

We don't have the luxury of starting over with new cities, and current political and economic realities leave no room for major, all-encompassing solutions. How, then, can our society and our municipalities begin the process of developing metropolitan agriculture in our cities?

The change that must occur will be incremental and accumulative, guided by the development of new technology and by shifts in our perceptions and paradigms that define how we want to sustain the biosphere and ourselves.

Both the private and the public sectors will have a role in making change. Some change will be driven by the marketplace and some will only come as the result of government mandate and incentives. Government policy and capital will likely be the primary force, with private institutions and individual entrepreneurs being the doers that will take the risks.

Discussed below are a variety of tools and approaches that can be used to create change in some related areas. This listing is not comprehensive, but suggests the diversity of means to be considered as we move to create self-sustaining cities.

### The Municipality

Metropolitan leaders can take a page from the modern history of industrial development, characterized by an active partnership between business and government, and establish 'metropolitan agricultural development commissions.' As originally proposed by Edward Thompson, Jr., these commissions can function in a semi-autonomous fashion, much like the New York Port Authority. Funds raised by sales of agricultural development bonds can be used as a source of credit for urban farmers, or this capital can provide for the development of diversified farms through more institutional approaches in the metropolitan areas. The commission could act as a broker to assist in the transfer of land parcels, and could capitalize new farmers in the process. A vital aspect of the commission would be to take the lead in promoting local farm products and in developing integrated metropolitan markets for local produce.

Dust, odors, and noise are common complaints faced by farmers with urban or suburban neighbors. The city government itself, in conjunction with the state, can develop and support legislation that will protect farmers from undue harassment from nearby citizens protesting the 'nuisance' of farming. So-called 'right-to-farm' laws are needed to reduce pressures on farmers, and adequate measures have to be developed to ensure that farmers themselves take substantial precautions to reduce the nature or impact of potential nuisances.

### Federal Measures

In March 1982, the Urban Jobs and Enterprise Zone Act was introduced into Congress. It has been criticized as providing scant benefits for the urban poor while furnishing large windfall tax advantages for big business. However, this approach may offer a tool of value for the establishment of metropolitan agriculture. The tax shelters provided may enhance the ability of agricultural entrepreneurs to attract investors. In this case, society, working through the urban community, may wish to carefully regulate the ownership and organization of such ventures to ensure that equity issues and overall social goals are being met by the program. The enterprise zone approach, coupled with public/private partnerships, could be used to establish intensive, highly developed minifarms in place of rubble-strewn lots and abandoned buildings.

### Education, Research, and Technical Assistance

An obvious role for government at all levels is education, research, and the provision of technical assistance services.

The U.S. Department of Agriculture, the university systems, and the Cooperative Extension Service, with a few exceptions, have barely begun to recognize the need for metropolitan agriculture. One outstanding exception is the U.S. Forest Service, which has actively developed and supported urban forestry initiatives over the last twelve to fifteen years. Research areas that deserve high priority are those that will upgrade technical aspects of urban food production.

Agricultural-extension agents knowledgeable in metropolitan agricultural situations will be indispensable. Not only will they have to possess the horticultural and other technical knowledge necessary, but they must be able to work in the diverse, and sometimes difficult, social arenas in many of our urban neighborhoods.

The city school system can play a major part in developing a citizenry open to, and supportive of, metropolitan agriculture. Gardening in schools can start at the elementary level and continue as the student advances through the system. In the high schools, horticultural training can be combined with management and financial coursework, thus preparing the managers who will be needed to make a highly intensive, sophisticated food system operate successfully.

### Working Models

Prototypes of intensive, well-run farming operations can demonstrate possibilities and function as real-time laboratories and training centers for urban agriculture.

The model farm can represent a partnership of sorts between government, which would supply funding, and a private institution or group developing and running the project. The farm can be located right in the middle of town, or on the fringe of the city, where more land is available.

Crops grown will be selected not only for horticultural suitability but for popularity, in order to attract people to the farm site, thereby increasing public exposure and understanding of urban agriculture.

The model farm, while requiring substantial subsidy, might just be a catalyst and a source of inspiration to would-be farmers and consumers alike.

## Conclusion

Agriculture in our cities will only begin to flourish when the external factors that govern its economic viability change. The changes will not be sweeping and rapid, but incremental, usually localized, and often transitory.

Government policy will continue to have a major role in shaping the future of urban agriculture. The 'cheap-food policy' of the U.S. government for the past fifty or so years must change. When environmental, cultural, human health, and structure of agriculture (farm size, concentration, etc.) issues are given equal consideration with short-term economic efficiency, we will begin to see a major shift in government policy. An important side effect should be an increase in the price of food as we begin to pay the true cost of food directly, instead of having prices masked by hidden subsidies and myriad indirect costs. The excessive cost of the huge subsidy programs, through which the benefits go to relatively few, will likely be the target of an irate citizenry in the near future. The dismantling of these programs and the redistribution of subsidy benefits will provide a key opportunity to enhance the growth of urban agriculture.

But the unfortunate reality is that forests can grow old and good ideas wither while waiting for the government to act. And once it does move, it can be ponderous and not very sensitive to fine adjustment. We are better served as a society when citizenry can initiate action on the local level, be it as individual entrepreneurs, organized citizens' committees, community development corporations, or regional research and educational organizations. Political control or influence in municipal and county government is vital in the effort to bring ecological sensibility to the management of natural resource systems in and around the metropolis.

Jobs and business development are sorely needed in our cities. Small-scale, intensive agriculture can be the focus of an important part of urban economic development. The development of new employment along with a locally controlled food supply offer excellent opportunities to bring new stability to people in our urban areas.

We cannot hope for our urban areas to be completely self-reliant in food or to maintain ecological integrity in all things. But as the metropolis makes a place for nature in its midst and its environs, and as ecological cycles are rebuilt and reconnected, the city can find sustainability and a new future.

# Real Possibilities in the Transportation Myths

*Fred A. Reid*

A new awareness of the problems of our cities and their transportation systems came from the resource limitations of the '70s. This awakening caused more balanced and conservation-oriented planning, transit service expansion, and improved auto efficiencies. In transportation, many of these developments were turns toward old ideas. Some, like increases in electronic dispatching and control, and the appearance of new vehicle types somewhere between the auto and the bicycle, conjure up new futures. The disaffection with public systems in the '80s has seen us turn away from many of these transportation ideas. But the resource pressure, costs, and blight of our conventional auto system remain. The transportation initiatives of the '70s were in the right direction, but the opportunities are now being lost. We're again witnessing calls for more and faster highways and bigger cars.

We did not do a good enough job with our opportunities in the '70s. We came closer to the implementation of many transportation ideals than we ever had before. Transit was expanded greatly, even into the suburbs that had been designed around the auto. Dial-a-Ride and personal rapid transit were operated in full scale demonstrations. Several large commuter rail systems were built. Many auto-free zones were implemented.

However, many of these systems turned out to be much more expensive than the conventional auto system. Many even used more energy. Some were simply not used. We must look harder at the lessons of the innovations over the last two decades if we are going to promote anything similar. This is especially true in times of easier money and relaxed resource limitations.

There are new and better possibilities for transportation and the land-use planning that fosters it. Examples that will be shown in this chapter include:

- Conventional transit in high-density areas.
- Extensive transit interfacing with personal vehicles.
- Sharing of rides and vehicles.
- Smaller impact, more differentiated personal vehicles.
- Clustered community development.
- More differentiated and traffic-managed road types.

Since transportation encompasses more than people's immediate communities, it is easy to underestimate the extent of its requirements. We need to have a basis for defining travel requirements and judging between the utility of alternative systems.

But how can we judge? The most basic criterion is to satisfy what transportation is used for: serving all our activities away from home. These activities have been catalogued by researchers and planners. They exhibit many patterns independent of environment and time. But some of these activity patterns may change with different land-use plans.

This chapter will first draw on the data and research of household activity patterns associated with metropolitan travel. It will look at how these patterns have changed. Estimates of future changes in these patterns as a result of resource availability and sustainable city planning will be made. Three broad categories of myths — the Transit Society, the Zero Congestion City, and the High-Tech Vehicle Solution — will be scrutinized in the light of past experience.

## People's Activity Patterns

Employment, recreation, and other activities are very important to people's decisions on where to live, and transportation is their access to these activities. The figure pictures the distribution of these activities in two ways for a typical U.S. household. The percentages (the width of the arrows) show the percent of person-trips from a household that are made for local shopping, eating, school, civic activities, getting to work, and non-home social/recreational/cultural purposes. The mileages (lengths of the arrows) are the typical distances of trips to these activities. The percentages shown can be seen as proportions of the national average of 18.3 one-way trips per capita per week made for each activity category in 1977. Thus, the average individual makes 5.1 trips/week to local shopping, educational activities, etc. These data come from dozens of national and metropolitan surveys of people's travel and activity behavior over the last two decades.

About half of waking activities are spent in the home, but about 54 percent of the remainder are spent an average of ten miles away. Less than 30 percent of trips are within the range usually associated with one's immediate community (less than five miles).

With the kinds of opportunity we have in a modern metropolitan area, people have come to think of the place where they live not just as their home, not just as their immediate neighborhood, but as the area they can reach with transportation. People even have a continually broadening concept of what their activities can be. Transportation development has been key in enabling this expansion of activities and opportunities, for good or for bad. Most people seem to have embraced this trend. People's concept of what they want in life, their idea of where they have chosen to live, is largely this picture of activities.

Not only do people reach out from their homes to these activities, but their very ability to have homes in a large metropolis has depended on their ability to find and commute from areas of reasonable housing costs. Housing costs always increase near increasing employment

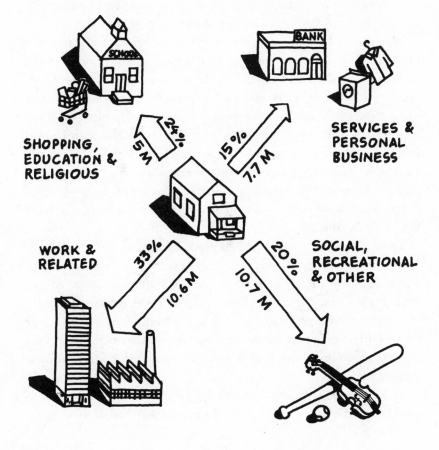

The diagram shows the percent of total household trips each group of activities represents and the average distance traveled for each.

169

concentrations. Transportation has played a very important part in providing affordable housing.

National statistics for many cities of many different economic and social conditions show that the proportion of time spent traveling to these types of activities is remarkably stable over cities. Trip distances are not. Distances have increased greatly throughout the twentieth century. They also tend to vary with the size of the total metropolitan area that people live in. Small metropolitan areas of about 250,000 population (Sioux City, Iowa; Orlando, Florida; Springfield, Illinois; Nashville, Tennessee) tend to have only half the trip distances of the big ones. Distances are higher again in rural (low- density) areas. Some of the older eastern cities are exceptions, notably Philadelphia. But New York, Washington, and Chicago are right up there with Los Angeles and San Francisco, leading the nation in trip lengths. Household trip distances, and thus transportation energy consumption, tend to be proportional to overall metropolitan size, probably due in part to the large numbers and the spread of activities. Trip purposes and particularly trip-making frequencies depend on extreme socioeconomic factors. Cities with high percentages of poor or old people have shorter trips, fewer work trips, and smaller overall frequencies of trips (but not the two-to-one differences across the range of city sizes above). The most stable factor, even across world cultural boudaries, has been the time out of each day that people devote to travel: about an hour-and-a-third on the average weekday.

Many observers ask if people's travel won't decrease under resource limitations. The profound lesson of the great gasoline price increases and shortages of the mid and late '70s is how little difference they made on travel. While gas prices rose 400 percent between 1973 and 1980 (actually only 60 percent, correcting for inflation), auto travel per capita decreased only 5 percent. Preliminary statistics indicate that it may have been back up to 1973 levels by 1983. Personal transportation costs are only 20 percent of all expenses. We apparently are not going to see more than a temporary halt or slowing of the growth rate in travel unless we have future energy or economic crises much worse than those of the '70s.

Transit patronage increased 20 percent between 1973 and 1980. However, noting that transit comprised only 3 percent of all trips before 1973, the increase amounted to only 3/10ths of one percent of its national share. During this time, transit service, measured in vehicle miles of service per capita, increased 6 percent, reversing a 30-year decline. (These figures are extrapolated from Federal Highway Administration and American Public Transit Association annual statistics.)

Short of major traumas, people are going to continue to want to travel to all the activities and services they can afford. If there is going to be any change in people's basic travel patterns it will be in trip distances and overall frequencies, rather than elimination or reduction of purposes. We should still expect that people must get to all of these activities.

# The Myths and the Possibilities

Growth and crises over recent decades have fostered ideas for solving transportation problems. But since many of these — high-speed rail and suburban transit are notable examples — have contributed much less than their claims or investment, they have become regarded as transportation myths, in the negative sense of the word. Costly failures should not be repeated.

But there is also value in myths aside from the lessons of their idealism. Though they may be oversimplifications of solutions, they show us clear ways. And they spin off forms or derivatives that are effective. Urban rail experiments show us that we cannot make it pay except in the highest-density areas. They taught us that lighter rail on old rights-of-way have much wider value. Dial-a-bus failed as suburban transportation but illustrated the potential of shared rides in selective corridors and services for the elderly and handicapped. These aspects of the myths should also be illuminated.

The remainder of this chapter will examine the three general categories of persistent transportation myths listed before. It will show where their often pure applications have been delusions or counterproductive. But from each we can pull elements or derivatives that are real possibilities for improving transportation and the quality of our cities with lower resource costs. Some of these are possible within the established framework of metropolitan planning. Other more powerful advantages will be seen when applied to sustainable land-use planning.

Before discussing the first myth, I will estimate some of the possibilities for beneficial change in people's basic activity patterns that can come about with sustainable planning.

We are reaching saturation in auto ownership per capita. We are not able or willing to bring more of our population into the mobile middle class. We may be reaching saturation in our ability to increase the capacity and speed of travel faster than population growth. This (essentially highway) performance has increased steadily all through this century, and has been a major factor in travel growth. But our tolerance for taking greater proportions of our land for transportation is low; and even if our technology could beat freeway or subway speeds, we are still essentially limited by urban arterial streets to ac-

171

cess these systems. If it weren't for this factor, travel would probably continue to increase as long as real incomes grew. In smaller metropolitan areas, there is still room for travel expansion.

The main thing that sustainable planning can do to reduce travel consumption is to bring people's activities closer to home and create a community that attracts them more than distant commercial and recreational activities.

The cycles of the '70s showed us that the least important trips were those to distant recreational and commercial activities. Thus, as sustainable communities provide a more natural environment, and as sustainability encourages city-sized clusters of business and commercial activity that can support many of the more specialized services and cultural activities normally found in distant city centers, travel pressures will be reduced. Development of more clustered, community-scale centers, rather than strip or corner stores, will reduce travel by encouraging multiple purpose trips.

There are apparent counterpressures in retailing economics and the media at present: more centralized, specialized, and volume stores. Paul Hawken's chapter discusses how these may be short-lived and spawn more sustainable forms such as catalogue sales and quality emphasis. Developments of more local services should be timed to capitalize on periods of price pressure on transportation and reaction against centralized marketing.

## The Mass Transit Society Myth No. 1:

This very pervasive myth suggests that if we provided good transit service everywhere, it would be possible to return to the sizable transit usage of the past — '1900 writ large.' In the 1970s, this myth extended transit into the suburbs. People ask 'Why can't today's knowledge produce a system at least as good as eighty years ago?' But 1900 was not such a transit utopia. Nor are today's travel requirements so limited. There are several important problems with the myth for today. First, most of our metropolitan areas now have a decidedly different, lower-density pattern incompatible with economical mass transit coverage. Our activities, associated travel needs, and service standards are much greater. And transit is not the energy-efficient answer to tranportation that many people think, except in the denser parts of our big cities.

In 1900, we did not use the land around our urban centers the way we now do. The horse was not the convenience or the cost competition to transit that the auto is today. Suburban land was relatively inaccessible and low in value. Cities were built densely around transit lines within walking distances of activities. If the auto had not been invented, we would have continued to build dense areas or corridors.

The land component of housing costs in the bigger cities would have grown even worse than it has because of the inaccessibility of land between outlying transit corridors. The auto lets people reach a larger percentage of suburban land economically. Given this possibility people will neither buy the more expensive urban housing nor live at its densities.

Sustainable planning presumes a larger proportion of clustered densities compatible with transit. However, land costs and the potential access to all of it by personal vehicles mean the land will be used at low densities as well. We are likely to continue to have most of our population at lower, non-urban densities.

Transit cannot serve low densities economically. It even requires substantial subsidy at the medium densities surrounding most of our metropolitan cores. At densities of the order of six housing units per acre along the lines serving smaller urban centers, it takes a 67 percent subsidy to sustain transit. Support of one-third of operating costs by fare revenue has come to be the minimum standard for transit systems — the law in California. It is sometimes argued that these or higher subsidies are justified by transit being inherently more efficient — economically, environmentally, and in terms of energy usage. This is only true at high residential densities. At lower densities, the cost required to operate sufficiently frequent service and ample routes to attract riders grows to high multiples of the fares people will pay. Many behavioral studies have shown that transit service has to be frequent and closely spaced to attract even 10 percent of an area's trips. The cost to provide this level of service does not go down with population density. It is dominated by driver labor.

Transit is usually thought to be unquestionably more energy-efficient than autos. However, if the energy necessary to construct, maintain, and access transit is taken into account, our urban systems are only a little better than the average 1985 auto production. Some forms of transit, such as in the suburbs, are dramatically worse.

The table compares the full energy consumption required for travel by different modes of U.S. transportation in the mid '70s. Also shown are consumption estimates for improved autos. The numbers are primarily from a Congressional study in 1977, updated by several recent sources.

The first column in the table shows national average vehicle occupancies for all trip purposes (except for commuter modes). The second column shows the average energy per mile to move each vehicle type divided by the corresponding occupancy. This 'operating energy' is what is usually stated as the efficiency of a transportation mode. The third column adds the prorated energy expended in the construction of vehicles, roadbeds, and facilities; in the maintenance and operations overhead; and to access and egress the modes (all in the Con-

The table shows average occupancy, energy per mile per person, and total energy per mile (including maintenance, infrastructure, etc.) for differing transit modes.

| MODE | (Occupancy) | OPERATING ENERGY INTENSITY | LINE-HAUL ENERGY | FULL SERVICE ENERGY |
|------|-------------|---------------------------|------------------|---------------------|
| 1975 Auto (11.6 MPG) | (1.5) | 7,860 | 10,160 | 10,160 |
| 1985 Auto Std. (27.5 MPG) | (1.25) | 4,748 | 6,137 | 6,137 |
| Small Electric Auto | (1.25) | 4,688 | 6,048 | 6,048 |
| Carpool | (3.3) | 3,670 | 4,740 | 5,450 |
| Vanpool | (10) | 1,560 | 2,020 | 2,420 |
| Dial-a-Ride | (2) | 9,690 | 12,310 | 17,230 |
| Heavy Rail (New) | (23) | 3,570 | 4,550 | 6,580 |
| Light Rail | (23) | 3,570 | 4,280 | 5,060 |
| Express Bus | (13) | 2,610 | 2,820 | 3,070 |
| Fixed Route Bus | (7) | 5,393 | 5,827 | 6,344 |

gressional study); plus a 50-year allocation of residential garage construction energy to the auto modes. The units of this 'System Energy' column are also converted to a more familiar number: gallons required per thousand passenger-miles. System energy changes some of the relative efficiencies, making buses more efficient and rail even less efficient relative to the 1985 auto standard.

The table shows that it would take only a 20 percent improvement in the 1985 standard autos to equal the efficiency of 1975 bus systems. Rail transit averages only 10 percent better than the 1983 national stock of autos, and much worse than the new ones. Other data from 1977 show light rail consumption to be very close to the rail average. The last row shows how poorly transit performs beyond its optimal territory. An increase of the order of transit's present share of national travel (3 percent in 1977) would in large part be at consumption levels as big as those of the feeder buses. It certainly isn't justified to subsidize transit outside of dense cities on the basis of energy efficiency alone. Pollution effects probably parallel energy efficiency. Van-pools appear to be by far the most efficient travel mode in the table. But this advantage would deteriorate rapidly, due to falling occupancies if they were expanded beyond the closely grouped trip-ends of their current rider market. Car-pools defined as vehicles containing three or more occupants comprise 16 percent of all trips nationally — five times those in transit. Their large potential base and excellent energy efficiency suggest the expansion of carpools produces benefits in energy reduction second only to improvements in vehicle fuel consumption.

The potential for improvements in transit energy efficiency through better vehicle propulsion efficiencies is not as great as the factors discussed above. A 1983 study showed the best examples of rail to be 31 percent better than in the table — about equal to the commuter auto example. It showed the best bus potential to be a 10 percent improvement. Operations streamlining, particularly for rail, may be a bigger potential, but this is not going to make large-order differences in the relative efficiencies of the modes.

## Real Possibilities for Transit

In view of the large dollar and energy costs of misapplied transit, it is extremely important to limit transit to where it serves well and to find other solutions elsewhere. Independent of sustainable planning, transit is efficient and economical at high densities and should take precedence over auto modes there. Other universal applications are the stressing of van-type subscription paratransit for commuting to all employment concentrations, and convenient interfacing of transit to autos for most trips into very high-density areas.

Transit can be energy efficient only when operating between residential densities above approximately five dwelling units per acre and employment or commercial areas over about one million square feet.

At residential densities above approximately eighteen units per acre along transit lines to commercial centers of several million square feet, transit is preferable on cost as well as energy grounds. Even at this density, it will only have a service level advantage over auto if roads and parking policies are prevented from being given their typical priority to autos. There would be more social advantage in restricting general private auto access to very concentrated centers, allowing permits to emergency vehicles and necessary VIPs. This would achieve better transit service for everyone and a more attractive environment.

Exclusive lane provisions for buses and paratransit are a more likely way that transit may be given the advantage it returns to a city. Washington, Los Angeles, San Francisco, and many other cities have exclusive busways in significant corridors into their central cities. Many cities have reserved lanes for buses in the central areas. Denver and Portland have gone a bolder route. Selected streets and malls have been given over exclusively to transit. These are the precursors of auto-free zones, 'campuses,' or groups of these areas, connected and served internally by shuttles or people movers.

Creating sustainable land-use patterns can add considerably to the efficient realization of transit service. To the extent that it concentrates development in clusters and discourages uniform, low-density spread, it will add to the area of efficient transit. At six units per acre, transit passes an energy-efficiency threshold over autos for lower density areas. As a more public- and pedestrian-oriented environment is produced, transit is encouraged. It is important to keep the above thresholds in mind in sustainable planning.

Another bright possibility in conventional transit is the expansion of express bus service, especially in the 'park-and-ride' configuration. This form of rapid transit has the most favorable energy and cost position of any mass transportation. There are many areas where high-speed rail has been chosen (probably because of its politically valuable symbolism) but express bus is cheaper, more energy-efficient, and can provide better service. Express bus with exclusive lanes will often give better residential-to-activity- center service because its stops are closer to actual trip ends, its smaller vehicle size allows more nonstop distance, and it has a much smaller energy overhead in construction and operations. Viewed broadly, express transit extends from van-pools, through subscription buses, to articulated buses operating between park-and-ride lots and activity centers. The greatest hopes for expansion lie in catering to particular central city activities.

A badly overlooked possibility is the potential for convenient and beneficial interfaces between transit and auto modes. The majority of our metropolitan areas will remain primarily auto territory. But many trips, especially for work, major shopping, and entertainment, will go into good transit areas. If these centers and corridors into them are to avoid being choked by cars, we must expand many more interfaces to transit from trips originating in auto-superior areas.

There has been much more effort in coordination within transit networks than between them and autos. Park-and-ride areas can become increasingly important in providing efficient and less costly service. Cities could lessen internal burdens by buying land at remote points on express bus and rail lines for park-and-ride. These areas should be distributed well out near trip origins, or placed crucially at points of advantage over straight auto trips, such as at heads of exclusive bus lanes, at bridges, or other points of constriction. Parking areas at the fringe of central auto-free zones or collections of such zones or central areas well-connected by transit would also cut signficantly into autos shuttling around central cities. Parking areas for van- or carpooling are a worthwhile alternative to greater highway or transit expenditures. One can imagine major parking-lot/transit terminals at the portals of central auto-free zones, such as in Venice and Dubrovnik.

Another aspect of transit interfacing that is particularly important in sustainable architecture is the pedestrian link. Site planning has for years been dominated by interfacing the auto to buildings. At low densities, this is appropriate. At high densities, it is a great mistake. It is even impossible to gain convenient auto access. Parking takes so much space that great walking distances to cars are the result. Transit can bring many more people closer to dense activities, especially if it does not have to fight for access with car traffic and parking.

The orientation of sustainable architecture toward the pedestrian and the natural environment is especially compatible with this crucially important pedestrian link to transit. San Francisco and many other cities have begun to recognize this in their zoning which favors the transit-pedestrian-building link over the parking link. Laws there and even in outlying cities do not require the same parking-to-floor area ratios in dense centers and near transit nodes as elsewhere. Requirements and incentives favor the pedestrian and transit link.

Though this pedestrian link is most important at the destination end of transit trips, it is also important in dense residential developments, where we hope to realize significant numbers of transit and pedestrian trips. It has been even more the practice there to bring the auto and its storage right to our door. Aside from the environment this creates, if our autos are at our right hand we will seldom use transit. Though convenient auto access is necessary for heavy groceries, it is not necessary for storage. We can even trade off temporary vehicle convenience for more remote storage, while increasing access to transit and visitors. Again, these are the same objectives of sustainable architecture. This site-planning aspect of transportation will be examined further in the section 'Real Possibilities For Roads,' below.

## Myth No. 2: The Zero Congestion City

This contrasts with the other myths in being an ideal not of reformers but of the present-day establishment. It is a dream of the perfect freeway network — the complement to the twentieth century's largely successful dream of the perfect personal vehicle. It is thought to be the channel of economic prosperity. But uncrowded conditions are incompatible with a busy, successful city. Everyone knows that popular activities mean crowds. People will always fill popular spaces. They even consider it desirable. Businesses do. That's why they locate in crowded places. People will fill roads to popular places until it 'costs' them too much in terms of congestion. This cost for access to dense activities is appropriate.

As the number of autos has grown nearly equal to the adult population, and as our cities have grown without limit, the zero-congestion ideal has become unattainable. In the established parts of urban areas congestion, pollution, and environmental blight are as much the experience as access to pleasing activities. This creates the tremendous political power of the congestion issue in transportation. Much of the move for transit comes from a hope of restoring the free movement of autos.

In a developing metropolis, we can only temporarily have congestion-free roads. Further development and pursuit of activities will always fill transportation to the tolerance limit of the traffic. Except in declining or constrained areas, more transportation capacity means more development and congestion. We're not relieving this by our road building, we're only encouraging more activity. While it's true that before the 1970s highways became better movers of people, the result was not to save people time, but to make our urban areas bigger. More people were able to commute further to jobs for a while. But it only got worse with greater consumption of energy and impacts on the quality of life. Businesses thrive on accessibility, but not with the costs associated with ever-increasing metropolitan size and complexity. Manufacturers fled the large eastern cities. In the west, they are increasingly moving to the smaller cities.

Even though urban growth experience has taught planners that congestion cannot be relieved, they still often go beyond providing only the capacity necessary for approved growth — maybe in the hope of getting ahead of the problem. Large, economically attractive metropolises are condemned to lower tranportation service levels. (Transit service can never beat uncongested auto levels.) If growth is allowed, planners must see that this means worse service, greater costs, and negative impacts on the quality of life. If the benefits of growth are seen to be worth it, only adequate capacity should be provided.

Efforts might better be spent managing the existing capacity — removing subsidies, for example, in parking costs and bridge tolls to discretionary trips, deliberately designing close to capacity rather than to free flow on roads. This is gaining some planning adherents in many urban areas. Parking and congestion prices should both be allowed to be at the real-cost levels to avoid subsidizing travel. This will avoid building up a deception and 'debt' of growth that will get out of hand if it continues. The cost of transportation should be more apparent to the users, and travel should be priced according to its expense. This activity is rife with subsidies on all sides, transit as well as highway. It has contributed enormously to excess travel and energy consumption. Interstate highways have a 90 percent federal subsidy, transit, 66-90 percent at several levels of government. Though the funds are often from user taxes, the path between source and use of funds is so complex that the planners don't even understand or consider it a variable in decisions.

Managing our transportation capacity will break the congestion cycle, but leave us still moderately congested. Can anything else be done? There are still some possibilities for managing travel better than results from conventional metropolitan sprawl land-use planning. And there are further improvements possible in the impacts of travel by micro transportation management. The first will be discussed below under land-use possibilities, the second as new road possibilities.

## Real Possibilities for Land Use

In economically strong cities, congested roads are a given. Improvements are possible in the 'quality of the congestion' more than in its elimination. It's better to read on a train than to fight traffic for the few minutes saved by car. But the land-use conditions that would make transit a competitor to autos are rare in our cities. Large-scale applications of sustainable, cluster-developed communities, surrounded by open or low-density areas would provide such an environment. This is the same concept as has been suggested for years by Lewis Mumford's writings and the many movements for open space, agricultural preservation, and quality of urban life.

The garden city cluster concept provides for development primarily in dense, transit- and pedestrian-priority communities. Autos would be used primarily for nonwork trips between communities and within smaller communities.

But this pattern of development runs counter to some strong economic forces. Land next to intensely used land is valuable for use. Environmental or social forces beyond economics will have to prevail if this is going to change significantly. However, there are economic and social forces that are moving things in this direction. The costs and social economics in ever bigger metropolitan areas are forcing commercial centers to be developed in distant suburbs. The costs of low-density housing construction have forced more cluster development. Unfortunately, this has usually not happened until all the intervening land has been developed to a fairly high density, diluting the possibility of focusing transit on its efficient territory.

If sustainable planning can enhance these trends by showing more of the advantages of community-scale clustering, we may get closer to the rewards of the 'greenbelt city' ideal. It must show the housing-cost and environmental advantages of cluster residential development. It must show the economic and social advantages of balanced activity, community-scale development. These patterns can be approached by infill, but they will be most feasible in newly developing areas, especially beyond the perimeter of urban areas. The Chino Hills plan for San Bernardino County and the Marin Solar Village new town plan are good examples.

There is bootstrap potential for saving transportation resources in these patterns. Separation of communities and clustering give much more favorable access to local services, allowing the development of broader community services that would not survive in the ubiquitous accessibility of sprawled services.

If we are not going to uniformly fill in between clusters, it will be necessary to demonstrate some strong arguments for holding significant percentages of land in very low density use, agricultural or recreational preserves.

## Real Possibilities for Roads

We can control the growth of congestion within the cores and in the outlying clusters of our metropolitan regions by managing road capacity. Since it is only temporarily possible to relieve congestion, we should leave it at a naturally limiting value such as the commonly used traffic-engineering level of service 'D', often the standard in large cities.

Tolerable operating speeds: 31 to 70 percent of the stoplight cycles having one or more vehicles waiting through more than one signal cycle at peak periods.

If greater capacities are built, they will soon be reduced to this level if we are not always spending for capacity for the next stage of growth. Failing to manage our road capacity like this — that is, not allowing a natural 'congestion price' to occur on roads — constitutes a subsidy of unnecessary travel and an inducement to additional growth. Sometimes the latter is desired. But this should be 'up front' in planning. It may not be what the planners, much less the constituency, want. It may cause relocation of activities in an undesired pattern.

Planners in the '60s argued that we should increase our accessibility throughout metropolitan regions. It has not worked. With sustainable planning, we can increase accessibility to activities by bringing them closer to people, balancing our communities better. We should concentrate on making our dense environments more livable. Auto priority roads can be phased over to transit, first by giving lanes to high occupancy vehicles (HOVs) at peak hours, later going to majority or exclusive HOV streets, and finally to malls or areas of auto restriction as density demands this space for pedestrian, transit, commercial, and emergency vehicle access. Parking areas may be phased into transit stations and delivery depots, with good connections to newly remote parking areas.

Though the typically lower densities of residential areas will not use such strong measures, those areas with the greatest densities will also benefit in environment and cost of transportation by managing traffic and giving some priority to transit and pedestrians. This will be especially necessary as we let road congestion rise to a 'natural price' to preserve the environment in residential areas.

Residential developers have long known this. They often provide limited access into and narrow winding roads within their better projects. Many large private institutions impede or regulate traffic with limited access, speed bumps, and narrow streets.

The neighborhood traffic management plans of Berkeley, California, the Chelsea district of London; and Seattle, Washington, are trying to create at least a separation of heavy-traffic environments from lower-traffic neighborhood environments. This is done by discouraging, if not preventing, through traffic. The walking, bicycling, and living environment is thus safer and encouraged, even if not completely free of conflicts with autos.

The traffic management plan in Berkeley was carried out to protect neighborhoods in a direct response to overflow traffic from an intentionally limited arterial capacity. It is a very ambitious plan, limiting or preventing through traffic on dozens of streets in all of Berkeley's fifteen neighborhoods. Approximately one hundred street diverters, closures, intersection islands or circles, and other devices were used to create a degree of isolation of neighborhoods from through traffic not unlike what exists in a hilly area with winding or dead-end streets. The plan was hotly contested by a minority through two referenda and to the California Supreme Court.

It survived all these tests and has a strong following among residents of neighborhoods that experienced reduced traffic. There is a process for improving it and making it more permanent. (It has been implemented since 1976 in a temporary form with concrete bollards and boards, first for a trial period but later for want of funds to install curb delineated versions.)

The plan was initially conceived in combination with a much increased transit service grid, which then could not be financed. Thus, arterial street congestion initially worsened and has remained bad in some areas. Adjustments have been made mostly favoring the resident over the commuter to Berkeley. Local employers have instituted van pool and park-and-ride plans. Transit service has been slightly increased. After a period of little growth, the city is expanding commercially in the '80s.

The plan seems to be a success in terms of its support. A study made within a couple of years of its implementation showed the number of accidents to be down in the city. There is a movement in the city and the state for a subtler plan to create a completely different 'slow streets' category for some of the most heavily bicycled streets in Berkeley. The original plan has created and encouraged more cycling. It has increased property values on many protected streets, but at the expense of a worse environment on the arterials.

Economic trends both in housing and transportation — smaller autos, the evolution of cycle-like vehicles, and higher costs — require us to reexamine our roadway system, at the housing unit as well as the neighborhood scale. We will not be building rows of single-family houses with twenty-foot-wide garages, strung out along streets standardized for 4,000-pound cars. We will be building clusters and rows of houses with common green space, planned and constructed in neighborhood units. Developments such as Baywood Village, Harbor Bay Isle in Alameda, California, Village Homes in Davis, California, and Park Merced in San Francisco (now thirty-five years old) separate living and even travel spaces (paths to neighborhood facilities) from the conventional road system. Garages are clustered, using less road and storage space and intruding less into the residential and recreational areas. These trends can be further developed to encourage more walking to nearby activities and services and to create a neighborhood environment that will attract residents to activities closer to home.

Researchers at the College of Environmental Design at the University of California, Berkeley have designed examples of street environments which allow vehicles full access to residences but clearly differentiate the spaces closest to homes as people territory; the vehicles are the intruders on these access ways, not the playing children. Existing areas are retrofit by narrowing, winding, and landscaping streets and preventing through traffic. In an interesting Dutch example, vehicle access to homes is only on driveway-like raised paths, paved more like a playground than a street, serving a number of homes each. Drivers entering these areas clearly see that they are in a foreign and low-speed environment.

This concept answers the question of how we provide reasonably close access to homes by emergency, service, and visitors' vehicles, and the family car filled with 100 pounds of groceries, when we are separating the major road and parking system from doorsteps.

## Myth No. 3: The High Tech Vehicle Solution

This myth has appeared in many forms. High-speed rail as the savior of our cities has been the most tenacious, for all its costs and limitations. The automobile has been the most successful, even with its costs and impacts. The electric vehicle was the hope in the '70s. Telecommunications as a substitute for travel, especially to office jobs, is the current one. The ideas behind most of these myths are valuable components of our tranportation system; but as panaceas for or focuses of our plans, they often do more harm than good. With their clear ideal and apparently great power, they take our attention off what service we need to perform and what are its full costs.

High-speed rail is the worst example of misplaced attention in plan-

182

ning. We had rail speeds at the turn of the century as high as those of the new metro systems hailed in the last decade. The bullet train in Japan is a great burden of maintenance and expense. The Northeast Corridor Metroliner had similar maintenance problems. BART failed miserably to realize its automation objectives for reducing operating costs. It has the same proportion of labor costs as bus systems. Its overhead operations energy is much higher than the rail average.

Rail is economical and energy-efficient only on long multiple-accessed or very dense corridors. High speed is only important on the longest ones. An auto with average long-distance occupancy is cheaper and more efficient than average-occupancy rail. Express buses are better on these measures in metropolitan areas except where the very high-capacity commuter rail cars can be justified. Rail is certainly not a widely applicable answer to our urban transportation needs.

Electric vehicles (EVs) have been promoted because they emit no pollution, appear compatible with a future based on renewable electric generation, and they symbolize small, clean, simple travel. With the electric generation methods that will be feasible for many years to come, the table shows that EVs are no more efficient than fuel-engine cars of the same size. The inefficiencies of electricity generation, transmission, and battery storage are as bad as those of gasoline refining and auto engines. Of the three possibilities for future generation, only solar could make EVs better for energy and pollution than fuel cars. But solar electric generation is the least developed, and is not certain to dominate power production in the long run. If solar and coal-electric generation prove to be more expensive than nuclear, commitment to EVs might strongly encourage a nuclear future. It is even possible that if solar electric or nuclear rates become low, another race for bigger, more powerful autos could result. Technology is no panacea.

An EV future based on solar, or even coal, is attractive compared to the present. But the basic objectives of size and even overall pollution control must be the guides. Otherwise the blight of generation facilities, power lines, and batteries will just be transferred from one place to another in our land. Size (or weight) is the appropriate focus on the personal vehicle.

The focus on EVs may also divert us from looking at the overall land-use and transportation network system. There are powerful forces for any new technology to substitute directly for an old one. EV development to date has been principally in vehicles larger than the leading new fuel-engine autos. Battery limitations may never allow EVs to be as lightweight as fuel-powered vehicles. We may be able to achieve better efficiency and utilization of roads with smaller non-EV technologies.

Telecommunications (TC) and microcomputers are spurring suggestions that they may significantly substitute for travel to work and to shop. The electronic office, with its networks connecting scattered video work stations, and experiments in cable or telephone line shopping like Teletext are bolstering these visions. It certainly is possible to imagine the trend in discount catalogue or 'off sale' stores going to on-line video shopping.

The trouble is that, although this may all happen, it won't make as much difference as imagined, and the demand for other travel will fill any reduction. There are still many reasons why people will still be required, and even want to go to a workplace. People shop for social and educational reasons, and of course to touch the product.

TC was speculated by studies in the '60s in the U.S. and France to have the potential for a 15-20 percent substitution for urban travel. We forget that there has been a large expansion of telephone, cable, and microwave services since the '60s, and that TV in the '50s represented a great expansion. And there's the original telephone! Travel increased throughout in spite of these developments. The net result estimated in a Canadian study was a 1 percent **increase** in trip making, ignoring the population growth effects. A 1982 conference on Transport and Telecommunications is even more conservative than the Canadian study. It concludes with the following statements: 'There are reasons to expect much less than a 20 percent reduction in work trips — principally economic and other impediments to working at home. There are no conclusive arguments or evidence that overall travel will decrease due to TC.' The participants agreed that there are many obstacles to simple substitution, that there are reasons for TC to induce as well as to substitute for trips, and that there is a tendency of other trip purposes to expand to fill any time saved. There are no clear, strong influences of TC on decentralization. The participants did point out that much more investment capital is being put into TC than into transportation, and that there are economic arguments for substitution, particularly in business.

The conference further estimated that the main influences of TC on transportation will be in public information and reservations for conventional transit and paratransit, including car-pooling; in increasing transit operations efficiency; in better traffic management; and in significant substitution for mail.

## Real Possibilities for High Technology

Technology should be thought of as a servant, a component of a desired future or service, not as a simple solution, ideal, or focus in itself. Trip time, energy, cost, and environmental objective are better measures of good transportation than speed or clean technology.

Even though we have a dramatic law on auto fuel efficiency, we do not yet realize the effect it will have for even greater change. The efficiencies of 1985 autos are double those of 1975. Since the law only requires an average efficiency, we will probably have over a four-to-one range in the fuel operating costs of 1985 cars — $600-$2,400 per year in 1981 dollars — plus greater differences in other ownership costs. Non-fuel costs of auto ownership have risen almost equally with fuel. With the efficiency mandate, they will increase more rapidly than fuel-use costs. These will be powerful infuences on people to buy the smaller of the cars on the market.

All this means less fuel use, lower costs, less pollution, less vehicle storage and road space, less obtrusiveness, and less of a power image for autos. These are large changes because of the levels of the new efficiencies and the continuing economic pressures. The benefits will be larger than those gained from all our efforts to substitute transit for autos. Such changes in the personal vehicle will continue to be the biggest leverage for improvements in transportation. Even with a manifold increase in cluster development compatible with transit, we would still have a great majority of all trips in autos, as transit only comprised 3 percent of U.S. travel in 1980.

This, of course, will still leave us with autos, their roads, and storage systems. However, the decrease in auto size and the emergence of cycle-like vehicles open the possibility for beneficial changes in these facilities. Communities and developments that realize these potentials and cater to new smaller vehicles — for example, by making parking spaces for them most convenient, recovering land from previously larger parking and road space standards, and building disincentives for the larger autos — will reap more than the average benefits of downsizing. The small-car potential has barely been tapped.

As fuel and other auto prices continue to rise beyond 1985, there will be more room at the low end of the market for competition from less conventional vehicles: mopeds, powered tricycles, small electric cars, etc.

There is a great motivation for the emergence of small vehicles such as powered tricycles. This gives a qualitative decrease in the space required for transportation. It has been pointed out that if significant numbers of these vehicles replaced conventional autos, and if existing road lanes could be marked alternately for two of the smaller vehicles, much of road capacity could be doubled.

A related new potential for more efficient auto utilization is rentals, including community-based or co-op systems. Auto cost pressures as well as tax laws are favoring a major shift away from ownership toward leasing. Because of tax depreciation and write-off laws, leases can be lower in cost than ownership. The same is true of rentals. Organizing this on a neighborhood co-op basis gives advantages of local tailoring and economic sharing. This could be integrated with housing site plans, and even made a part of the common property or other services or finances of a housing development.

Neighborhood apartment house-based auto rental operations are being tried in at least two areas of the U.S. The Mobility Enterprise in Lafayette, Indiana, designed by a research team headed by Thomas Sparrow at Purdue University, began in 1983. For a monthly fee, less than owning two cars, it offers full use of a micro car like the Honda CRX or G.M. Cutlass, plus an average hours-per-month allotment of and immediate access to a shared fleet of larger cars. Experience has shown that the sharing is practical and economic because people are able to preschedule a lot of their use. The economies come from the fact that the size of the car used is tailored much more to the needs of the trip, as well as from the sharing.

The STAR (Short-Term Auto Rental) experiment began in 1984 in a large apartment/condominium development in San Francisco, sponsored by Crain and Associates of Los Altos, California. A variable sized fleet of cars is available on a 24-hour basis in the regular garage of a housing complex. It aims principally at displacing ownership of a second, large car, or one by the occasional but convenience user. Participants are billed monthly according to usage. The hope is to demonstrate that there is a demand for this lower-cost, yet more usage-based charging system for transportation. The experiment is in an area also rich in transit.

If rentals or shared ownership were organized so as to make use just as convenient as it is now, the main effects would be a smaller number of more intensively used cars rather than less fuel consumption or traffic. Yet, even a smaller number of vehicles, stored more in clusters, would be an environmental improvement and a better use of resources. Large vehicles would not have to be used for small one-person trips. Such rental operations could be the basis for introducing micro vehicles not practical as family cars. The range of selection of vehicles, even recreational and utility types, could be a major public attraction to such systems.

The direct effect of Telecommunications on travel will not be large. However, significant secondary effects can be expected. Work trip volumes may be replaced by recreational trips, actually just accelerating an existing trend. Trips for these two purposes are currently about the same average length, but recreational trips have much higher vehicle occupancies. Thus, we may expect less vehicle trips as a result of shifts in the proportion of these two trip types due to TC. Also, we may see shifts in peaks to weekends.

Big secondary effects will come from TC's facilitation of the use and operation of less conventional forms of transportation. Forms of pooling cars, vans, and taxis, especially in their dynamically scheduled versions, will be able to provide much faster and better customized information, scheduling, response, and billing to their users. Fleet operations can be optimized and economized also. The same is true for auto rental operations.

It is possible to imagine a new type of business evolving out of the present ride-sharing, paratransits, local auto rental, and/or taxi businesses that offer transportation or vehicles as needed, as convenient as a touch-tone phone or simple terminal in every home.

## *Summary*

In the transportation sector, sustainability means lower energy consumption, low cost, and compatibility with sustainable land-use and life- styles. The most important possibilities for this sustainabiity are in the expansion of the following trends.

1. The trends toward lower-impact personal vehicles and their road systems:
   - Smaller, more efficient vehicles matched to their trip purpose.
   - Larger vehicles trending toward neighborhood rentals or pools.
   - Growing shared-ride or vehicle-rental agencies, businesses, and co-ops.
   - Residential site planning for smaller (vehicle) garage space, narrow roads at homes, more pedestrian and bike paths, and large vehicle storage away from residences.
   - Growth of 'slow streets' and of mixed-use, textured and Woonerf street designations and designs.
   - Traffic management for the safety of people and microvehicles in residential areas.
   - Highway and street capacity and expansion policies matched and staged more closely to the needs only of planned growth.
   - More differentiated road system speed and weight standards.
2. The trends toward more efficient and increased shared use of residential land:
   - The expansion of cluster and high-density housing development.
   - The recovery of unnecessary garage and access road space (with sustainable transportation) for environmental and aesthetic qualities at these densities.
   - The clustering of a balance of commercial services with higher-density residential clusters.
3. Refining the effectiveness of transit, parking, and traffic policies in dense commercial areas:

- Increasing the emphasis of transit in dense urban cores relative to suburbs.
- Decreasing the traffic and parking accommodation there.
- Increasing the proportion of street capacity for transit and high-occupancy vehicles in cores and major corridors.
- Increasing the transit-pedestrian zone convenience there.
- Increasing the auto-to-transit convenience at core perimeters and with express transit park-and-ride nodes.
- Increasing the emphasis on private subscription vans and buses.

# A Short History of Twentieth Century New Towns

*Peter Calthorpe*

Many U.S. cities are the product of ideal design rather than organic growth.

Washington D.C.
Savanna, Georgia
Santa Fe, New Mexico

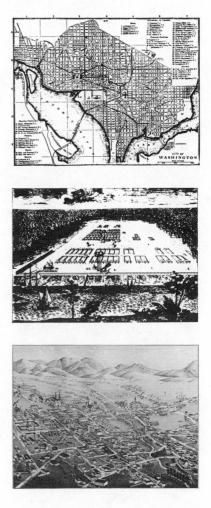

Until the twentieth century, new towns represented a way of occupying and controlling new terrain. Some grew organically while many, such as the Roman garrison, the French Bastille, and some Greek cities were pre-planned. In the U.S., many cities were the product of designers and planners: Washington, D.C., the product of the Beaux Arts school of planning; Savannah, Georgia, an abstract checkerboard of parks and houses; Santa Fe, New Mexico, an example of Spanish planning regulations. Farther west, most U.S. cities grew from the surveyor's grid—a kind of unconscious town planning.

With the Industrial Revolution, urban congestion and rural depopulation reached crisis levels. Starting with the social reformers of the nineteenth century, Engels' criticism of industrial workers' housing, and Ebenezer Howard's Garden City proposal, the purpose of new towns shifted from a means of occupation or escape to a response to industrialization and its ill effects. These ill effects, though changing throughout the twentieth century, are still the impetus behind new towns. Pollution, sanitation, economic health, and the quality of working peoples' lives have always been and still are the motivation for planned growth. New technologies have certainly generated new urban problems and new possiblities. Coal heating and residential overcrowding led to extreme air pollution in the nineteeth century. Today, cheap oil and the auto are having the same effect. But beyond pollution, new ecological and social issues have arisen which have not been addressed by the new towns movement. Planned com-

189

munities always seem to lag behind the issues, solving yesterday's problems while aggravating today's.

Some nineteeth century reformers responded to the poverty, urban overcrowding, pollution, and social decay by proposing a return to a pre- industrial technologies, romanticizing the Medieval structures, crafts, and guilds. Much of John Ruskin's writing, William Morris' work, and the pre-Raphaelites reflect this attitude. Though unsuccessful at turning back industrialization, their basic sensibility was to have a lasting effect on the British new town movement. Their picturesque aesthetic with its curving streets, Ruskin's advocacy of the gothic as an indigenous, craft-based architecture, and their village-scale social vision can be seen in the garden cities and much of twentieth century English landscape design. The Romantics' social ideals of political decentralization and worker control of production, as in the guild system, was translated in Howard's proposal into the idea of cooperatives which commonly owned and governed the town and its land. However, Howard eliminated the Romantics' notion that scientific progress must be abandoned to maintain social equity, human health, or environmental stability.

State socialism and its town planning ethos, as expressed by the modern movement in Europe in the 1930s, was another response to the social and physical effects of industrialization. Unlike the garden cities movement, this vision affirmed industrialization, claiming the old urban forms were frustrating its potential. The Romantic's decentralization was replaced by efficiency, progressive technology, and centralized political structures. The new technologies and techniques produced by industrialization, the auto, airplanes, steel construction, etc., are embraced by plans which placed efficiency first and individuality last. Cities were seen as machines which had to undergo radical change in order to be in harmony with the new technologies.

The post-World War II new towns are the bastard sons of these earlier, ideologically pure movements. Robbed of their radical political and social structures, the form of these new towns and urban redevelopments, with a few exceptions, have earned almost universal disdain and prompted the current rejection of the use of new towns.

The history of twentieth century new towns can be and has been examined from many perspectives: economic, political, social, and aesthetic. This chapter will try to highlight several aspects which relate to sustainable communities: first, the technical and planning features which reinforce ecological stability and second, the treatment of common space and shared facilities.

Born of industrialization, most twentieth century new towns were coping with an unheard of material abundance, economic growth, and the transformations of new technologies rather than a sense of physical limits or ecological balance. Expansion and progress were considered inevitable and new towns were designed to make the modern world more efficient, not to reduce its consumption of resources. Unintentionally, the earlier new towns provide models of pedestrian and mass transit plans primarily because they pre-date the auto. Significantly, the garden cities tried to reintroduce agriculture and open space in a way that is extremely relevant today. Garnier's Cite Industrielle is laid out with perfect solar orientation and access, but was done so for health, not energy, reasons. The post-World War II towns in some cases dealt with broad ecological issues, but ultimately focused primarily on social and economic efficiencies. New towns designed for ecological stability would certainly be a new chapter in the evolution of town planning.

The second perspective used to review these new town proposals is the shifting treatment of public space in relation to a new architecture and new technologies. It is here, I believe, one can locate the primary failure of new towns. Lacking the remnants of common space and community which are scattered throughout our older cities, the twentieth century design ethic and new towns planners failed to create the common space so elusively essential to human well-being and community. As industrial production and consumption tended to amplify the individual, modern architecture and planning ignored public spaces in its preference for expressive buildings. New towns, without historical buildings, old squares, and mixed-use streets, lacked the memories and commons to bind a people together. We now are beginning to understand the need to preserve the past, nurture the common ground, and respect the environment. These are concerns which unfortunately were largely lost to the later new towns movement.

## Ebenezer Howard: The Garden Cities Movement

The European Enlightenment of the eighteenth century and its notion of progress gave rise to the scientific revolution and its commercial partner — industrialization. Implicit in the revolutionary movements that followed in the nineteenth century was the notion that these breakthroughs could bring about the improvement of human life—through scientific method, land planning, political revolution, economic reform, mass production and specialization.

The population of Europe grew in the nineteenth century from 180 million to 400 million. The population growth corresponded to an equally significant population shift, bringing thousands from the countrysides to the cities. In England, those early urban immigrants were the first witnesses to what have become the persistent tragedies of modern life—poor housing, poverty, lack of sanitation, rural depopulation, pollution, and congestion. These conditions gave birth to a generation of philosophers, writers, architects, and social thinkers whose work ranged from a denouncement of industrial progress to attempts to redefine and organize modern industrial societies.

The garden city movement, originating in England in the early twentieth century, was one of these attempts. Led by Ebenezer Howard, the garden city movement sought to describe not only the physical characteristics of an ideal urban form, but also to define an economic, political, and philosophical basis for modern life.

Out of the French Revolution came the early socialist writers such as Henri de Saint-Simon (1760-1825) and utopian planners such as Francois Marie Charles Fourier (1772-1837). Fourier proposed reorganising society into 'phalanges,' each containing about 1,600

French Francois Fourier proposed new towns much like palaces to house 1,600 people.

people in a common building. This community would own and work around 5,000 acres of land, as well as run small businesses. One building would house a fairly self-sufficient town. His benign socialism, though clearly not expressed in his palatial architecture, was manifest in common ownership and pay structures: the worst jobs would receive the best pay, and vice versa.

In England during the same period, Robert Owens (1771-1858) attempted to defuse political unrest with proposals that did not transfer the basic ownership of business, but provided for better working conditions and housing through the building of new towns. His experimental communities at New Lamark Mills proposed villages of 1,200 people at a density of about one acre per person built around one basic industry. The villages were to be laid out in a square enclosing a common open space within and allotment gardens and industry without. While some activities were to be communal, such as cook-

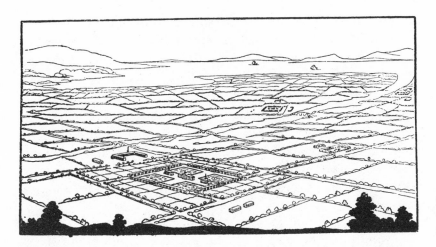

Robert Owens in England proposed villages for 1,200 people in which private industry would dominate.

ing and eating, the industry remained in private hands, i.e., Robert Owens'.

In a more radical version of utopian planning for welfare capitalism, James Silk Buckingham made a proposal for a new English town of 10,000 inhabitants to be named "Victoria." Buckingham advocated the private construction of model towns to absorb the unemployed and to offer a benign living and working environment. Out of 10,000 acres of land, 1,000 acres were to be concentric squares of buildings containing factories, housing, public baths, kitchens, laundries, and schools. All the buildings were to be the property of a corporation owned in part by the inhabitants. Profits of the corporation, after dividends were paid to outside investors, were to be divided proportionally among the residents.

These schemes distill the essence of the plan Ebenezer Howard was to put forward as the Garden City over fifty years later. Each proposed an integration of agriculture and industry in a new town

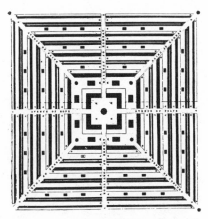

"Victoria", a new town for 10,000, was advocated by James Silk Bulkingham as a way to absorb the unemployed from England's overpopulated cities.

(Above) plan; (left) perspective.

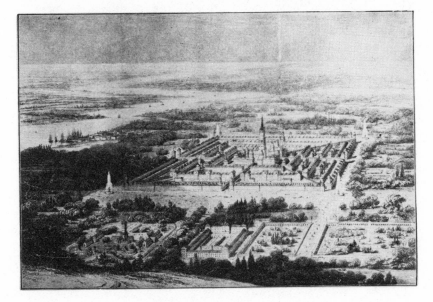

193

in which financial equity was shared with its inhabitants. The goal was to redirect the industrial pattern of growth for the benefit of the workers, to relieve congested cities, and to revitalize depressed agricultural zones. They differ from Howard's towns primarily in form; their's was a rationalist vision of architecture: classical in nature, geometric, and abstract. Their rectilinear forms didn't respond to site characteristics or sun path, i.e., their form suppressed individual expression in favor of common identity. Both Fourier and Owens conceived of the town as a single building, a single pure form in the landscape, a classical palace turned into a kind of communal village.

The arts and crafts movement led by John Ruskin (1819-1900) and William Morris (1834-1896) in England, provided a counterpoint to the rationalists' optimism about technology, progress, and its expression in classical forms. Their vision was a return to a fourteenth century medieval ideal in which the wealth was more evenly distributed, but the town remained gothic and picturesque. The craft guild was to be the primary social unit. Ruskin's ultimate effect, however, was not on social structure but aesthetics. His messianic criticism of classical forms and support of the organic vernacular of the gothic set the direction for an art, landscape, and planning movement which continues to this day. This tradition had a significant effect on Howard's garden cities through the work of Raymond Unwin, his first architect and planner.

Ebenezer Howard's proposals were diagrammatic and didn't predetermine form or styles. He advocated a new town of 32,000 people on 6,000 acres, of which 5,000 were to be held as an agricultural reserve. His goals were clearly stated: "To find for our industrial population work and wages of higher purchasing power, and to secure healthier surroundings and more regular employment." Unlike Buckingham's proposed new towns in which the residents were equity partners in local industries, residents of a garden city were its landlords. Their share of the wealth would be extracted in land rents as "change in land values created by the community will be enjoyed by the community." All the land would be owned cooperatively, and all would pay rents. This income would cover the primary debt service, costs of improvements, and finally, health care and pensions for all workers. Howard had combined public ownership of land with private enterprise, thus satisfying all political groups. The town's revenue would be the increment of land value, brought at agricultural costs and developed to urban standards. This was certainly not a revolutionary platform, but a simple way for the working class to share in economic growth: "A peaceful pathway to real reform."

His diagram of the garden city had a single focus and was sym-

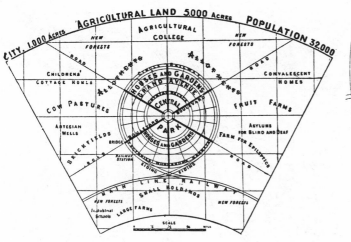

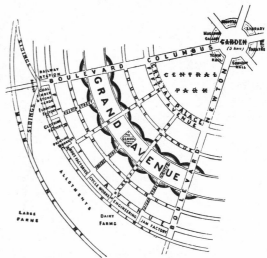

metrical. The ring configuration placed a large park at the center with public buildings at its core. Around the park was to be a "crystal palace" (derived from Paxton's glass house for the Great Exhibition of 1851): a glass arcade to house the shopping area, sheltered from rain in summer and acting as a winter garden the rest of the year. It was perhaps the earliest proposal for a shopping mall. Beyond the crystal palace were rings containing houses with gardens in which variety in architectural style rather than unity was to be reinforced: "...though proper sanitary arrangements are strictly enforced, the fullest measure of individual taste and preference is encouraged." A "Grand Avenue" of 420 feet divided the residential area from the ring of work places and industry. All machinery (home heating and lighting) was to be electric. Beyond the industrial area was to be a rail line circling the town, beyond which were allotment gardens, followed by large farms. Some farms were to be cooperatives run for the city, while others would be run as private businesses.

The first realization of the garden city idea came with the formation of the Garden City Pioneer Company in July, 1902. Their purpose was to build a new town at Letchworth, a small village of fifty inhabitants, located just thirty-four miles north of London. The company bought 3,822 acres of land and retained Barry Parker and Raymond Unwin as architects and planners. Unwin had been involved with the garden cities movement since its inception, espousing the idea that the form of the town must be the product of the site, and that housing should not be built at densities greater than twelve units per acre. Most of Howard's diagram is translated in the Parker/Unwin design. The civic buildings are placed at the center (in this case on the highest ground) with park areas around; the housing develops along radial streets with blocks of houses forming rings around the core. In a less orderly way, the shopping street curves

Ebenezer Howard's new town proposal was diagrammed (left) as a circle with green belt agriculture surrounds and rail linkage to other new towns.

A detail of Howard's new town (right) placed a park and public buildings at the center with retail and housing separated from industry and work at the periphery.

195

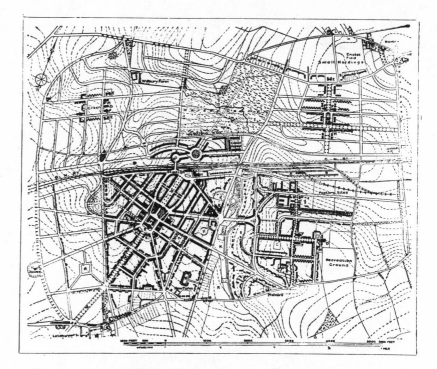

In 1902 Barry Parker and Raymond Unwin produced a plan for the first of Howard's new towns, Letchworth. It interpreted Howard's diagram placing park and public buildings at the center with housing streets radiating out.

away from the train station and the industrial buildings are scattered around the periphery. Of the total area finally purchased (approximately 4,500 acres), 1,500 acres was planned for the town, 135 acres for industrial use, and the remainder for allotment gardens and farms. Of this, one-third became pasture with approximately eighty dairy and fruit farms, nine large farms of 252-842 acres, and seventy-one acres of allotment gardens.

The actual town of Letchworth never achieved the symmetry or clarity of the plan. Construction began with housing around the existing village to the east of the new civic center site and proceeded with several experimental blocks of workers' cottages. Many homes were built by private individuals, thus providing variety but also deviating significantly from the original plan. The public buildings were to be constructed last, when the larger population could afford the costs. This left the town without a center, deflecting its focus to this day to the retail street connecting the rail station with the housing around the existing village.

Letchworth was successful, however, as a community. The land remained in common ownership in spite of several attractive offers by businesses to purchase rather than lease land. The agriculture never diversified to the extent desired and the farm co-op eventually failed, but the local market for dairy products remained strong and the tradition of private kitchen gardens grew. The industrial component became the keynote of the town's success, incorporating over forty-one businesses of great variety in scale and product.

The end of World War I accelerated the demand for new hous-

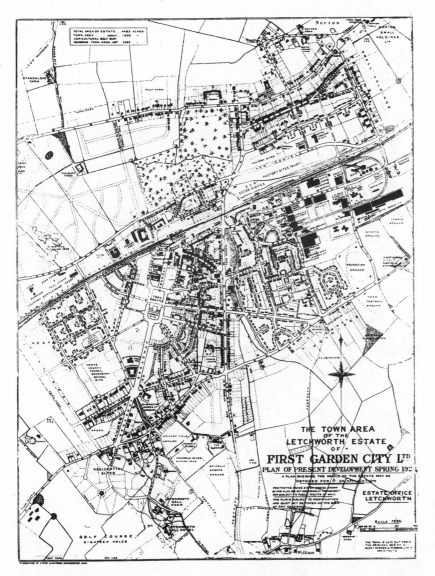

By 1924 Letchworth had grown but not according to plan; the public buildings at the center of the town had been delayed, the housing scattered, and retail shifted.

ing in England. To meet this need, Howard took on the construction of a second garden city at Welwyn, a village even closer to London than Letchworth. The central concepts of the garden city were retained but modified in scale and focus. The agricultural component was to be smaller and the town's autonomous identity modified to act as part of London's growth rather than as a nascent community. The preliminary announcement of September 1919 was called "A satellite town for London." Its description challenges suburban sprawl and claims autonomy within London:

The town will be laid out on garden city principles, the town area being defined and the rest of the estate permanently reserved as an agricultural and rural belt. Particular care will be taken, in the arrangement of the town, to reduce internal transport and transit, whether of factory and office workers, or of goods, to the practicable

197

minimum. A population of 40,000 to 50,000 will be provided for, efforts being made to anticipate all its social, recreative, and civic needs. The aim is to create a self-contained town, with a vigorous life of its own independent of London.

Louis de Soissons masterplan for Welwyn shows the town with small agricultural belts and curving residential streets. The central parkway terminates in the civic center and parallels the existing railroad line.

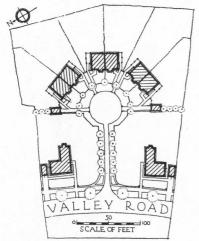

Soissons introduced the concept of the "cul-de-sac" residential street off the primary connecting streets.

The site consisted of 2,378 acres twenty-one miles from London (only fourteen miles from Letchworth). Louis de Soissons developed the diagram master plan in 1920 by combining concern for the topography of the site with the order of existing railroad lines. A central parkway running parallel to the rail was to unify the site, with civic buildings and park at its head and the commercial center to one side on an approach to the train station to be named Howard's Gate. The industrial zone was located across the tracks to the east. The rural belt was held to only 608 acres. In fact, the emphasis of the town is clearly on the housing. It is in this plan that varieties of the "close," or "cul-de-sac," were first developed. The housing was the first built, as the plan of 1924 shows. The industrial area followed and remains successful to this day, but the commercial area collapsed into a smaller zone, and, as in Letchworth, the civic center never materialized.

After World War II, the New Towns Act of 1947 in England was largely based on Howard's vision and was to launch one of the largest satellite town programs in the world. His thinking influenced progressive elements in the U.S. during the 1930s through individuals such as Lewis Mumford and Clarence Stein, and some of Franklin D. Roosevelt's policies of regional development.

But, it is important to note the failings and problems of the garden city concept. Though the garden cities succeeded in a real mix of housing, workplaces, and commerce, it was a mistake to believe they could be autonomous. The larger economic forces around them finally determined their internal economic structure. Facing forclosure in 1934 as a result of the Depression, Welwyn was forced to give up the inhabitants' ownership of land to a private concern. Similarly, the country's general food market and competition from farms forced Welwyn's "new town agricultural guild" to fold during the agriculture depression of the late 1920s. The guild, a co-op organized

(Left) A detail of the original plan for the central sections of Welwyn.
(Right) The town as built in 1924 with the residential areas filled out but the civic and retail areas undeveloped.

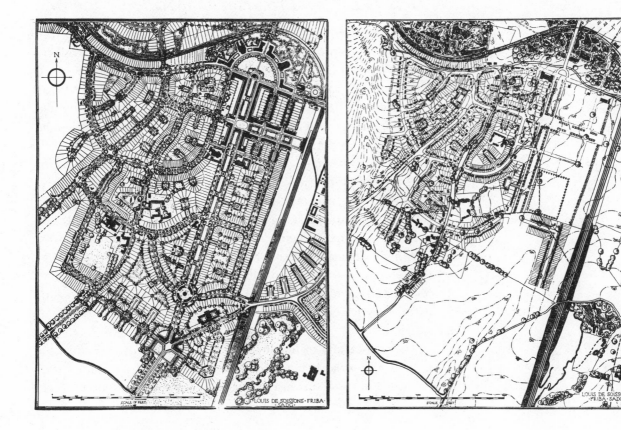

to provide diverse and high quality foods for the town, suffered from an endemic problem of new towns: how to survive with a partially established consumer market. The same proved true with some of the civic amenities never fully realized because of their dependence on a full population and economic base.

The garden cities success lies in their industries, which served the larger marketplace and in their retail areas, which always grew in direct relation to the growth of the town. In fact, though not designed as such, the retail areas always became the center of the town. The housing also demonstrated the ability to improve, through planning and design, the living conditions of England's working class. Finally, the common ownership of land and common idealism generated strong feelings of community and general responsibility. Howard's proposals and garden cities had a profound effect on planning throughout the twentieth century and are particularly relevant today. As a stand against both congestion and sprawl, his concepts are relevant to the environmental movement; as social reform they can be meaningful in relation to the current housing stress; as compact mixed-use towns, they represent a solution to transit problems; and their vision of incorporating agriculture offers an alternative to our large-scale agribusiness.

## Toni Garnier: Precursor of Modern Planning

Toni Garnier (1869-1948) produced a plan for an ideal industrial town in 1904, a product of his student work at the French Academy in Rome under his Prix de Rome Prize. He continued to develop it until 1917 when it was published as a two-volume work called **Une Cite Industrielle**. Unlike Howard's, his vision was never literally realized, but many of his concepts and formal examples effected the evolution of modern architecture and planning.

He selected a hypothetical location in the south of France and an industry, metalurgy, around which to construct a town of approximately 35,000 (Howard's proposals were for 32,000). His was a rational, functional vision of a city clearly zoned: a residential zone with a civic center, schools, and recreation; a train station quarter with higher density housing and retail next to an existing village; the industrial area with train and water access; and a separate zone for a hospital and sanitorium. This segregation of uses was intended to allow for expansion of each zone as well as compatibility of activities.

The political and economic structure of the city was clearly socialist in nature, Fourier being an obvious influence. All the land was to be owned in common with the city administering slaughterhouses, flour mills, bakeries, dairies, and pharmacies, as well as the more typical responsibilities of water, waste, and standard maintenance. In an extremly utopian gesture, police, jails, courts, and churches were omitted as unnecessary in a town with such equality and economic justice. In another radical proposal, the city was to be energy independent, constructing and operating a dam for hydroelectric power. As with Howard's plan, the city was to be all electric: trams, heating, water, and industry.

Another powerful philosophical influence on Garnier was the turn-of-the-century movement for regionalism and decentralization. These theories, as advanced by Patrick Geddes (1854-1932) in England and by others throughout Europe, had a strong impact on Howard as well as on Garnier. Geddes's theory of regionalism maintained that development should follow the local occupations and customs. The regionalist movement stood for preservation of provincial characteristics, government decentralization, regional universities, conservation of historical monuments, and support of local arts, crafts, and industries. Garnier's city accomplishes many of these goals, preserving the old village near the station, creating a semi-autonomous city government and a local industry (mines in the region) and using local materials for construction.

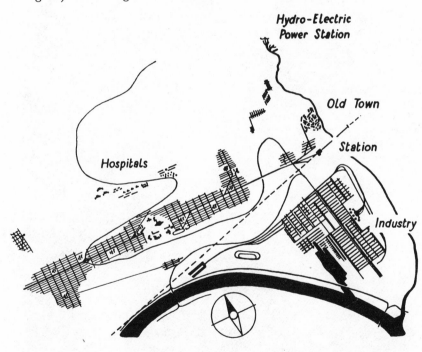

Hydro-Electric Power Station

Old Town

Station

Hospitals

Industry

Toni Garniers' plan for a new town of 35,000, "Cite Industrielle", showed a clear zoning of areas and uses.

The form of the town is the product of environmental principles and a classical planning tradition. The whole city is laid out in relation to sun, wind, topography, and transportation: "A main-line railroad passes between the factories and the town, which is located above on a plateau. Higher still are placed the hospitals; they, as well as the city, are sheltered from cold winds (hill to the north), and have their terraces oriented to the south.'' In the residential area, orientations and spacing of the dwellings probably constitute the first solar access code. Every room is to have at least one window ''to allow the direct rays of the sun to enter.'' The zone is laid out in long east- west blocks so all buildings can face south. The houses cannot shade one another: ''the minimum distance between two dwellings in the north-south direction is equal to at least the height of the building situated on the other side.'' Additionally, the streets are configured and landscaped to allow solar access, north-south streets are twenty meters wide and planted on both sides, the

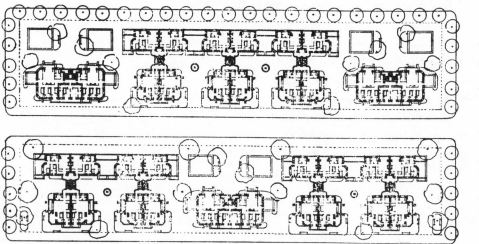
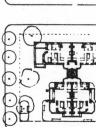

Plan and perspective of one of the higher density residential sections of "Cite Industrielle". The street layout represents zoning for solar access with large south aspects, minimal shading, and sensitive tree placement.

east-west streets have no trees when thirteen meters wide and trees on the south side only when nineteen meters wide. These seem to be the perfect formulas for passive solar planning, but the intent at the time was health not heat. Sun and ventilation were thought to be the cure for many of the industrial urban ailments— consumption, tuberculosis, etc. The placement of the hospital expresses Garnier's concerns clearly.

The hospital for "Cite Industrielle" is located above the residential areas with each room facing south. Its overhangs, balconies and overall layout is a model for passive solar design.

The town is innovative as a design statement as well. The two trends in planning at the turn of the century, the romantic and classic traditions, were locked in a false confrontation. The classic tradition was represented by the academic school, enshrined by the Ecole des Beaux Arts in Paris (where Garnier was trained), and manifested by Georges Eugene Haussmann's rehabilitation of large sections of Paris at the mid-nineteenth century, Otto Wagner's proposals for Vienna, and even work in Bath, England. This work used axes, symmetry, uniformity, and classical forms to create monumental urban spaces. The counterpoint was provided by Ruskin, Morris, and Camillo Sitte (1843-1903), advocating the gothic vernacular as a set of design principles. Sitte's book, **City Building According to Artistic Principles**, is an analysis of medieval urban spaces; their casual, asymmetric, picturesque qualities. Unwin, for the garden cities, welded the two traditions by employing the grand axial forms of the Beaux Arts school for the public sections of the town, and the intimate, curving, and site-specific qualities of the romantic tradition in the residential areas. Garnier transcended these planning styles to generate a new formal tradition: modern planning and architecture.

The romantic and classic traditions may appear contrary, but they share one basic trait: the public space—either street, square, or plaza—is the dominant form. The buildings are subservient. Though less true of the romantic, both traditions use urban buildings as the

Garnier's treatment of buildings as objects in the landscape rather than "street walls" marked a dramatic shift in design perspective.

"walls" of great outdoor "rooms," with the facades ornamenting and unifying, and public art "furnishing" these rooms. Garnier's plan expresses a totally new sense: the building becomes the object, not defining the public space, but situated in it. The residential areas have no private yards, but paths which wind casually through the blocks, and building offsets and jogs which deny the rectilinear form of the street. Within the overall structure of a grid the buildings become autonomous forms placed in a park-like setting. The plan juxtaposes a romantic composition of buildings and landscape against the rational framework of the street. The civic center, when compared for example to Unwin's plan for Welwyn, reinforces this interpretation. The great assembly hall, though on the primary axis of the town, is clearly a dominant object in the central park, rather than its containing edge. This formal shift from building as edges to buildings as objects is one of the foundations of modern architecture and planning.

Garnier's Cite Industrielle was never constructed, but its influence was broad. Corbusier met Garnier and was clearly influenced by his work, as were most of the protagonists of the early modern movement. In fact Garnier's plan, with its human scale, site-specific qualities, and attention to orientation, is of greater interest now than much of the modern proposals for high-rise cities. Its sense of regional autonomy, and use of local power, solar access, landscape order, and rational transportation mix are significant today.

All the environmental issues that plague the 1970s and 80s had obviously not arisen in the same form at the turn of the century. These plans address a different dimension of the impact of industrialization. Both Howard's and Garnier's plans address the social implications of industrialization—the effects on the working class, their physical health and their equity in the economy at large. From a purely environmental standpoint, they address health more than resources. Solar access and the orientation of buildings has more

A comparison of the "Cite Industrielle" civic center and Welwyn's civic center shows the moderist's tendency to emphasize the building function rather than the urban form.

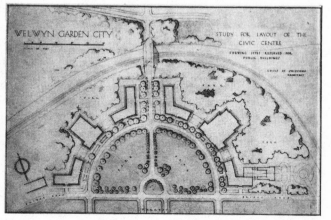

to do with the healing effects of the sun than its heating effects. The use of landscaping is an aesthetic born of a desire to escape the industrial city, rather than the more current proposals for an edible landscape to augment food production or complete biological cycles for waste treament.

Agriculture is reintegrated in their plans more as a way of completing the cultural mix of the town than as an attempt to renovate farming practices. At the turn of the century, the corporate farm, petrochemical fertilizers, unecological water use, and energy consumption in farming were not problems. The depopulation of agricultural areas was a problem, both because of the loss of food production and because of the congestion it created in the cities. It was as an attempt to balance rural and urban life that the garden cities movement and Garnier's industrial city proposed a reintegration.

Even with these differences in mind, it is clear that the proposals put forth are extremely relevant to our current condition. They propose a mix of activities which would reduce our dependence on the automobile and, thereby, its negative environmental effects. Their plans are pre-automobile and built primarily around railroad and light rail systems for inter-city transit. This reinforces a compactness that had been the tradition in Europe. Both plans' sensitivity to their site in terms of orientation, overall topography, and climate are obvious cornerstones for work that would be relevant today.

And finally, their emphasis on civic amenities as necessary for social health is a cause that needs to be redeveloped in our time. Their socialist leanings, such as distributing the equity of land and labor, is also of some relevance today. We live in much more conservative times. Capital and resources are more entrenched now than they were at the turn of the century. But the question of major investments such as public utilities, transportation systems, and overall land use, still lies within the public domain. The rationality of our decisions in these areas and their ultimate equity and life- cycle economic effectiveness should be the responsibility of all citizens. The environmental movement cannot truly succeed by merely attempting to limit and repair the effects of profit-oriented industries. The regionalist and decentralist philosophy present in these plans is perhaps still relevant to our current political struggles.

## Le Corbusier and the High-rise City

It is obvious that the traditional urban forms, either classic or romantic, were unadaptable to the needs and growth generated by the Industrial Revolution. The efforts to create workable urban forms demonstrated by the Garden City and Cite Industrielle were expanded and radicalized by the modern movement. These expansions took two directions. On the one hand, Le Corbusier (1887-1965) in Europe moved further along the City Industrielle's rational layout and autonomous building configuration by utilizing the high-rise building as a way of creating density. At the other extreme, Frank Lloyd Wright, in his Broadacre City, used the modern development of the automobile as a way of spreading the city over vast land areas at extremely low densities. Both of these extremes were built on the modern concept of form in architecture and planning; the building is an autonomous object maintaining responsibility only to internal functions, rather than the old urban tradition in which the building defined the public space that it fronted. They were both built upon innovations brought about by industrialization—the technologies of the airplane and the automobile, the structural implications of the steel frame, and ultimately, the environmental opportunities of mechanical and energy systems which could defy the local climate.

Corbusier produced a plan in 1924 for a show in Paris of a new city of three million inhabitants. Later, he published **The City of Tomorrow** as an elaboration and explanation of this earlier work. He named his proposal Ville Radieuse, the radiant city. His plan is built on two philosophical foundations. The first is the absolute supremecy of Cartesian order in which geometry is the ultimate expression of the evolution of man's mind and the pure result of the scientific revolution and industrialization: "Geometry is the means created by ourselves, whereby we perceive the external world and express the world within us." Corbusier's almost religious adherance to the notion of the rectilinear is consonant with his belief that it expresses the inner nature of industrialization, i.e., standardization, repetition, and linearity. "Machinery is the result of geometry. The age in which we live is therefore essentially a geometric one." These principles of geometry, derived from the primary notion of the horizontal and the vertical, are applied to city planning as an expression of rationality above and beyond any environmental or regional influence. This is certainly a powerful extension of Garnier's grid city. The plan for Washington, D.C. is a clear precursor to Corbusier's city plan. However, these earlier plans in some way accomodated natural forces, events, or historical landmarks. In Corbusier's mind, however, the abstract order was to be absolute.

The second foundation of his philosophy of planning rested in his interpretation of mechanization. Mechanization was to be the criteria of the city as well as its savior. The necessary means for efficient production in an industrial economy was the primary criteria of his proposal. Speed of transportation, the efficiency of building location, and the straightforwardness of mechanical utilities are all discussed at greater length in Corbusier's works than the complex-

206

ities of human life and social interaction. Similarly, the solution to the demands of industrial production lay in their own products. The automobile and the airplane were modern technologies employed to reinforce modern production. The standardization of buildings is an expression of mass production. The use of high-rise buildings, perhaps the most striking and radical aspect of his plan, is made possible only by advanced technologies. In a sense, Corbusier felt the vindication of the city lay in supporting—in fact, amplifying—industrialization, rather than attempting to modify, compromise, or redirect its course.

The goals for Corbusier's new city were clearly stated:

1. We must decongest the center of our cities.
2. We must augment their density.
3. We must increase the means for getting about.
4. We must increase parks and open spaces.

Three of these goals were obviously shared by the garden cities movement and, in a less explicit manner, Garnier's plans. The desire for greater density, however, runs counter to most of the garden cities movement which only saw the solution to congestion in lower densities. Corbusier's manipulation of the high-rise seems to represent a technical sleight-of-hand, decongesting the city, while at the same time increasing its density by moving vertically. The effects of this shift are profound and have indelibly affected the course of twentieth-century architecture.

In producing his idealized city, Corbusier, like Garnier, chose a hypothetical site. However, his selection is very telling. The site is consciously neutral, absolutely flat, with no specific climate or region. He even indicates that any major environmental event, such as a river, should be kept well without the limits of the city.

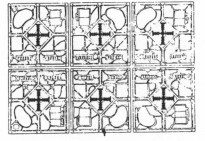

Corbusier's plan and perspective of highrise urban development radicalizes Garnier's rational plan. The buildings are now completely free of street configurations, floating in a park-like setting.

The social makeup of the city, however, is fairly explicit. He categorizes the city's population into three groups. Citizens who live and work in the center of the city, the high-rise section, are the people he is later to term "the captains of industry"—those in a natural hierarchy who control and manage production from the top. The second zone and type of population are suburban dwellers. They occupy an outer industrial zone and do not come into the city, but live in areas much like the garden cities of Howard. The third is a "mixed sort" who live in the peripheral garden cities but commute into work. This basic stratification, from higher density to lower, is not unlike Howard's earlier concentric plans. The difference is that residing at the center is an elite class of modern technocrats and bureaucratic institutions, rather than, as in Howard's plan, a civic center available to all.

His primary mechanism of ordering the city is through the configuration of streets. This is developed along extremely rational lines out of a concern for efficiency. He first dismisses the romantic, age-old quality of the gothic street, calling them donkey ways. He highlights their inefficiency for moving at the speed and quantities the industrial culture needs. "The corridor street should be tolerated no longer, for it poisons the houses that border it and leads to the construction of small internal courts or wells." His is a vision, like Garnier's, in which the buildings no longer follow the public domain but are set apart as independent objects. The scale at which this takes place in Corbusier's plan is greatly exaggerated. For him, the straight line and the Cartesian grid are the only framework for a city: "But the modern city lives by the straight line. The circulation of traffic demands the straight line. It is the proper thing."

He classifies traffic into three categories: heavy goods, lighter goods, and fast traffic. He then develops three types of road systems which are superimposed stories, once again exploiting the notion of verticality. Below ground is the street for heavy traffic, for commerce loading and unloading. At the ground level would be ordinary streets taking traffic in every desired direction. And finally, at an upper level would be a great cross access running through the city for fast one-way traffic, the equivalent of our freeways. There would also be a subterranian rail system connecting the garden cities to one central station. The scale of the city block is determined by the speed of traffic. A module of 400 yards—four football fields—between intersections is used as a way of reducing congestion by reducing the number of intersections in the overall city. Deriving the scale of the block from the nature of traffic, he sets a scale for the buildings, architecture, and dwellings well beyond the norm for pedestrians. In fact, there is little in the plan that implies that there could be any pedestrian motion, and almost no discussion thereof.

(Opposite) Corbusier's masterplan for a city of 3 million, is zoned from high density 60 story towers at the center to lower "ribbon" housing blocks at the periphery with "garden cities" and industrial centers removed from the city proper.

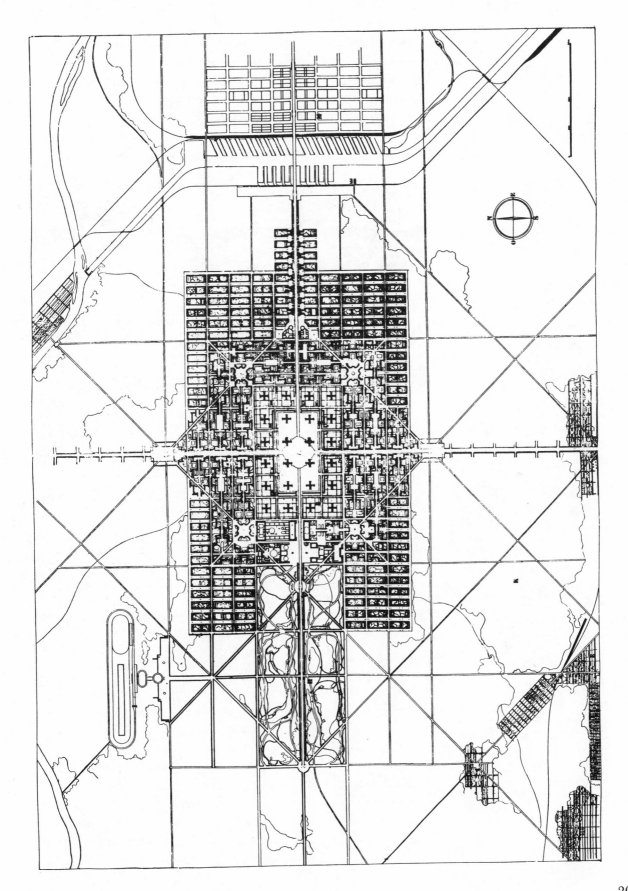

209

Within the grid are to be placed twenty-four skyscrapers of approximately sixty stories. These skyscrapers produce a density of approximately 1,200 inhabitants to the acre. As a comparison, the average density of Paris is 146 inhabitants per acre and of London is sixty-three. The overcrowded quarters of Paris reach 213 and of London, 169. These high-rise towers are then surrounded by zones of luxury dwellings on residential blocks with set-backs. These are

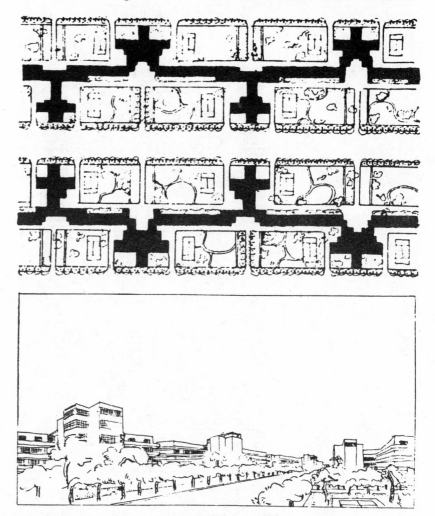

Corbusier's proposal for lower density housing is built on long East-West blocks, 6 stories high, with open park areas between the housing and streets.

built at approximately 120 inhabitants to the acre and are six stories of stacked two-level dwellings. A third type of housing, residential blocks in a cellular system, is also proposed further from the center for a different income group at about the same density.

The abstract and regular quality of these three types of dwellings defy any sense of orientation or topographic inconsistencies. They are meant to be representative of the products of industry; a standardized, efficient, and functional place to live, but incapable of modifications for climate, local interest, or personal identity. Corbusier describes the effect he is designing very clearly: ''The result of a true geometrical layout is repetition. The result of repetition is a standard. The perfect form.''

Surrounding these buildings of standard form are large blocks of open space. In the central high-rise area, 95 percent of the ground is open for parks, restaurants, and theaters. These open spaces are not intended as productive areas for small allotment gardens or local farms. They are purely a neutral visual space meant to provide light and air to the buildings placed in their center. The concept of massive open space was one of the most attractive elements of Corbusier's plan, and ultimately, one of its greatest failings. Open space at this scale rarely supports any kind of truly active or functional uses. Conversations, play, gardening, games, promenades, and courting are activities which need the juxtiposition of human activities and shelters in close proximity to the open space. In a sense, Corbusier's open space is as neutral and standardized as the buildings, lacking a clear sense of purpose and diversity. They are meant to be inhabited in an abstract rather than social way.

When compared to the turn-of-the-century utopias, Corbusier's plan bespeaks a significant shift of ideology. Rather than championing an improved life for the workers, the plan effectively champions a more efficient environment for industry. There is no mention of a greater equity or economic share for working people. In fact, their segregation is heightened and clear statements are made as to the position of an elite ruling class. Health and sanitation is a justification used by Corbusier, but no mention is made of other environmental concerns. Rather than the decentralist philosophies that drove Garnier, Corbusier's plan heightens centralization by the shear magnitude of the proposal and the scale of the institutions that would occupy it. There is, as was stated, no response to the local region in terms of customs or history. There is also no mention of agriculture.

Around the central city, separating it from the industrial quarter and the garden cities, was to be a protective zone, an area not unlike Howard's greenbelts. This was an area in which all buildings were to be prohibited and would consist of woods, fields, and sports grounds. The industrial area is ambiguously defined in much the same terms as the central city. Corbusier's version of the garden cities, acting as lower density satellite suburbs, would be built along the same geometric principles as the center. Although Corbusier's stated intention is to place machinery at the service of man, the plan clearly indicates the opposite. In this case, the city comes to serve the machine before its population.

Lewis Mumford was later to summarize Corbusier's work as the anti-city:

"The first mistake was the overvaluation of mechanization and standardization as ends in themselves without respect to human purpose. The second was the theoretical destruction of every vestige of the past, without preserving any links in form or visible structure between past and future, thereby overmagnifying the importance of the present and at the same time threatening with destruction whatever permanent values the present which might in turn create and nullifying any lessons might be learned from its errors. This is the error of the disposable urban container. Finally, Corbusier's concept carried to its extreme the necessary reaction against urban overcrowding: the mistake of separating and extravagantly over-spacing facilities whose topographic concentration is essential for their daily use."

Corbusier's plan in many ways represents the source of the environmental crises we face today. The creation of a freeway network that has now grown into a transportation nightmare, squandering land and energy and producing air pollution and congestion. Buildings which do not respond to their climate or place create energy demands that we now must struggle with. The absence of a concern for the integrity of the natural environment generates a tradition that is yet to be overcome. Finally, the anonymous quality of the city and its lack of social coherance underlies many of our current urban dilemmas.

It is only in the later half of the twentieth century that the failures of progressive social systems became manifest and the limitations of the seemingly benevolent technologies, such as the automobile, began to produce their negative side effects. The belief that all problems could be solved through rational deduction and all social needs satisfied through relatively scientific processes has also eroded. Certainly we now have a more complex understanding of the unquantifiable interdependancies that make up the diversity and integrity of human settlements.

## C.I.A.M. and the Modern Movement

Corbusier's early utopian schemes opened the door to many new urban design and town planning possibilities. Less extreme plans followed as the modern movement developed functional analysis for cities and buildings. Where the garden city had been in some sense a return to a pre-industrial framework, the modern movement took up Corbusier's vision as a courageous step into the future, employing the products of the industrial culture to effectively solve its problems.

In 1928, the Congress Internationale de Architecture Moderne

(C.I.A.M.) was formed. It was a group of progressive architects and planners from throughout Europe who joined together to analyze and redirect development in Europe. Their congresses were convened with detailed analyses and proposals for many urban centers throughout Europe. Their most famous product, the Charter of Athens, was developed in 1933 while the congress was convened on the steamship Praxis II en route from Marsille to Athens. This manifesto standardized much of what Corbusier had articulated in his earlier plans, but made it flexible, adaptible, and more acceptable. Gone were the fixation with geometry and the overriding concern with a complete master plan. In its place were a whole series of design principles applicable to various European circumstances. C.I.A.M. continued through 1937, at which point the war interrupted the progress of this renowned group. Their work, however, was taken up after World War II and was used extensively in the reconstruction of Europe and as a philosphical basis for much of the urban renewal that later took place in the United States.

Their basic criticism of urban growth was that it was antifunctional: "The city of today is largely the product of modern machine development. As applied to the city, however, the machine technique has been employed only as a means of exploiting the old city framework. Therefore, it carries within itself the elements capable of destroying the concentrated metropolis it has helped to create."

The C.I.A.M. analysis of the city was broken into four primary categories of function: Dwelling, work or production, recreation, and transportation. Most European cities were analyzed in their existing forms using scale drawings and standardized symbols. In the functional area of dwelling, their primary criticism (along with all the other new town planners) was of overcrowding and congestion. Their focus on slum clearance was the precurser to many of urban renewal programs that swept U.S. cities in the 1960s. C.I.A.M. documented the quantities of sub-standard housing in many of the cities across Europe and the United States. In the mid 30s, of the 7.5 million people in New York, 1.8 million—or nearly one in four—were living in what they called antiquated tenements or substandard housing. C.I.A.M. assumed that the slum could not be remodeled. In their eyes, renovation and rehabilitation was impossible in a building configuration that was basically unsound and unsanitary. "The only remedy for this condition is the demolition of the infected houses and the reconstruction upon the reclaimed land of sanitary dwellings surrounded by open areas so that air and sunshine can penetrate into their rooms without hinderance." Certainly, the correlation between disease and urban area was very strong. In Detroit, the city average for cases of pneumonia was seventy-four persons per 1000 population. In the slum areas the number reached 217. For tuberculosis, the city average was seventy-five, whereas the slum average was 488.

C.I.A.M.'s proposal for reconstruction of slum areas was built upon modern traditions of architecture. The dwelling was to be independent of the street. Orientation and spacing of the buildings were to be calculated in terms of solar access, and open space was to blanket the surroundings of every dwelling. Their criticism of dwellings which border street lines had to do with noise as well as exposure to sunlight. "As a general rule if one side of the street receives the necessary sunlight in the most desirable hours, the sunlight condition on the opposite sides are different and often bad." They demanded a minimum amount of exposure to the sun for all residential structures regardless of their location or class. This, once again, was a call for a solar access regulation. Unfortunately, their interpretation of solar access often resulted in the layout of apartment blocks with a long access north to south, in order to eliminate the troublesome north-side dwelling unit. These orientations provide some sunlight for each part of the building, either morning or afternoon. The fact that the sun was inneffective for heating and perhaps would produce a cooling problem was not a primary concern.

They claimed that low density development, as proposed in the garden cities, would be uneconomical, antithetical to civic life, would devalue land, increase traveling distances, and make community services uneconomical. Their solution lay with Corbusier's vision of tall housing towers surrounded by a park. "They [uniformed planners and architects] do not realize that modern housing plans properly conceived on a large scale could provide for high densities without overcrowding." C.I.A.M. also disregarded medium density mid-rise as a compromise not particularly economical in terms of land development nor as effective in terms of open space. The key to their plan for housing, as to Corbusier's, was the park land between the high-rise housing. Walter Gropius, a member of C.I.A.M. and one of the founders of the Bauhaus school in Germany, did a series of fairly sophisticated studies relating the height of buildings to their spacing with regard to solar access and views. His studies found that useful living space would be considerably greater using high blocks rather than lowrise, as the amount of land given over to building footprint is reduced in the higher form.

Walter Gropius' sun angle studies further justified increased densities by showing more open space for increased building heights and spacing.

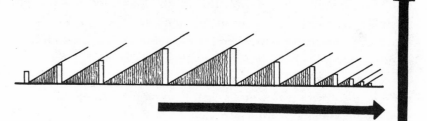

214

Another key concept developed by C.I.A.M. was the neighborhood unit. Large housing complexes were to be broken into super blocks within which a whole range of neighborhood services could be provided. The neighborhoods were meant to have day nurseries, kindergardens, public libraries, indoor and outdoor recreation space, as well as some private enterprises such as cinemas, local stores, garages, and a small dispensary for emergency health uses—all within walking distance. The primary traffic routes were to bypass the neighborhood, penetrating only at the periphery.

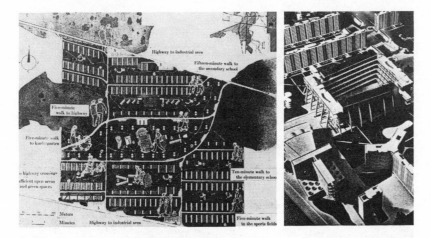

Designs of "neighborhood" scale development became a primary planning tool of post World War II projects. High rise or mid rise apartments were floated in green space with civic services and retail scattered about.

These neighborhood units became a primary planning tool of the post-World War II era in both Europe and the United States. They differ significantly from the earlier utopian schemes in that they segregate the primary commercial and industrial areas away from the dwelling zones. Furthermore, there is no mention of the reintegration of agriculture at this particular scale.

C.I.A.M.'s proposals for recreation are thoroughly humane in their intentions and very generous in size. But, the scale of such spaces ultimately was to defeat them by overlooking the more complex qualities of human sociology: the need for territoriality in open space, the need for activity generators along the edges of open spaces, and the need for adequate surveillance to maintain safety. All are lost in these mega-parks. Many such schemes have been built since World War II, and almost every case became a wasteland, a no-mans land, often dangerous and unmaintained. Although the quantity of buildings and the scale of the open space quantity and function seem deceptively successful, the qualities of these spaces and buildings have proven unsuccessful. What is overlooked in such a functional analysis of urban planning is human scale, the texture and complexity of daily activities, the diversity of interactions, and the synergy of various activities.

Similarly, their proposals for work areas are flawed. The availability of raw materials, suitable labor, transportation facilities, and accessibility to markets are the primary criteria for siting large industrial areas. In their view, climatic conditions were no longer of primary interest as artificial climates could be produced anywhere. Air conditioning could solve these problems. Furthermore, in their view the modern highway and trucking services free industrial zones and work places from any need to be connected directly on a regional or town scale. "If a constant flow of traffic can be maintained between the main focal points of the city and the industrial areas the distance between them need not be extremely short."

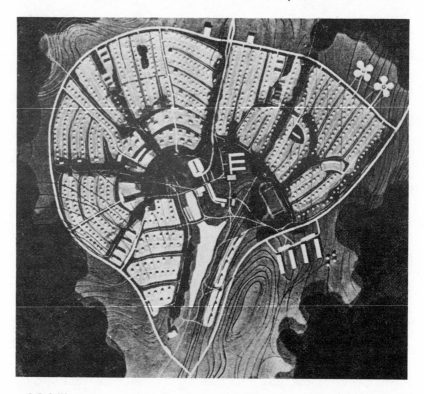

Highway new towns were little more than bedroom communities. Auto's allowed the complete segregation of work and house, as land use zoning became the norm.

Mobility was seen to be the great liberator in this domain — mobility of power, labor, and goods. Electricity could supply power to any location. The automobile meant that labor could be moved easily. And commercial vehicles made possible the world-wide transportation of goods. In order to reduce commuting time but not necessarily deny mobility of workers and goods, zoning of cities for specific areas of use was proposed. "Industrial areas and those planned for other functions should be separated by open spaces." Such industrial zoning has become the standard planning tool ever since. Once again the scale of the unit, in this case the industrial zone, seems to be the primary flaw. Similarly, the segregation of commerce and white collar workers into skyscrapers is a solution of superficial success. Certainly these early modern visionaries were correct: In order for these large scale entities (office high-rises, large industrial zones, super-block dwelling units) to function properly, large spaces between them have to be allocated and gridded off with high-speed transportation. Its final execution tends towards the arterial street system we have today. In their minds, the freeway and cloverleaf interchange were a positive and necessary evolution of the transportation system.

## Frank Lloyd Wright and the American Utopia

Frank Lloyd Wright's Broadacre City forms a very interesting contrast to both Howard's and Corbusier's vision. Foremost, his plan demonstrates the culture- bound character of personal vision. Howard's vision is certainly born from an idealization of the English village and the integrity that it represented. Corbusier's vision of the grand city was certainly built from the strength power and future promise of Paris. Wright's vision is built out of a truly American tradition, that of the homestead, the autonomous and free individual. It is a rural and pioneering philosophy largely expressed by the likes of Jefferson and Emerson. In his proposal, the city as a centralizing force disappears completely. His is a more radical decentralization than Howard's, actually eliminating the center. For Howard, the

Wrights' vision of a horizontal city in which work, agriculture, and home were integrated was built on a grid freeway system with personal helicopters.

217

focus and building block of the community was the neighborhood; for Corbusier, it was the high-rise; and for Wright, the individual home and the family that it represented. In his plan, all aggregations of power and wealth are eliminated; the individual, their labor, and their private land become the foundations of the culture. Cooperation is a secondary attribute, and economic and political centralization a transgression.

Wright claimed Broadacre City was built on three primarily modern changes. First was electrification, which meant not only the decentralization of power, but the expansion of long range communications allowing the disengagement and the disassociation of daily activities. His second major change was mechanized mobilization. He lived in a time in which the automobile represented a radical and positive innovation. Once again, this high-speed private transportation further amplifies the opportunities for decentralization. In Howard's plan, the pedestrian is still the measure of the community, and clustering is necessitated by the distances that could be easily walked and by the nature of railroads which demand one station for each community. Wright embraces the automobile as a symbol of progress in the same way Corbusier embraces the highrise. They both envision helicopter taxis and freeway systems gridding their cities with totally new dimensions. Wright explained, "It is significant that not only have space values entirely changed to time values, now ready to form new standards of movement-measurement but a new sense of spacing based upon speed is here." This sense of space is present in both Corbusier's and Wright's plan. The difference, however, is extreme. Wright is proposing an extremely low density development in which each individual is connected directly to the land. Corbusier is proposing high density development within this new order of space, built upon high-rise construction and a marked lack of individual expression.

Wright's third modern change was *organic architecture*. This was his definition of a correct and honest architecture—not an architecture of vernacular forms or handcrafted artisans, but an architecture rational in its conception, mass produced and efficient, simultaneously varied and site-specific. His vision of architecture represents another departure in our concept of form. In his expression, the building, still free of public space, becomes part of the landscape rather than an object within it. This is quite different from the picturesque aesthetic in which the architecture remains distinct and vernacular. His notion of organic architecture certainly contained much of the climate-responsive and passive solar design currently popular. Many of his Usonian houses were direct gain type passive solar, using the optimum orientations, plenty of glass area, and thermal mass in the form of masonry and slabs. His commercial buildings, the Johnson's Wax building comes to mind, are essays in natural lighting. Wright never fell prey to the "building as machine" ethos, in which mechanical systems camouflaged a range of design errors. He was inventive with heating systems, developing some of the earlier radiant floor slabs. For Wright, organic architecture was an integration of climate, land, structure, machines, and foremost, man's spirit.

Wright first proposed Broadacre City in a series of lectures at Princeton University in 1930. In 1932 he published **The Disappearing City**, a description of his plans. And, in 1935, he had a large showing of a model at Rockefeller Center in New York. The Depression in a sense fueled Wright's utopian efforts by demonstrating the fallibility of the then current urban systems and by validating radical proposals. And Wright's proposal was truly radical. His is more than a plan for a city of the future built around the automobile. It is an expression of a deep philosophical commitment to a self- reliant individual, to a kind of democracy and individuality that he felt had

Broadacre city, first revealed in 1930, represented a new interpretation of modern architecture. Rather than buildings isolated from public space and distinct from the landscape, they became integrated with the land, part of an agricultural form rather than a picturesque landscape.

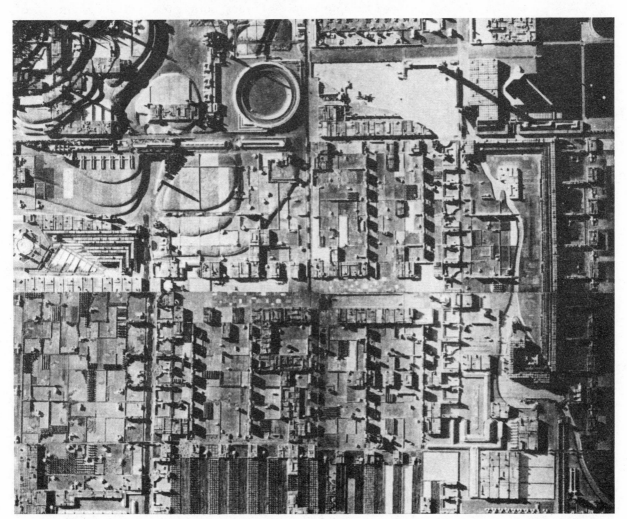

219

been lost. For Wright, Broadacre was a stand against centralization, against oppression and all its forms — whether in goverment, industry, or banking. The politics and economics of his proposal were derived largely from Henry George's work in the late nineteenth century. His book, **Progess and Poverty**, which also influenced Howard, maintained that land ownership was the key reform necessary to create a more equitable and just society. Once land had been redistributed and everybody had a sufficient quantity (and nobody was allowed more property than they could actually use), a laissez-faire, free-market economy would necessarily produce a benign society. The conflict between labor and capital could be eliminated if its root inequities of land ownership were eliminated. For Howard, this transfer of land ownership was to go from large private interests to a cooperative. The community was to receive the final ownership. For Wright, the individual became the recipient, and the homestead was to be reborn.

Wright expressed his disdain for the economics of centralization by declaiming all forms of rent, both in terms of land, money (i.e., interest payments), and ideas (i.e., royality payments for inventions). Wright felt the elimination of landlords of all types would vindicate the best of our individuality. The economic structure that had "…made of the man a piece of cheap speculative property…" would be eliminated. In his proposal for Broadacre City, each household would have at least one acre of property. Others would have more. There would be no specialization of labor in Broadacre City. Each person would be part farmer, part businessman, part artist, and part factory worker. Nobody would live off the manipulation of other peoples' labor or the value of goods. There would be factories and offices in Broadacre City which could be either cooperatively or privately owned. However, the most significant traits of the businesses would be that they were small and decentralized — effectively subserviant to the primary economic unit, the household. "The true center in Usonian democracy is the individual in his true Usonian home."

The form of Broadacre City has no center; it is designed without hierarchy, without zoning, without specialization. It is a formal presentation of integration at every level. Households become part farms, part workshops. The roadside market or main retail area is a mix of restaurants, private booths, craft shops, gas stations, and recreation area.

The civic center, "an attractive and mobile objective — perhaps situated just off some major highway — noble and inspiring" is an integration of golf courses, racetracks, zoo, aquarium, botanical gardens, art museums, libraries, galleries, etc. Lacking urban mix and density, Wright reduces the scale of each activity so it can be spread throughout the city. Large schools, which he calls "knowledge factories" which turn "perfectly good plums into perfectly good prunes," must be divided into small units, ideally twenty-five students per school. Similarly, design centers dedicated to his organic sense of experimental industrial design and craft, would dot the landscape. Although there are distinct areas in Broadacre City given over to certain types of uses, these do not constitute any typical zoning because the uses are always combined.

As with Garnier and Corbusier, the street grid, however large, is still the primary ordering device for Broadacre City. Not so much an abstract principle, the grid for Wright is a framework to interact with the land. Around his prairie home near Chicago, the farmland maintained the linear quality of the original section survey, the genesis in America of both the rural and urban form. Like Corbusier, Wright postulated a freeway system complete with specific designs for overpasses and a new type of motor car. Freeways 'bright with wayside flowers or cool shade trees, joined at intervals with modern air-rotor fields (helicopters) from which site noiseless transport planes, like modern taxicabs, take off. Giant roads now themselves great architecture' Also like Corbusier, Wright segregates the heavy traffic—trucking and cross country transit—onto the converted railroad right-of-ways. Nowhere, except at the buildings, is the grid broken down to a pedestrian scale. All transit is high-speed, and all destinations are distant.

Wright's custom designed autos and silent flying taxis connect a decentralized matrix of destinations. A city with no center, each building in Broadacre has mixed use functions at a residential scale.

Wright creates order in this diffuse landscape by continuing the street grid at a finer scale into his buildings and landscaping. This ordering of plants as well as buildings is antithetical to the more naturalistic landscape that Garnier used within his grid. In this, Wright is amplifying the formal implications of agriculture as a means of unifying architecture and landscape. This unity is neither superficial nor merely visual. A majority of Broadacre's open space is intended to be productive farms. Unlike the Ville Radieuse park areas with their curving paths and random plantings as a counterpoint to the towers, Wright's open space is all either private homesteads, larger farmland, or public recreation centers. Unwin's plans reduced agriculture to a green belt whose form was independent of the city, and landscaping within imitated natural rather than cultivated forms.

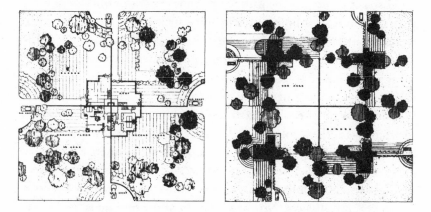

The heart of Broadacre city is the usonian home. Each home was to have at least one acre of land for agriculture, with workshop and office space integrated with the living areas. The financial autonomy of the household unit is Wright's foundation for a just and healthy society.

A back-to-the-land ethic is the backbone of Broadacre City and the functioning farm was to be a part of every persons's life. During the Great Depression, this vision was not too far-fetched. Many people grew to distrust the industrial future and sought to re-establish their rural past. Many saw homesteading as a national solution to widespread unemployment. Roosevelt institutionalized these sentiments in 1935 by creating the Resettlement Administration to aid the back-to-the-land movement. Wright's city is born of this ethos— that national and individual salvation lay in reconnecting people to the soil. Although his grid is as scale-less as Corbusier's, his open spaces would not fall prey to the same kind of abandonment. They were the economic and cultural center of his decentralized city.

Broadacre City may appear to be a model for suburban sprawl— and the Usonian house the antecedent of the ranch house—because its image of decentralization validated much that was to come in the post-war growth. But, the seeds of suburbia were cast long before with the railroad suburbs of the 1890s and much of the housing in the 1920s. Wright's vision is more radical and has never been realized. But it is flawed in much the same way as Ville Radieuse—the distance between areas destroys the opportunity for chance meetings, casual on-the-way stops, for local characters to emerge, and for child care to become a non-institutional concern. The distances isolate the family, and all the electronic communication or helicopters cannot reconnect it. Broadacre City is an ecological vision without community.

## The Practice of Built New Towns

In contrast to the relatively extreme and unbuilt diagrams of Broadacre City and Ville Radieuse, many new towns of various size and purpose have been constructed in the twentieth century. After World War II, some were to follow the model of Ebenezer Howard's garden cities, others more modernist principles. But in total, these settlements are much more persuasive than is popularly known. A partial listing in **New Towns, Their Origins, Achievements and Progress**, by Osborne and Whittick, identifies approximately 750 new towns in seventy-four countries. As of 1976, England had close to one million people living in new towns with 915,000 jobs. It is estimated that the U.S.S.R. has between 1,000 and 2,000 new towns, of which 400 are apart from the metropolitan areas.

Acting as a bridge between the garden city movement of the turn of the century and the post-World War II new towns of Europe, a small group of planners, architects and historians formed the Regional Planning Association of America in 1923. The most notable of their group were Lewis Mumford, Clarence Stein, and Henry Wright. Their advocacy of humane housing patterns akin to Howard's garden cities produced in the 20s and 30s some of America's most progressive planned communities.

Although Stein and Wright, as architects and planners, never completed a new town such as Letchworth, their Radburn, Sunnyside Gardens, and Chatham Village were fragments which clearly set new directions for America and Europe. Radburn, the best known product of the Stein-Wright partnership, was intended to be a full garden city in the Howard tradition. But several key aspects were missing. The green belt was never purchased because of cost and location. The designated industrial areas were never developed, partially because of the Depression (Radburn's first homes were completed in 1929), and partially because the sites were unattractive to business due to poor transportation. Radburn was to be an innovative bedroom community rather than a new town.

Most of the ideas developed at Radburn can be found in Welwyn Garden City: the use of the cul-de-sacs, curving streets to match the topography, the variety of housing types, and neighborhoods serviced by small retail areas. The innovation at Radburn was in large part a reaction to the automobile. As Stein was to say, "The Radburn idea was to answer the enigma, how to live with the auto or, if you will, how to live in spite of it." The design principles he lists as formative are all coping with the new phenomena of the

Radburns' plan, by Stein and Wright in the late 20's, popularized the then common "cul-de-sac" with a network of green ways which connected the housing to recreation centers and schools. Designed as a suburb, the plan lacked industrial or commercial elements.

automobile: the use of superblocks with interior greens and cul-de-sacs; specialized roads for different uses; complete separation of pedestrian and auto traffic, with interior paths and overpasses at streets; house plans turned toward the internal open areas rather than the street. This segregation of auto and the pedestrian, along with the common open spaces linked to schools, recreation and retail, is the heart of the Radburn plan. Additionally, the concept of neighborhoods popularized by Clarence Perry, was fully developed here. The complete plan for 25,000 people involved three neighborhoods of approximately 7,000 to 10,000 people. Neighborhood size was determined by school population. Each of these neighborhoods was to have its own shopping area, school, and park recreation area.

Ultimately, only one neighborhood was to be completed. The entire town plan, however, had called for a central high school, community center, and playing fields located at the intersection of the proposed three neighborhoods. A large commerical center was to be located at the edge, near a proposed interstate highway to serve a regional market. The neighborhoods were to be built at a one-half-mile radius and the complete town at a one-mile radius. This larger vision was to be destroyed by the Depression, but the completed section proved a great success nonetheless.

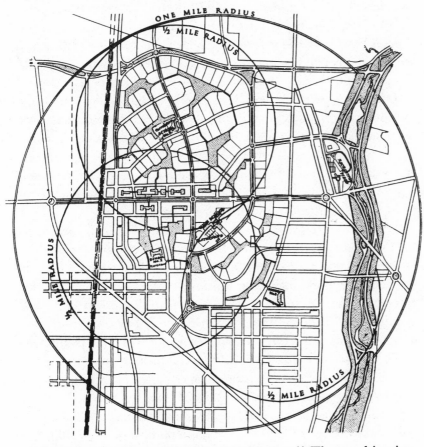

Radburn's unrealized masterplan involved three neighborhoods each with schools and minor rental areas. An unrealized larger commercial center and high school was to be common to all.

"Radburn is above all a town for children." The combination of pedestrian paths, parks, schools, and recreation facilities created a wonderful environment for kids. The safety of the area has been well documented with only two road deaths in its first twenty years. Although the plan called for higher density apartments near the service centers, the house plans were dominantly family-oriented. The community therefore became largely populated by young families who were white-collar commuters. These similarities, along with the pronounced common space, created a strong community identity which persists today.

From an ecological perspective, Radburn's contribution lies in re-establishing the pedestrian environment and reducing auto dependence. But lacking in the primary destinations of work places and large retail districts, the area is a suburb with a large commuting

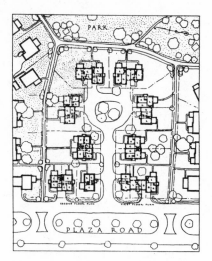

The housing at Radburn was designed primarily for families. The front door faced the greenway and path system with the auto accessing the "rear".

The diagram for Stockholm's satelite new towns showed gradations in housing density from a central shopping area with a subway stop to greenbelt. Schools and gardening areas are at the periphery. The highway and industrial areas are shared between several new town centers.

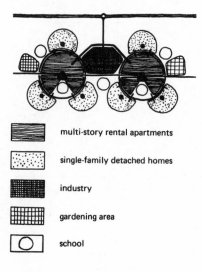

multi-story rental apartments

single-family detached homes

industry

gardening area

school

population. Its low-density housing with generous green spaces affords the opportunity for climate-responsive design, but the building orientation is random and doesn't use solar energy to any advantage. It succeeds in developing a great sense of community, but makes no effort to redistribute equity in land ownership or cooperatives. There is no effort to integrate food production, biological recycling, or energy production. Born of a different time, its objectives—a safe, healthy place for young families— set the direction for the next thirty years of planning for the suburban environment.

After World War II, demands for housing in Europe and America were phenomenal. Several European countries—notably England, Sweden, and Finland—instituted massive new town developments. In England, over thirty new towns have been built to date, housing over one million people. In the United States, major population shifts were underway. Before 1940, only 17 percent of the population lived in suburban areas; by 1975, 30 percent were suburban. In America, suburban development became a kind of private-sector new town program, lacking the balance and planning of the European efforts, but still providing for the same needs.

Although there are many examples to choose from, three new towns can serve to demonstrate the range of these post-World War II experiments. In Sweden, a series of satellite towns has been developed around Stockholm, linked by its rail system. Vallingby is the preminent example of this master plan, housing over 55,000 people on 2,251 acres. In the United States, Levittown was constructed at the same time (around 1950) for a similar population of 67,000, but spread over 5,750 acres. Not really a new town, Levittown nonetheless represents a pre-planned community, missing only employment opportunities. Finally, Milton Keynes in England represents a larger effort, and is perhaps more autonomous than the other two. Started in 1967, it now has a population of 77,000, but when complete, it is projected to reach a population of more than 250,000 over its 22,000 acreas. Each of these examples shows different tendencies in housing, transportation, and ecology.

By far the most progressive of the three examples is Vallingby. Developed by the City of Stockholm on city-owned land, rather than by private interests, it came about as a conclusion to many earlier experiments. Having completed neighborhood-scale projects in the 40s involving civic center infills and self- help housing, the City of Stockholm planned a series of satellite towns in the early 50s which incorporated higher density housing, significant retail areas, balanced job opportunies, and mass transit. With a tradition of progressive planning influenced by the English garden cities and Lewis Mumford's watershed book **The Culture of Cities**, published in 1938, the city, under the direction of Sven Markelius, set its primary urban goals in its 1952 general plan for Stockholm. It called for suburban districts of ten to fifteen thousand population along the subway lines, each with a commercial and cultural center. To reduce auto demands, housing was to be within 550 yards of the subway stops. Open space and parks were to separate these areas, with access roads weaving through them. Several of these neighborhoods would be larger, with populations of 50,000 to 100,000, and would contain a full range of urban services. Vallingby became the first of these ''area centers.''

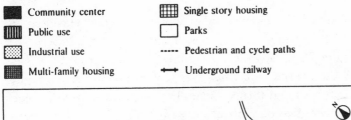

| | Community center | | Single story housing |
|---|---|---|---|
| | Public use | | Parks |
| | Industrial use | ----- | Pedestrian and cycle paths |
| | Multi-family housing | ←→ | Underground railway |

The specific plan for Vallingby shows a successful realization of the diagram with a thriving retail center, much used open space, and a high percentage of people living and working within the town.

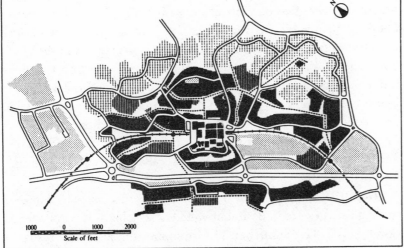

1000   0   1000   2000
Scale of feet

The design principles employed at Vallingby have been proposed many times before, but rarely have they been so successfully executed. The plan attempted to balance employment and housing in the ''walk-to-work program,'' much advocated in Sweden since the 20s. In 1965, Vallingby had 14,000 jobs, of which 44 percent were filled by local workers representing 24 percent of the town's inhabitants. Earlier in 1956, 70 percent of the jobs were occupied by local workers. This shift was generated by a housing priority system for local workers, which was abandoned by 1957. There were simply too many people jealous of this preferential treatment for it to be maintained any longer. Additionally, by the time the majority of industry moved in, the housing was completed and occupied. The city-wide housing shortage made housing turnover unlikely, and therefore, workers began commuting rather than trying to relocate. Nonetheless, the ratio and proximity of jobs when compared to other developments is extremely successful.

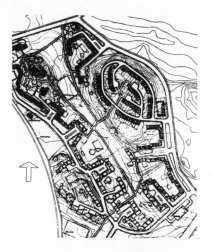

Vallingby's residential neighborhoods have much the same character as Radburn but use higher density housing types and more compact floor plans. The greenways and paths link each area to the retail center and subway system.

A second design principle involved preference for the pedestrian. This had several expressions: a highly developed path system complete with overpasses at every major auto street and intersection; clustering of the majority of housing near the subway station and retail area; constrained parking opportunities to discourage short trips. Once again, the planning efforts brought comparative success, with 36 percent of the total trips made on foot, 27 percent made by public transit, and 30 percent by car. This from a population with approximately the same auto ownership ratios as the United States!

Not unlike Radburn, the layout of Vallingby favors the pedestrian, is linked together more by a series of open spaces than by roads, and is grouped into neighborhood zones. It differs from both Radburn and the garden cities, however, by employing much higher housing densities and forms. Several towers and four-story block apartments ring the commercial center at Vallingby, and the lowest density housing form is rowhouses for families. In the modernist design tradition, the buildings are autonomous objects in the landscape and are sited more by land form than street form or solar orientation. The urban street grid is gone. The curving arterial and super block configuration provide the infrastructure. Additionally, the civic and commerical center is serviced by subterranian roads for deliveries, as well as by the surface roads, pedestrian overpasses, and subterranian trains. C.I.A.M. had called for a similar segregation of traffic.

Overall, Vallingby is an unquestionable success. The housing waiting list attests to its desirability, and as sociologist David Popenoe documents in **The Suburban Environment**, this attraction is shared by a broad spectrum of the Swedish population: ''It works well for the young family, especially if the family is not too large or desirous of personal private space. It works even better for older families because it is especially well-suited to the needs of teenagers and working women. For parents whose children have left home, it provides a maintenance-free dwelling, close to desired services and facilities, and often close to the children themselves. It seems to work just as well for singles and young couples with no children and for many pensioners.'' This social success is matched by the success of its retail, recreation, transportation and industrial efforts. Although the form and technology are completely different, it seems to fill many of Ebenezer Howard's fondest dreams. In fact, the land is publicly owned and, when combined with the welfare state programs of Sweden, we see a partial fufillment of Howard's economic goals.

From an energy viewpoint, Sweden in general is extremely progressive and Vallingby demonstrates why. On the whole, an average Swede consumes only 55 percent of the energy used by an average

American with a similar standard of living and industrial profile, and a more severe climate. Cogeneration is one of the principle reasons. At Vallingby, waste heat from a local power plant is delivered to the houses via a district heating system, doubling the efficiency of the electric power plant. Additionally, the buildings, though not solar, are extremely well-insulated. Finally, a reduced use of the auto and higher percentage of mass transit use, coupled with the more compact urban forms, significantly reduces energy use in the transportation sector.

Levittown stands in sharp contrast to Vallingby. Although built at the same time and about the same size (67,000 ultimate population), its context and principles are entirely different. Foremost, it was planned and built for profit by a private concern, rather than by a public body. Levittown inherited many of the planning ideas of Radburn, but lacked its garden city ideological roots. There was no thought of building jobs into the town, its location was selected near employment centers. The Fairless Works of United States Steel are nearby and Philadelphia represents a possible commute. Although

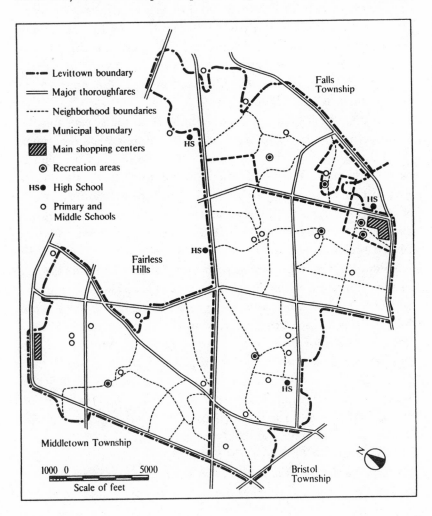

Levittown, the quintessential suburb, was designed around neighborhood units with schools as its primary focal points. Ultimately providing 17,000 single family homes, the plan made no attempt to separate car and pedestrian or create jobs on site.

this omission seems to make Levittown a simple suburb, its size makes it the tenth largest city in Pennsylvania. It was finally to have 17,300 single-family homes spread over 5,750 acres on 1,300 streets. One of the area's largest shopping malls, called "Shop-a-rama," was constructed with over sixty stores. Recreation areas and schools became the primary focal points of its plan.

Levittown employed the Radburn idea of superblocks, but eliminated the auto-pedestrian separation. The superblocks were broken into several neighborhoods of about 430 homes. The primary arterials were kept to the edge, with curving interior streets to break the visual scale of the plan. Most streets intersected in T-forms for safety. There is little diversity in housing type as reflected in the relatively homogenous population. Levittown works for one type of family: young married couples with small children. Once again, sociologist Popenoe summarizes, "In the early years of Levittown the teenager, the elderly person, the widowed and divorced female head of household, the working class woman living in tight financial straights and cut off from relatives, were unfamiliar figures. Today they have become common and the environment is not as congruent with them as with their predessors. For adults in anything but a fully-functioning, economically secure family system, Levittown may be an invitation to trouble; it provides great opportunity to the self sufficient family but little sustanence and support to the family which is not self sufficient."

The true orientation of the community is to the streets and the automobile. Those too young or too old to drive are at an extreme disadvantage. Given that the sight is flat, the form of the plan is largely arbitrary. In the tradition of the energy-rich 50s, the houses are poorly insulated and have no sense of solar orientation. Although progressive at the time and economically very successful, Levittown represents the planning source of many of our current environmental and social problems.

Milton Keynes in England accepts many of the trends represented by Levittown, but expands and rationalizes the results. Foremost, its plan accepts the dominance of the auto and the public's preference for lower-density housing. Designed in 1967 with an area of 22,000 acres, located forty-five miles from London, Milton Keynes represents a new generation of town planning at a new scale. Like Levittown, the city is built of a grid of arterial streets, specifically placed at five-eighth-mile intervals, and requiring approximately one hundred miles of new road construction. Within these super "superblocks" of between 250 and 300 acres are "environmental areas" of approximately 5,000 people. The housing densities are considerably lower than Vallingby, ranging from ten units per acre to six units per acre, of which about 50 percent are rental units and

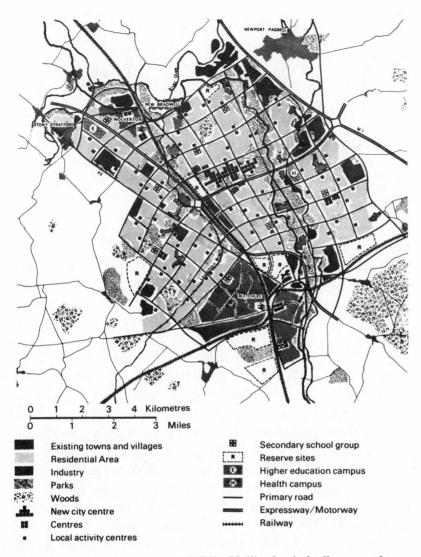

Milton Keynes is a new town designed for the auto. Structured on a grid of arterial road ways, each square has several clusters or housing, and small shopping "activity centers" linked with pedestrian open space. Secondary schools, industrial areas, and a larger shopping mall style "city center" are segregated in certain areas of the plan.

| | Kilometres |
|---|---|
| 0  1  2  3  4 | |
| 0  1  2  3 | Miles |

| | Existing towns and villages | | Secondary school group |
|---|---|---|---|
| | Residential Area | | Reserve sites |
| | Industry | | Higher education campus |
| | Parks | | Health campus |
| | Woods | | Primary road |
| | New city centre | | Expressway/Motorway |
| | Centres | | Railway |
| | Local activity centres | | |

50 percent privately owned. While Vallingby is built around one primary center with increasing densities to encourage walking and mass transit, Milton Keynes is a matt of distributed activities to avoid the auto conjestion generated by such focal points. It does, however, encompass and respect several existing villages which form cultural and aesthetic focal points. Additionally, a "city center" regional shopping and office area is under construction and will contain one of the largest covered shopping malls in all of Europe. It is designed primarily for automobile access.

Although Milton Keynes' densities and auto-orientation are close to Levittown, the similarities stop there. Within each block a pedestrian open- space network provides convenient access to "activity centers," which form bridges over the arterials. With over two hundred locations designated throughout the plan, these activity centers contain a variety of uses potentially combining shops, schools, pubs, daycare facilities, recreation areas, and bus stops. These con-

231

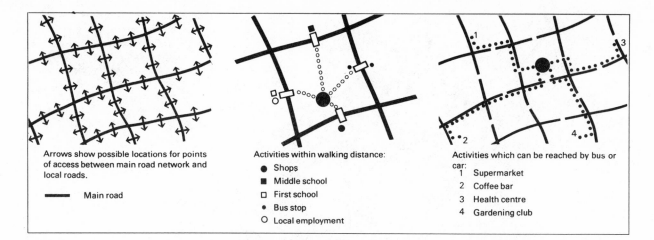

Arrows show possible locations for points of access between main road network and local roads.

━━━━━ Main road

Activities within walking distance:
- ● Shops
- ■ Middle school
- □ First school
- • Bus stop
- ○ Local employment

Activities which can be reached by bus or car:
1 Supermarket
2 Coffee bar
3 Health centre
4 Gardening club

Milton Keynes has a standard hierarchy of arterial and secondary roads. The pedestrian greenway link bridges over the arterials which are reinforced with busstops, schools, shops, and some local employment.

nection points provide a pedestrian focus, within 150 yards of any house, to what would otherwise be a typical suburban pattern. In another major departure from Levittown, Milton Keynes has effectively attracted industry and office-type employers, as well as a major health center and a major university. The location of the employment opportunities in a distributed fashion was calculated to reduce commuting distances and time.

The housing plans at Milton Keynes vary greatly, expressing the avowed flexibility and plurality of the master plan. Ranging from barrack-like rows of rental housing to the socially-sensitive designs of the Eaglestone neighborhood designed by Ralph Erskine, the quality of the environment is largely a product of the quality of the designers. Seventeen percent of the total area is designated as permanent open space, woods, and recreation areas, and community centers are planned at each activity center. Although not as energy efficient as Vallingby, Milton Keynes represents a degree of social diversity and concern beyond the typical suburb.

## Sane Suburbs, New Towns, and Urban Gentrification

New towns, and comprehensive planning for that matter, have been recently considered a failure. The urban renewal programs of the 1950s and 60s have left a bloody trail of destroyed neighborhoods and unsuccesful housing blocks. New suburban towns such as Reston, Virginia and Columbia, Maryland have proven uneconomic for private developers, and boring to young urbanites. The architectural quality of many of the European new towns has contributed to their image as sterile and unnatural places.

Many of these negative traits are irrefutable. The modern movement tended to discount the psychological and social complexity of the environment in favor of rational and functional criteria. New

232

towns inherently disconnect people from local history and the symbols of their past. They all seem to ignore ecology, climate, and the natural qualities of place. It is no wonder people prefer the messy confusion of older, unplanned areas.

Jane Jacobs, in **The Death and Life of Great American Cities**, led the rebellion against the modern planning principles of C.I.A.M. and new towns. Her work is an eloquent portrait of the social success of the old urban patterns that they rejected. In her eyes, the congestion and mixed use of these patterns, along with the affordability of old buildings, creates a vitality and community lacking in suburban and planned areas. The unplanned proximity of activities, the chance meetings, and to a certain degree, the anonymity of the city, create a culture which cannot be simulated.

Her work came full circle from that of the turn-of-the-century idealists: from a rebellion against the confusion and decay of the industrial city to an idealization of its reinhabited form. Hers is a stand against the scale-less superblock, the segregation of activities and people, the demolition of history and old associations, and the mechanization of buildings. And, she is right. But her proposals for urban preservation can only go so far, especially in growth areas such as the sunbelt which have no significant urban environments upon which to build. In America, the question of a better suburban pattern remains unresolved.

Leon Krier, an architect from Brussels, has become a radical champion of her theories in Europe. His is a vision honoring the historical qualities and use patterns of Europe's predominantly urban world.

Leon Krier's plan for a new quarter in Brussels shows the fine grain fabric of a walkable urban environment built on the traditional elements of street, square, and pre-industrial city blocks.

233

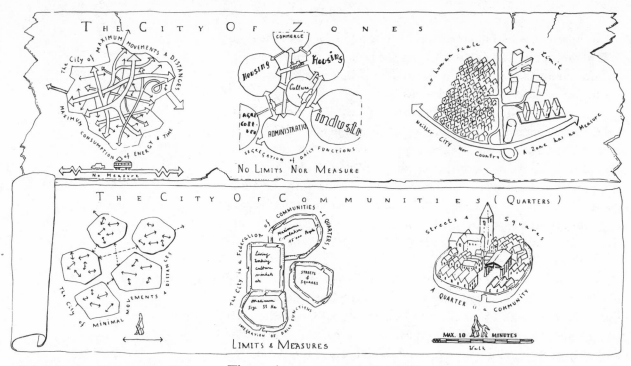

Krier's drawings diagram two radical opposites: The 20th century tendency towards functional zoning made possible by the auto and a mixed use urban quarter scaled by the pedestrian and conceived as a complete community. He challenges the modern notion of technical progress while advocating a return to the traditional form of old European cities.

There, in contrast to the U.S., such urban preservation and revitalization, rather than suburbanization, could be a general solution. Krier's design principles stand in stark contrast to both modernest and new town practices; the pre-auto city block returns, pedestrian plazas and squares replace park-like open space, mixed-use buildings line the street, piecemeal infill replaces large-scale demolition, the urban "quarter" replaces land-use zoning, and low-rise buildings prevail. This is a return to utopian rather than practical planning. The auto is banished from the city, and common space and community re-established. His architecture returns to traditional forms and techniques.

In the U.S., such sentiments quickly lose their integrity, degraded to a kind of stylistic nostalgia. Confronting real social and environmental issues gives way to fashionable gentrification of old urban neighborhoods. Meanwhile, most growth continues in sunbelt suburbs, in patterns which bear little resemblance to any of the proposals outlined in this chapter.

This is the crux of the problem: Planned communities must be judged in contrast to suburban sprawl, not idealized urban environments. For the U.S., new towns are relevant because, though unconsciously, we continue to build them. A housing subdivision, shopping mall, and industrial park with a freeway network is an unnamed new town. Whether it is the best form socially, environmentally, and economically, should continue to be questioned. The value of this short history of new town planning is merely to outline the progression of ideas and experiments, and demonstrate the broad range of alternates.

# Index